ANXIOUS JOBURG

ANXIOUS JOBURG
THE INNER LIVES
OF A GLOBAL SOUTH CITY

EDITED BY NICKY FALKOF AND COBUS VAN STADEN

WITS UNIVERSITY PRESS

Published in South Africa by:
Wits University Press
1 Jan Smuts Avenue
Johannesburg 2001

www.witspress.co.za

First published 2020

http://dx.doi.org.10.18772/22020106284

978-1-77614-628-4 (Paperback)
978-1-77614-632-1 (Hardback)
978-1-77614-629-1 (Web PDF)
978-1-77614-630-7 (EPUB)
978-1-77614-631-4 (Mobi)

Project manager: Catherine Damerell
Copyeditor: Russell Martin
Proofreader: Lisa Compton
Indexer: Sanet le Roux
Cover design: Hybrid Creative
Typeset in 10 point Garamond Pro

CONTENTS

ACKNOWLEDGEMENTS

This book emerges from a project titled 'Urban Anxieties in the Global South', which has been generously supported by a Friedel Sellschop early career award from the University of the Witwatersrand and a National Research Foundation Thuthuka Early Career Fellowship, both awarded to Nicky Falkof in 2017–2019. The book itself has been further supported by the Andrew W. Mellon Foundation-funded Governing Intimacies project, also based at Wits University. Most of the chapters included here were developed during an August 2017 workshop in Johannesburg, co-hosted by Wits Media Studies and the Wits Institute for Social and Economic Research (WiSER). Thanks to Roshan Cader at Wits University Press, to Srila Roy at Governing Intimacies, and to Sarah Nuttall and Najibha Deshmukh at WiSER. Thanks also to Anton Kannemeyer for the use of his images, to Eric Worby for advice on ethics, to Mehita Iqani for providing an intellectual sounding board, to Carli Coetzee for valuable conversations about anxiety, to Job Mwaura for his work on the original conference, to Valerie Killian for her administrative support, and to the two anonymous reviewers who read this book before publication, whose generous and insightful comments have made it far better. Cobus and Nicky would like to acknowledge the contributors for their continued willingness and enthusiasm through many rounds of revision, and for offering such powerful chapters to this volume. Special thanks to Baeletsi Tsatsi, Antonia Steyn and Naadira Patel for their creative contributions, and the associated conversations, without which the book would not be what it is. We are enormously grateful to our respective partners, Lebogang Mogashoa and Joe Walsh, for their patience with our unusual interests and their invaluable behind-the-scenes input into this book.

LIST OF FIGURES

CHAPTER 8 SHIFTING TOPOGRAPHIES OF THE ANXIOUS CITY

CHAPTER 9 PHOTOGRAPHY AND RELIGION IN ANXIOUS JOBURG

CHAPTER 12 INNER-CITY ANXIETIES: FEAR OF CRIME, GETTING BY AND DISCONNECTED URBAN LIVES

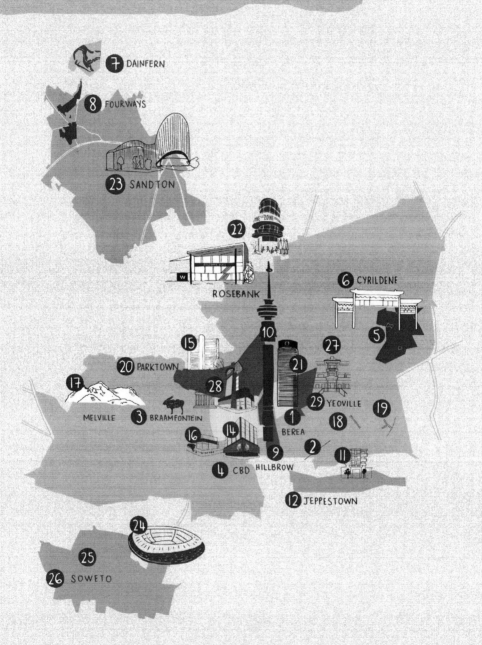

MAPPING ANXIETY IN GREATER JOHANNESBURG

ILLUSTRATION BY NAADIRA PATEL

7 DAINFERN

8 FOURWAYS

23 SANDTON

22 ROSEBANK

6 CYRILDENE

5

10

20 PARKTOWN

15

21

27

17 MELVILLE

28

29 YEOVILLE

19

3 BRAAMFONTEIN

18

16

14

1 BEREA

9

2

11

4 CBD HILLBROW

12 JEPPESTOWN

24

25

26 SOWETO

PRETORIA

30 DESMOND TUTU REFUGEE CENTRE

GREATER JOHANNESBURG

PRETORIA

SANDTON

KEMPTON PARK

JOHANNESBURG

SOWETO

13 KEMPTON PARK

31 DRIEFONTEIN

32 BARBERTON

359 KM

33 MSINGA

424.6 KM

FOREWORD

For black people Johannesburg has always been a place of toil and misery. Especially in the early years, as its mine dumps and tall buildings were just beginning to rise above the veld, Johannesburg gave its black denizens no choices. By the turn of the century Africans were pushed into the city from as far afield as Malawi and Mozambique. Soon they were trapped there, victims of taxes and labour systems designed precisely for that purpose; victims too of the vast distances between where they had come from and where they now found themselves.

Africans in Johannesburg were quickly squeezed into new urban selves, hemmed in by the city's enormity even as they suffocated in the tight and narrow spaces of its dormitories and shacks. They had mainly grown up in kraals and on farms, and suddenly they were here in a place of summer lightning and winter frost. Country boys remade as miners were forced to spend their days underground with their backs bent, digging up this precious metal that made white men rich. As they walked the city on their days off, they quickly learned to bow their heads and duck their chins, to avert their eyes to stay safe when they crossed paths with men who had recently decided to call themselves 'white'. Johannesburg was a place where black people learned to make themselves smaller than they had ever had to be.

In the United States of America, the Great Migration that unfolded after the Civil War spelled a new chapter of freedom for black people in that country. In the wake of the failed Reconstruction era, as freed slaves realised that their white compatriots would not easily share power with them, former cotton pickers and tobacco sharecroppers began to move off the land in great numbers. Cities like Atlanta, Chicago and New York represented liberty for black people. They were places where the dignity of former slaves and their descendants might be restored as they escaped the blood and memories that had thus far defined their experience of the New World. While there are many commonalities shared by the US and South Africa – two societies that exemplify stubborn and long-running experiments with white supremacy – the story of the city as a site of freedom is not one of them. In South Africa, cities were not a chosen future. Johannesburg in particular was part of a new era of enforced labour; cities were the very opposite of freedom. If all cities in the country that became the Union of South Africa were wretched, Johannesburg was the most wretched. It was the epicentre of misery, the heart of a new form of southern African bondage. Black people were not drawn to the city by a desire to be free – they were forced there by a set of exploitative practices that had been engineered across Africa but perfected in the southern part of the continent. These practices made it impossible for Africans to stay where they were, on the lands to which they had once had unfettered access.

It is important not to romanticise the pain and labour and grit that defined life in the big city from its earliest days, long before the formal advent of apartheid. It is true that black people made the city bearable. They helped to create places like Sophiatown, cultural zones of pleasure and joy. But this does not mean that they arrived in the city in pursuit of these experiences. The fact that black people turned some aspects of city life into something joyous does not justify the indignity of having been forced into the urban areas in the first place. The development of a rich nightlife and of the music that came to define the city from the 1950s onwards is evidence of the genius of African creativity. Indeed, it is no accident that Soweto grew alongside Johannesburg. The township was the meeting point for people who had very few options, and over time it turned into a place where black people remade themselves in the image of everything they would need to be in order to survive. Soweto's brilliance is evidence of the same cultural strength that enabled African diasporic communities from Barbados to Brazil to retain the self-confidence that helped them survive unimaginable degradation.

But this is a book about Johannesburg rather than a book about Soweto. A book about Soweto would be a different beast, a more unequivocal thing. A book about black Johannesburg – one that encompassed Alexandra and the grey zones where race mixing was tolerated – would not be steeped in anxiety. These books – and there are many – are celebrations or lamentations. They catalogue and they mourn and they track triumph.

No serious publication about Johannesburg can boast such certainty. Johannesburg's story is laden with guilt. The weight of its wealth and the injustice of how that wealth has been maldistributed make analyses of Johannesburg much more fraught exercises. Indeed, the title of this book says it best. In the lingo of the present, anxiety is 'peak Joburg'.

As this book illustrates, there are many things about Johannesburg that make it an ideal city to study. Like any good metaphor, it stands in for so many other places. With its freeways and dense traffic it is like Los Angeles. Its townships juxtaposed with neighbourhoods like Houghton make it sometimes feel like São Paulo. And as it tries to remake itself, evicting immigrants from crowded, old and often still magnificent buildings in order to create sterile, soulless hipster oases, parts of the city increasingly feel like gentrified Brooklyn.

Yet for those of us who love it, Johannesburg's magic is its adrenalin. In Johannesburg you never know what nightmare waits for you around the corner, and if you believe in karma this is part of the city's charm. It is impossible to believe that everything that went before – the gold, the wealth, the silicosis and the appalling injustice of it all – has not yet been avenged. Even at its swaggiest, the city is always looking over its shoulder. It has always struck me as apt that the City of Joburg brands itself as 'a world-class African city'. The identity crisis is evident, the anxiety about what this place actually is, is palpable. Is Johannesburg African or should it not be? Is the city global, and what kind of aspiration is that? Is the city rich enough for its dreams? Who is this city talking to? Who is it for?

As Falkof and Van Staden write in the introduction to this book, 'Joburg is not the most worried, most dangerous, most unequal or most precarious of the burgeoning megacities of the south. The visibility of its multiple anxieties does, however, provide an important insight into the volatile shifts of contemporary urban life.' Those of us who love this city do so precisely because it has found a way to embody the contradictions of modern life so exquisitely and so excruciatingly and because it makes so much of our angst visible. What better example is there of this than the young entertainers who dance at street lights and ask for money – beggar boys dressed like lions or cats, breakdancing and risking life and limb at busy intersections? They laugh mirthlessly. They are ghoulish, frightening and delightful, and they exist because the city that birthed them is so breathtakingly unjust. They remind us that, like all great cities, Joburg runs on audacity.

Those of us who love Joburg do so because these moments of audacity and pain are constant and inescapable, and so no one in Johannesburg can pretend to be innocent. We are devils all. This, more than anything else, is the city's magic. Johannesburg is a meeting place of the wounded; the place where clowns gather to laugh, where the stars collide with the star-struck, where fear bleeds into courage on a daily basis. In Joburg history is a guide but not necessarily a compass.

But for those who are looking for a compass, for those still hopelessly invested in the idea of the future, this book is a reminder that at their best academic literatures can offer a way forward if not a way out. There can be no better homage paid to this city – my city – than a book that traces the heart of the city's anxieties and maps Johannesburg's innermost landscapes. This book serves as an ode to everything that is unstable and unknowable and therefore everything worth loving and examining in this place we call Joburg.

Sisonke Msimang
January 2020

INTRODUCTION: TRAVERSING THE ANXIOUS METROPOLIS

NICKY FALKOF AND COBUS VAN STADEN

> Johannesburg became and remained, by default, an instant city, periodically growing and being torn down as the gold seams shifted course in one direction or another and the needs of its fickle residents changed … It is said that Johannesburg has been built up and torn down no fewer than five times since it first appeared on the Highveld in 1886. And each time it has re-emerged even uglier than before … No one has really been able to wrestle Johannesburg into any kind of civilized order. (Matshikiza 2004, 481–2)

Something odd is happening in Johannesburg. A city that for many years was used to illustrate disaster, decay and the failures of the post-apartheid promise is suddenly attractive. From being a place that wealthy tourists and destitute migrants alike warned their compatriots to avoid, Johannesburg has once again become desirable. No longer just a catalogue of potential dangers, the city has seen its longstanding aspirational qualities condensed into an atmosphere of edgy, global chic, epitomised by its place on the must-visit lists of fashionable media outlets like *Travel & Leisure* (Knafo 2017), which calls it 'Africa's hippest city'; *GQ*, which crowned it the 'new cool capital of the southern hemisphere' (Carvell 2015); and Culture Trip, which names it 'the one place you need to visit this year' (Jordan 2018). Joburg, as lifestyle writers say, is having a moment.

Enthusiastic journalists emoting about its hipster-friendly downtown can-not, however, avoid traces of the city's darker reputation. Notwithstanding its renewed cultural capital, Joburg remains South Africa's 'gritty urban metropolis' (Jordan 2018), a place where intense glamour intersects with intense poverty, where the ambitious and the volatile live cheek by jowl. Most importantly, though, it remains a place where people live in multiple, often conflicting ways. Optimistic portrayals of a tourist-friendly metropolis cannot account for the city's capacity to surprise, to unsettle, to make pre-carious. And yet it is part of the inevitable contradiction of Johannesburg that its parks, museums and coffee shops exist in awkward equilibrium with, not surplus to, its inner-city slums and peripheral informal settlements, its crumbling mines, its failing highways, its car guards, its security companies; and that it is renowned for both its potent dangers and its easy sociality and unexpected warmth towards strangers, which can seem so incongruent in a high-risk place. 'Johannesburg has always been a city of extremes, with the urban glamour zone of high-value real estate at one end … and the abandoned site of neglect and ruins … at the other, integrally connected in a symbiotic, unequal, and exploitative relationship of mutual dependency' (Murray 2011, xiv). Exposure to and immersion in such extremes seem to lead inevitably to emotional reactions: the multiple anxieties that characterise moving, work-ing, living and surviving in the city.

The contributors to this book are not the first to write about Johannesburg. Despite being marginalised as a global south, an African and a developing world city, Johannesburg has been the focus of some heavyweight scholarship, much of which is cited throughout this introduction. So why write about the city again rather than, say, Gaborone or Harare or Maputo?[1] What more do we need to learn about Johannesburg?

To echo Fredric Jameson (1995), writing on the global south is frequently called on to explicate the south to the north. Meanwhile, the north often sees its own experience as *the* human condition. The north is always ready for new writing about London or New York or Paris, no matter how micro the micro-trends or how repetitive the insights. It is exactly in the almost obses-sive examination and re-examination of these specific urban experiences that they become useful to those of us trying to understand what city life means elsewhere. That said, the limit to this utility lies in how a northern analysis of a Northern city cannot escape its location at the centre of global webs of power. Talking about London reverberates through Hong Kong, Delhi, Accra and Johannesburg, not least because colonialism left these cities sharing the same street names. But talking about Accra does not reverberate back to London, not only because of the inequality, racism and arrogance built into colonialism, but also because Accra has not (yet) gone through the same process of having its experiences mediated and globally circulated. City life in Accra is vital to its residents, but so far it has not come to define city life elsewhere.

Johannesburg, on the other hand, has established a particular set of mediated associations that connote specific experiences of being urban. It goes without saying that compared with the associations that delimit, say, Tokyo's brand of urbanity, Johannesburg's is distinctly more negative. Its place in the global imaginary is that of a troublesome metropolis. It reigns over indices of inequality, it makes other gun-ridden cities feel safe, it is always weaving its convolutions into ever more fiendish patterns.

The default instinct when faced with such complexities is to try and solve them. It can be difficult to avoid thinking of Johannesburg as anything but a list of problems – housing, water, infrastructure, Gini coefficient and particulate count. This pivot towards NGOism might signal real concern with the city's many inequities but it also reinforces the tendency of entities in the global north to keep tabs on, measure, rate and list the south. It is an instinct to keep the north safe behind its force field of concern, to look at – but avoid being touched by – the realities of daily life in the southern city. With this book we propose a different intellectual project, and a different act of reading. We want to write about what it is like to live in a global south city, and we are interested in Johannesburg because Johannesburg is interesting.

Johannesburg shares many realities with other cities in the south. It features luxury as well as slum tourism, gated communities as well as shantytowns, extractive and resource-heavy industry and business, unreliable infrastructure and public transport, mass migration, poorly regulated development, privatisation and neocolonial investment, youth unemployment and a vast gulf between wealthy elites and an increasingly marginalised poor. But in contrast to many cities, some of its problems are being mapped, not least because of longstanding international interest in the still-potent historical underpinnings of those problems. This mapping is far from comprehensive, and this book is an attempt to fill some gaps, but at least it is taking place.[2]

By treating Johannesburg as a viable template for city life, we want to open a door to other urban conversations, not only with São Paolo, Mumbai, Lagos and Shanghai, cities that already attract much outside scholarly interest, but also with Kinshasa, Lima, Dhaka and Manila, and with scholars who not only write about them but live in them too. We aim to provide a glimpse of life in a global south city not as a set of target areas but as an emotional topography, a landscape of feeling.

Johannesburg is a complicated place and it runs on complicated affects. Our attempt to link the landscape with the emotional life of the city is also an attempt to work through how irreducible the experience of living here is within the narrow parameters of Johannesburg's international image. The chapters in this book delve below existing mappings of life in the city to connect with some of the deeper experiences that too frequently are locked inside phrases that conceal as much as they reveal. 'Historical trauma', 'fear of crime', 'the legacy of apartheid' – just as Johannesburg's international image does not reveal the complexity of life here, these phrases obscure the complexity of the city's emotional existence and the powerful historical currents that have shaped it. It is only by focusing on the city as an ever-shifting physical *and* emotional landscape that we can start unpacking what Johannesburg reveals about urban life more globally. Through this unpacking we hope to offer insights useful to residents of other southern cities in order to move towards a wider acknowledgement of the global south city as the central urban experience of the twenty-first century, one that 'literally [embodies] the future of humanity' (Dawson quoted in Nuttall and Mbembe 2008, 4).

READING THE ANXIOUS METROPOLIS

Another pressing question that underlies the motivation behind this book is that of anxiety. Why select this particular angle to discuss Johannesburg? Why approach the city through the lens of a feeling rather than through, say, economics, urban planning, housing, employment patterns, transport, epidemiology, the various 'ways of seeing and reading contemporary African cities [that] are still dominated by the metanarrative of urbanisation, modernisation, and crisis' (Mbembe and Nuttall 2008, 5)? The answer, of course, is that once we shift away from an instrumental gaze that views Johannesburg as a problem to be solved, we begin to see that the condition of anxiety lurks behind *all* of these urban features. Anxiety impacts on how money is spent and invested; on what is planned and built; on who works and lives in what areas and in what ways; on how people and goods move around; on how and where people access health care, and concurrently on how disease spreads. Because cities do not emerge fully formed into a vacuum, because they are organic and sometimes mutant formations, the affective lives of those who inhabit them always impact, to some extent, on their shape. Anxiety is thus a surprisingly productive way to approach a discussion of many of the disparate elements and ways of living that characterise Johannesburg.

We chose to centre this volume, and the larger project of which it is a part, specifically on anxiety rather than on risk, affect or other related notions that play a role in the scholarly literature about quotidian life in late capitalism. While these ideas do appear within the discussions in this book, anxiety is their central connection. In psychoanalytic terms, anxiety neurosis appears against a background of 'general irritability':

> chronic anxiousness or anxious expectation [is] apt to become bound to any ideational content which is able to lend it support; pure anxiety attacks accompanied or replaced by various somatic equivalents … and phobic symptoms where the affect – the anxiety – is bound to an idea … which it is impossible to identify as a symbolic replacement for another, repressed idea. (Laplanche and Pontalis 1988, 39)

Anxiety is, then, a feeling, or conurbation of feelings, that is pervasive and consistent rather than reactive. It is free-floating and easily attached to disparate series of objects, or rather what Kopano Ratele calls 'objectless' (2001, 77). It has effects and symptoms that are bodily and visible, meaning that they impact on everyday experiences. It is characterised by the 'absence of any obviously privileged object, and by the manifest role of actual factors' (Laplanche and Pontalis 1988, 40): while anxiety may not be aimed at one specific cause, there are authentic factors that drive it. We can perhaps think of it as a ubiquitous *condition* rather than an intermittent *experience*, and one that, notwithstanding its potential to result in neurosis or pathology, has its roots in something that is empirically visible.

As we suggested above, anxiety – particularly as an urban and political state – is not simply an individual experience without wider consequences. The cultural theorist Sara Ahmed tells us that emotions 'are not "in" either the individual or the social, but produce the very surfaces and boundaries that allow the individual and the social to be delineated as if they are objects' (2014, 10). We can usefully apply this understanding to anxiety. As Derek Hook explains in his chapter in this book, 'Anxiety … cannot be limited to a circumstantial or simply intrasubjective affect; it entails an intersubjective dimension (with the Other) and it speaks as such to the underpinnings of the subject's most crucial identifications.' Following this lead, we approach anxiety as social and collective and as socially and collectively created and transmitted.

Such an appeal to psychoanalytical thinking does not imply an attempt to psychoanalyse the city, a Promethean task whose attempts are best left to artists.[3] Rather, we use anxiety as a narrative and metaphoric tool that allows us to collate a broad swathe of Joburg city life. Anxiety connotes something bigger than a single person's feelings: a set of emotions and experiences that relate to identity, self and otherness, in the city as elsewhere. Anxiety is also contextual and historical. People are anxious not just because of contemporary circumstances but also because they have been historically and structurally set up to be so. Given the heightened meanings of apartheid in the global imaginary, these conditions become particularly visible in Johannesburg.

Such urban anxiety is related to what AbdouMaliq Simone calls 'a coincidence of the unexpected'. The intense proximity of opposing features in African cities can produce a 'highly ambiguous sense of place' that 'amplifies the historical capacity of many African societies to configure highly mobile social formations' (Simone 2004, 1, 2). African cities, and the micro- and macro-societies that exist within them, have a particularly mutable tendency. They shift and change, they welcome and expel. Indeed, 'with its constant, restless evolution, Johannesburg resists all efforts at objectification, classification, and definition' (Murray 2011, xx). Residents of Johannesburg, like most urban African subjects – and, indeed, like many elsewhere in the south – must themselves remain flexible in order to move within the fluidity of the shifting city. This unfixity is linked to the anxious condition of consistent uncertainty: whether of home and safety, of status and belonging, of unfamiliarity or precarity.

Anxiety is important as a metaphor. The word itself can connote both an encounter with and a way of explaining certain kinds of urban experience. At the University of the Witwatersrand, where we have both worked, students seem to be experiencing an overwhelming epidemic of anxiety. The institution's already stretched mental health services have been pushed to breaking point in recent years. Every time a deadline rolls round, lecturers are accustomed to a rush of students requesting extensions on the basis of anxiety, either self-diagnosed or supported by letters from medical professionals across the spectrum, from campus health and discount inner-city clinics to pricey consultants at private hospitals. The term appears relentlessly in urban young people's self-narrativisations of survival and success – anxiety seems almost de rigueur as part of the educational experience. We are not, of course, suggesting that these feelings are not personally significant or authentically experienced. University students in Joburg have plenty of reasons to feel anxious. As well as facing housing shortages, fee crises and neighbourhood threats to physical safety, they are also exposed to the intense competition and fear of being left behind engendered by South Africa's ever-increasing inequality. All of these features suggest the social, epidemiological and global qualities of anxiety, both as something experiential and as something explanatory.

African cities are often characterised as chaotic and unmanageable failures, as places that do not work (Simone 2004, 1), with Africans as 'eternal recipients, absorbing certain elements from global culture and rejecting others' (Isichei 2004, 206). This is in contrast to the modern, civilised representation that is common to cities in the north, which are seen to create and export culture, in an echo of the divisions between what Simon Gikandi calls 'European modernity, epitomised by the rule of reason, and African primitivism' (2002, 140).

But this contrast between the soaring metropolises of the north and the mingled prelapsarian and dystopian nightmares of the south is a spurious one. Achille Mbembe writes that 'from its beginning in the late nineteenth century, Johannesburg has always imagined itself to be a modern city' (2008, 39). This imbrication in modernity has continued after apartheid, when Johannesburg 'leads a double life. The city is a paradigmatic exemplar of first world glamour and excess and third world impoverishment and degradation. It is simultaneously a global marketplace of speculative investment integrally linked to the world economy via globalizing space of flows' (Murray 2011, 2). Far from being an 'African problem', its manifestation as an anxious city marks its status as a site of globalisation. As Zygmunt Bauman explains, the 'culture of fear', which has anxiety as its correlative, is a particularly modern condition (2005, 2006, 2007), with roots 'in the changing nature of economic and political structures which leave us more and more exposed to whatever may befall us' (Critcher 2011, 268). The kind of hypervisible urban anxiety with which this book is concerned is a consequence and a symptom of modernity.

This is in sharp contrast to depictions of Africans as static and as 'funda-mentally and even essentially rural creatures' (Mbembe and Nuttall 2008, 5). South Africans, who often live extraordinarily mobile lives within national borders, may feel negative emotions in rural areas – but it is particularly when one moves to Joburg that these become transmuted into the beast that we call anxiety. A person acquires anxiety by becoming urbanised, by investing heav-ily in her or his city self. As a way of describing feelings that are considered legitimate within the space of a city, anxiety is both a driver and a result of physical and social mobility.

As well as being part of an experience of living in the city, anxiety provides a common language, a collective rhetoric, that allows us to talk to each other about how we live here. It is part of how Joburg narrates itself, in particular to itself. As the chapters in this book reveal, anxiety as a condition of globalised modernity is particularly visible, or perhaps audible, in Johannesburg, where all sorts of people, from refugees and township dwellers to wealthy subur-banites, discuss and acknowledge their feelings of nervousness, tension and precarity as a common feature of city life.

The chapters to follow are in general concerned with six overlapping themes: crime, race, gender, status, space and authenticity.

ARGUING THE ANXIOUS METROPOLIS

Much important scholarly work has been produced on questions of crime, violence and safety in Johannesburg (see, for example, Bénit-Gbaffou 2008; Comaroff and Comaroff 2016; Lipman and Harris 1999; Murray 2011). While this is not explicitly a book about crime, crime appears in many of its pages. Chapters by Derek Hook, Renugan Raidoo and Nicky Falkof are concerned in different ways with what Teresa Caldeira calls 'talk of crime' (2000; see also Sasson 1995), and how this impacts on social imaginaries and the built environment for the wealthy, mostly white people who populate Johannesburg's suburbs and gated communities. A significant body of litera-ture discusses middle-class fear of crime in global south cities (Caldeira 2000;

Ferraro 1995; Lemanski 2004; Spinks 2001). Indeed, in his chapter in this book Aidan Mosselson argues that 'the majority of urban studies and planning scholarship has generally treated fear of crime as a bourgeois concern'. However, as shown in his chapter and those by Khangelani Moyo and Lebohang Masango, crime and fear of crime play an equally significant role in the collective imaginaries and daily lives of poorer and upwardly mobile Joburgers, who live, work, raise families and socialise in townships and the inner city.

Jean and John Comaroff write that crime and criminality have, 'in this Age of Global Capitalism, become the constitutive fact of contemporary life'. They think of crime as 'a critical prism by which societies know themselves' (2016, xiii, xiv). Some might contest the classification of crime as the most important site of globalised social knowledges (white-collar crime, which has even greater social consequences than its violent street-level cousin – see, for example, the 2008 global financial crash – makes very little appearance in collective imaginaries). However, there can be no question that experiences, narratives, rumours and architectures of crime intersect in meaningful ways with the concerns of this book. As well as being a potent source of anxiety in itself, crime is intertwined with worries about class and mobility, with gender, race and status, with spatiality. Crime is often a placeholder for a range of wider concerns. It appears repeatedly throughout this book because it opens up a hole in something that is supposed to be solid. In empirical terms it reveals the failings of the promises of city, state and the whole edifice of post-apartheid South Africa. In social terms, the hysteria surrounding crime and fear of crime operate like a psychoanalytic symptom that reveals the structural instability that the subject is trying to paper over. This is not just a book about crime, but it does attempt to put crime within a larger framework of the multiple intersecting anxieties that infect city life in Johannesburg, as well as to show that crime is heterogeneous, hydra-headed, more than one thing.

According to Martin J. Murray, 'Perhaps no other city in South Africa bears the spatial scars of white minority rule as profoundly and self-consciously as Johannesburg' (2011, xi). The city was subject to an 'unusually complex, extensive, and coercive array of government-sponsored measures that distinguished South African urban arch-segregationism over the course of its century-long history' (Nightingale 2015, 232). This segregationary urge plays a significant part in who lives where in contemporary Joburg. The suburbs, zoned white under apartheid, have undergone a performance of nominal democratisation, with middle-class black, Indian and coloured communities and individuals moving into areas where they would once have been illegal.[4] However, despite international interest in so-called white squatter camps, townships and informal settlements remain largely populated by black people, albeit with a degree of class mobility that would have been near impossible under apartheid (Alexander et al. 2013; Nieftagodien and Bonner 2008). As a consequence of these longstanding conditions of space and inequality, most aspects of life in the city remain heavily inflected by race and concurrently by class. Race influences where a person shops, what kind of amenities she or he has access to, how she or he experiences street life, what kind of crime or precarity she or he worries about. As Njogu Morgan's chapter shows, one's choice of mode of transport is suffused with racial and class anxieties, while Joel Cabrita's interview with Sabelo Mlangeni shows how questions of race and mobility impact on religious practice in the city. Reading Renugan Raidoo's chapter, it becomes clear that even one's access to nature – albeit nature at its most aggressively managed – is mediated by race.

Chapters by Hook and Falkof examine this ongoing racialisation in its most blatant form by considering the varying privileges, power and paranoia of white South Africans, who retain disproportionate access to the country's resources and who voice their social anxieties at a disproportionate volume. But, as Mingwei Huang's discussion of domestic labour in Chinatown reveals, racial tensions and negotiations are by no means restricted to black and white urbanites. Race remains a hypervisible cultural formation, impossible to escape and difficult to ignore.

Other substantial markers of identity, which impact powerfully on the ways in which different kinds of people experience living in the city, include gender and sexuality. South African rates of gender-based violence are disturbingly high (see, for example, Jewkes et al. 2011; Moffett 2006; Rasool et al. 2003). Stories of violence against women in intimate and public spaces are hard to avoid, even though research has shown that most such incidents never make it into the news (Brodie 2019). Instances of so-called corrective rape – sexual violence aimed at queer women and justified as necessary to 'fix' their unruly sexuality – remain common (Anguita 2012). Certain kinds of spaces are never entirely comfortable for women: from public streets to taxi ranks, being female in Joburg means living with the constant awareness of incipient male violence. Baeletsi Tsatsi's delicate, disturbing Taxi Diary stories offer a small window into the everyday demands of being black, female and constantly vigilant while moving around Johannesburg. Huang's chapter reveals in painful detail the lack of status that can come with typically female employment like domestic work.

In some instances, female anxieties about crime and safety are inextricably bound up with aspiration, agency and class mobility. Cobus van Staden interrogates the violence aimed at black, female and queer fans at the Global Citizen concert, while the young women interviewed for Masango's chapter find creative ways to avert the violent potential of the compensated relationships that constitute their urban survival. In B Camminga's chapter, Johannesburg is a hostile and dangerous bureaucratic maze for transgender African migrants and refugees who dream of making their way to the more queer-friendly environs of Cape Town. Within the anxious city, being female, trans or queer adds another layer of concern to the everyday acts of living, working and moving.

These stories fit into the wider struggles that face all inhabitants under the city's particularly brutal version of capitalism. As is pointed out throughout this book, Johannesburg is one of the most unequal cities in the world. This inequality is not only a material issue, but also affects the way inhabitants understand their own positions in the city. The policing of status is structurally enabled, as is clear in Camminga's examination of the spatial obstacles affecting refugees and Raidoo's reading of how gated communities physically manifest class distinctions while also constructing nature itself. This delineation of space to concretise social hierarchies is one of the most dominant aspects of life in Johannesburg. Raidoo's and Huang's chapters show how these divisions help to maintain islands of wealth amid poverty. Moyo's chapter shows how zones of impassability safeguard vested interests even within impoverished publics, while Cabrita's reveals the way in which faith communities negotiate geographic barriers in order to retain a sense of unity and, concurrently, safety.

The imposition of human settlement on the landscape is always a fraught and violent process, but in Johannesburg it was perhaps more violent than most. The city is still bifurcated by buffer zones, highways and barriers aimed at slicing up a complex society into spatially and economically discrete units (Nightingale 2015). As Falkof's chapter shows, the psychic scars of these zoning processes impact on all the city's residents. Even as the end of formal segregation led to the slow and limited reintegration of the population, people still have to pick their way across a landscape designed to make that passage as difficult as possible. The current obsession with crime only adds to these hurdles. Johannesburgers impose endless inconvenience on themselves and their fellow residents in the name of avoiding crime, accepting and even welcoming the kinds of invasive security restrictions experienced by Mosselson's inner-city interviewees. Alongside these physical boundaries, Antonia Steyn's photo essay reveals a slippage in the landscape itself, and the way in which geographic positioning impacts on perspective and experience.

Despite government rhetoric about development and the growth of the middle class, Van Staden's chapter reveals that the split between rich and poor is becoming even more powerful, and echoes global trends of widening wealth gaps between a transnational elite and a global underclass. Even when these divisions are not externally imposed, Morgan's and Masango's chapters make clear that they structure the psychological life of the city. Choices around modes of transport and personal relationships reflect economic divisions as clearly as the barriers around malls. At the same time, Masango shows how the city presents an unprecedented chance for social mobility, albeit at a massive price. The women in her study do not passively accept these compromises, but actively devise tactics to avoid harm while maintaining their freedom.

Taken together, these chapters force us to ask what it means to live an authentic life in the city. How do you live who you are, go where you want, do what you hope to do, when so many barriers grow around you? When not only the ubiquitous walls but the very people in the city actively keep you trapped in you? How do you reconcile the contradictions between Johannesburg's threats and its generosity, the impromptu kinship that often informs city life? The tension between the need for something else and the constant reimposition of the same connects the disparate anxieties outlined in the book. Despite the canyons separating different lives in Johannesburg, the constancy of anxiety hints at how everyone feels bounded in a fractalised, spiralling-in-on-itself kind of way, where each individual not only feels fatally hemmed in, but ends up complicit in hemming in everybody around them. As the gears of these wheels within wheels bite harder, the city itself seems to judder, as if about to fly apart. But it never does. Instead, the overworked engine somehow keeps going, belching its haze of stories, and they soak through the pores of the people trying to get home before dark.

WRITING THE ANXIOUS METROPOLIS

There are many ways to talk about Johannesburg and many other parts of Johannesburg that could be written about. Some of these have been raised by writers like Lindsay Bremner (2004, 2010), Martin J. Murray (2008, 2011), Mark Gevisser (2014), AbdouMaliq Simone (2006, 2008), Noor Nieftagodien and Philip Bonner (2008), Sisonke Msimang (2018) and Christa Kuljian (2013). Edited collections like *Changing Space, Changing City* (Harrison et al. 2014) and *Not No Place* (Malcomess and Kreutzfeldt 2013) approach the city from the contrasting positions of social science and art, architecture and aesthetics. Perhaps most significant for our purposes is Sarah Nuttall and Achille Mbembe's edited collection *Johannesburg: The Elusive Metropolis* (2008), which was based on but expanded upon a 2004 special issue of the journal *Public Culture*. In the introduction to that volume they write that 'few commentaries on Johannesburg have been preoccupied with city form and city life, keys to understanding its metropolitan modernity' (2008, 11). *The Elusive Metropolis* was an influential corrective to this trend, particularly in its detailed concentration on the city's hidden elements. This book follows its lead in thinking in sometimes micro-focused detail about how it feels to live in Joburg now, and about what those feelings can tell us about global urban modernity in general and Johannesburg's place within it.

No single book can contain the entirety of a vast and mobile African metropolis. This one is necessarily incomplete: specifically, its possibilities are limited by the interests of its contributors, who are largely drawn from participants in a workshop held in Johannesburg in 2017.[5] Its lacunae include areas like the complications of township life under the pressure of neoliberal aspiration; the trap of debt and other financial concerns; political uncertainty and concomitant violence; the difficulty of finding and maintaining queer spaces in the city; problems of disease, medicine and stigma; and the roles of art, literature and music in city-making. Future work on such questions could do more to centralise the anxieties of the poor and marginalised to the exclusion of middle-class Joburgers, whose voices are louder and whose fears are thus, perhaps, easier to read.

What a single book can do, however, is provide a snapshot of some of the emotional landscapes of contemporary Joburg, from northern suburbs to inner city to informal settlement, from precarious migrants to respectable working-class families to glamorous, aspirational young people and nervous middle-class homeowners. These hypermodern anxieties and ways of being in the city do not answer the 'question' of Johannesburg but they do provide a vocabulary with which we can begin to ask it, and which could be equally valuable in thinking about other southern cities. Joburg is not the most worried, most dangerous, most unequal or most precarious of the burgeoning megacities of the south. The visibility of its multiple anxieties does, however, provide an important insight into the volatile shifts of contemporary urban life.

NOTES

1   Needless to say, important research is being done on these cities. While much of this takes a hard science or social science perspective, other work offers a 'messier' interdisciplinary/cultural studies approach that considers how cities work on multiple levels. See Akindele (2011) on the meanings of public signage in Gaborone, Chiweshe (2018) on soccer fans in Harare, and Baptista (2015) on how pre-paid electricity impacts urban life in Maputo.

2   See, for example, recent publications on migration and health (Vearey 2017; Vearey et al. 2017), sex work (Hlatshwayo 2019; Yingwana, Walker, and Etchart 2019), corruption (Hornberger 2018), public space (Heer 2017) and urban policy and planning (Bénit-Gbaffou 2018; Mosselson 2018; Myambo 2018) in Johannesburg.

3   The creative work of South African visual artists, writers and musicians like Niq Mhlongo, Nkululeko and Siyabonga Mthembu, William Kentridge, Mark Lewis and Tanya Zack, Lesego Ramopolokeng, Donna Kukama, Terry Kurgan, Senzo Shabangu, Jodi Bieber, Fela Gucci and Sabelo Mlangeni – interviewed in this book – offers a vital perspective on the city.

4   For ease of use, this book draws on the four main racial categories that were used under apartheid and remain in common parlance today. However, we must highlight both the colonially constructed nature of these classifications (and, indeed, the fiction of 'race' overall) and their impossibility of accounting for diversity of language, history and identity in South Africa. The category 'coloured' in particular is undergoing important interrogation by scholars and activists. These terms remain useful for our project, however, as this book is interested in how people define

themselves and those around them, much of which happens through resilient racial classification.

5　'Urban Anxieties in the Global South' took place at Wits University in August 2017. The event had an open call, was advertised widely and was designed to bring artists, graduate students and early career scholars into conversation with established academic researchers.

REFERENCES

Ahmed, Sara. 2014. *The Cultural Politics of Emotion*, 2nd edn. Edinburgh: Edinburgh University Press.

Akindele, Dele O. 2011. "Linguistic Landscapes as Public Communication: A Study of Public Signage in Gaborone Botswana." *International Journal of Linguistics* 3: 1–11.

Alexander, Peter, Claire Ceruti, Keke Motseke, Mosa Phadi, and Kim Wale. 2013. *Class in Soweto*. Scottsville: University of KwaZulu-Natal Press.

Anguita, Luis A. 2012. "Tackling Corrective Rape in South Africa: The Engagement between the LGBT CSOs and the NHRIs (CGE and SAHRC) and Its Role." *International Journal of Human Rights* 16: 489–516.

Baptista, Idalina. 2015. "'We Live on Estimates': Everyday Practices of Prepaid Electricity and the Urban Condition in Maputo, Mozambique." *International Journal of Urban and Regional Research* 39: 1004–19. https://doi.org/10.1111/1468-2427.12314.

Bauman, Zygmunt. 2005. *Liquid Life*. Cambridge: Polity Press.

———. 2006. *Liquid Fear*. Cambridge: Polity Press.

———. 2007. *Liquid Times: Living in an Age of Uncertainty*. Cambridge: Polity Press.

Bénit-Gbaffou, Claire. 2008. "Unbundled Security Services and Urban Fragmentation in Post-Apartheid Johannesburg." *Geoforum* 39: 1933–50. https://doi.org/10.1016/j.geoforum.2007.10.011.

———. 2018. "Governing Street Trading in Contemporary Cities: Anatomy of the Policy Instruments Used by the City of Johannesburg in the Post-Apartheid Era." *Urban Research and Practice* 11: 396–425.

Bremner, Lindsay. 2004. *Johannesburg: One City, Colliding Worlds*. Johannesburg: STE Publications.

———. 2010. *Writing the City into Being*. Johannesburg: Fourthwall Books.

Brodie, Nechama. 2019. "Femicide in South African News Media (2012/2013)." PhD thesis, University of the Witwatersrand, Johannesburg.

Caldeira, Teresa. 2000. *City of Walls: Crime, Segregation and Citizenship in São Paulo*. Berkeley: University of California Press.

Carvell, Nick. 2015. "Get Yourself to Johannesburg, New Cool Capital of the Southern Hemisphere." *British GQ*. https://www.gq-magazine.co.uk/article/best-things-to-do-in-johannesburg-south-africa.

Chiweshe, Manase K. 2018. "Frenemies: Understanding the Interconnectedness of Rival Fan Identities in Harare, Zimbabwe." *Soccer and Society* 19: 829–41.

Comaroff, Jean, and John L. Comaroff. 2016. *The Truth about Crime: Sovereignty, Knowledge, Social Order*. Johannesburg: Witwatersrand University Press.

Critcher, Chas. 2011. "For a Political Economy of Moral Panics." *Crime, Media, Culture* 7: 259–75.

Ferraro, Kenneth F. 1995. *Fear of Crime: Interpreting Victimization Risk*. Albany, NY: State University of New York Press.

Gevisser, Mark. 2014. *Lost and Found in Johannesburg*. Johannesburg: Jonathan Ball.

Gikandi, Simon. 2002. "Reason, Modernity and the African Crisis." In *African Modernities: Entangled Meanings in Current Debate*, edited by P. Probst, H. Schmidt, and J.G. Deutsch, 135–57. Oxford: James Currey,

Harrison, Philip, Graeme Gotz, Alison Todes, and Chris Wray, eds. 2014. *Changing Space, Changing City: Johannesburg after Apartheid*. Johannesburg: Wits University Press.

Heer, Barbara. 2017. "Shopping Malls as Social Space: New Forms of Public Life in Johannesburg." In *Cities in Flux: Metropolitan Spaces in South African Literary and Visual Texts*, edited by Oliver Moreillon, Alan Muller, and Lindy Stiebel, 101–22. Berlin: Lit (Schweizerische Afrikastudien).

Hlatshwayo, Mondli. 2019. "Precarious Work and Precarious Resistance: A Case Study of Zimbabwean Migrant Women Workers in Johannesburg, South Africa." *Diaspora Studies* 12: 160–78.

Hornberger, Julia. 2018. "A Ritual of Corruption: How Young Middle-Class South Africans Get Their Driver's Licenses." *Current Anthropology* 59: S138–48.

Isichei, Elizabeth. 2004. *Voices of the Poor in Africa: Moral Economy and the Popular Imagination*. New York: Boydell and Brewer.

Jameson, Fredric. 1995. *The Geopolitical Aesthetic: Cinema and Space in the World System*. Bloomington: Indiana University Press.

Jewkes, Rachel, Yandisa Sikweyiya, Robert Morrell, and Kristin Dunkle. 2011. "Gender Inequitable Masculinity and Sexual Entitlement in Rape Perpetration South Africa: Findings of a Cross-Sectional Study." *PLoS ONE* 6 (12): e29590.

Jordan, Alex. 2018. "I'm a Travel Editor and This Is the One Place You Need to Visit This Year." *Culture Trip*. https://theculturetrip.com/africa/south-africa/articles/im-a-travel-writer-and-this-is-the-one-place-you-need-to-visit-this-year.

Knafo, S. 2017. "Why Johannesburg Is Becoming Africa's Hippest City." *Travel & Leisure*. https://www.travelandleisure.com/trip-ideas/city-vacations/johannesburg-transformation.

Kuljian, Christa. 2013. *Sanctuary: How an Inner-City Church Spilled onto a Sidewalk*. Johannesburg: Jacana Media.

Laplanche, Jean, and Jean-Bertrand Pontalis. 1988. *The Language of Psychoanalysis*. London: Hogarth Press.

Lemanski, Charlotte. 2004. "A New Apartheid? The Spatial Implications of Fear of Crime in Cape Town, South Africa." *Environment and Urbanization* 16: 101–12.

Lipman, Alan, and Howard Harris. 1999. "Fortress Johannesburg." *Environment and Planning B: Urban Analytics and City Science* 26: 727–40.

Malcomess, Bettina, and Dorothee Kreutzfeldt. 2013. *Not No Place: Johannesburg, Fragments of Spaces and Times*. Johannesburg: Fanele.

Matshikiza, John. 2004. "Instant City." *Public Culture* 16: 481–97.

Mbembe, Achille. 2008. "Aesthetics of Superfluity." In *Johannesburg: The Elusive Metropolis*, edited by Sarah Nuttall and Achille Mbembe, 37–67. Durham: Duke University Press.

Mbembe, Achille, and Sarah Nuttall. 2008. "Afropolis." In *Johannesburg: The Elusive Metropolis*, edited by Sarah Nuttall and Achille Mbembe, 1–36. Durham: Duke University Press.

Moffett, Helen. 2006. "These Women, They Force Us to Rape Them": Rape as Narrative of Social Control in Post-Apartheid South Africa." *Journal of Southern African Studies* 32: 129–44.

Mosselson, Aidan. 2018. *Vernacular Regeneration: Low-Income Housing, Private Policing and Urban Transformation in Inner-City Johannesburg*. Abingdon: Routledge.

Msimang, Sisonke. 2018. *Always Another Country: A Memoir of Exile and Home*. Melbourne: Text Publishing.

Murray, Martin J. 2008. *Taming the Disorderly City*. New York: Cornell University Press.

———. 2011. *City of Extremes: The Spatial Politics of Johannesburg*. Durham: Duke University Press.

Myambo, Melissa Tandiwe. 2018. *Reversing Urban Inequality in Johannesburg*. Abingdon: Routledge.

Nieftagodien, Noor, and Philip Bonner. 2008. *Alexandra: A History*. Johannesburg: Wits University Press.

Nightingale, Carl H. 2015. *Segregation: A Global History of Divided Cities*. Chicago: University of Chicago Press.

Nuttall, Sarah, and Achille Mbembe, eds. 2008. *Johannesburg: The Elusive Metropolis*. Durham: Duke University Press.

Rasool, Shahana, Kerry Vermaak, Robyn Pharaoh, Antoinette Louw, and Aki Stavrou. 2003. *Violence against Women: A National Survey*. Pretoria: Institute for Security Studies.

Ratele, Kopano. 2001. "Notes on the Anxieties of Belonging." *Agenda* 16: 77–82.

Sasson, Theodore. 1995. *Crime Talk: How Citizens Construct a Social Problem*. Piscataway, NJ: Transaction Publishers.

Simone, AbdouMaliq. 2004. *For the City Yet to Come: Changing African Life in Four Cities*. Durham: Duke University Press.

———. 2006. "Pirate Towns: Reworking Social and Symbolic Infrastructures in Johannesburg and Douala." *Urban Studies* 43: 357–70. https://doi.org/10.1080/00420980500146974.

———. 2008. "People as Infrastructure: Intersecting Fragments in Johannesburg." In *Johannesburg: The Elusive Metropolis*, edited by Sarah Nuttall and Achille Mbembe, 68–90. Durham: Duke University Press.

Spinks, Charlotte. 2001. "A New Apartheid? Urban Spatiality, (Fear of) Crime and Segregation in Cape Town, South Africa." *Working Paper Series*. Development Studies Institute, London School of Economic and Political Science, London.

Vearey, Joanna. 2017. "Urban Health in Johannesburg: Migration, Exclusion and Inequality." *Urban Forum* 28 (1): 1–4.

Vearey, Joanna, Kirsten Thomson, Theresa Sommers, and Courtenay Sprague. 2017. "Analysing Local-Level Responses to Migration and Urban Health in Hillbrow: The Johannesburg Migrant Health Forum." *BMC Public Health* 17 (427). https://doi.org/10.1186/s12889-017-4352-2.

Yingwana, Ntokozo, Rebecca Walker, and Alex Etchart. 2019. "Sex Work, Migration, and Human Trafficking in South Africa: From Polarised Arguments to Potential Partnerships." *Anti-Trafficking Review* 12: 74–90.

TAXI DIARIES I: WHAT ARE YOU DOING IN JOBURG?

BAELETSI TSATSI

B aeletsi Tsatsi is a storyteller from Kuruman in the Northern Cape of South Africa. She moved to Johannesburg in 2013. She lives in Norwood, a suburb in the north-east, but works all over the city. Her experiences of Johannesburg are intimately bound up with her travels on minibus taxis, the most prolific form of transport in South Africa but also the most notorious, known for reckless drivers, disintegrating vehicles and chronic overcrowding. The stories she tells here began as part of an informal chronicle on social media, named #TaxiDiaries: part autobiography, part urban ethnography, part love story and part lament.

ONE

I get inside the taxi and sit in the front seat. The driver's wife is seated there. I know she's the driver's wife because it's not the first time we're riding together. I say hi with the hope that she'll see that it's me, but she greets back without taking her eyes off the thing she is looking at. She's looking at it the way people look at an artwork – with the hope of learning the artist's intention. I follow her gaze, and this is what she's looking at: a man at the Noord taxi rank sits gracefully on one of the fallen cement dustbins, almost like a queen, his barefoot legs crossed. He is wearing layers of tattered black clothes. His hair looks like an unwashed mop that has dealt with truths that couldn't be swept under the carpet. Parts of his body that are visible look like they were dipped in black oil and his back is up straight. One hand is on his waist, the way people position themselves when they're about to ask an offending question, and the other hangs at his side holding a zol [joint] that is burning away. His eyes are looking into the distance but he can't see. We keep watching him, me and the driver's wife. I'm amazed at how he sits there and offers himself as an exhibit.

TWO

The taxi driver speaks Sesotho with a heavy accent. 'I'm sorry I don't speak isiZulu,' says each word that he speaks.

THREE

It's cold. I'm wearing a vest and a jersey. A lady sits next to me, she smells of coconut lotion and something else, it's familiar but I can't remember its name. She greets, pays and takes out her phone. I can see without glasses, I don't wear glasses, also I'm nosy, so I steal a look. On the screen is a picture of herself wearing a church uniform, white and green, and she's striking a pose. She opens her WhatsApp and searches for Bheki. She taps on his name and looks at the screen. Seconds pass and then minutes. She exits her WhatsApp and more seconds pass, she looks into the distance and sighs. She opens her WhatsApp again, goes to Bheki and writes, *Athini amakhaza?'* [How is this winter?] She presses send, looks out into the distance, this time with a smile.

FOUR

Today's driver is a newbie from Newcastle. He wears a shirt that someone bought him for the Christmas of 2000. He is so nervous, and he shows it off: 'Look at me, I don't know where I'm going,' his attitude seems to say.

FIVE

I enter a taxi with dark windows and in the first row sit four men. The taxi is loud and everyone is speaking a foreign language. I hesitate before I sit down and I fall to the seat near me because the driver starts driving off. As we get into town, a man with a heavy accent that I can't place asks to get off after the robot [traffic light]. The said robot is orange, and instead of following road rules, the driver goes through, at this point it's red. The accent man doesn't get off and the driver asks, 'Didn't someone ask to get off?' The accent man speaks: 'Yes, but I am not getting off anymore. You passed a red robot with me. You don't know how to drive.' The driver grunts and from the grunt I know that had the accent man been close by, a hot *klap* [slap] would have landed on him and thrown him out of the taxi.

SIX

It warms my heart when a taxi driver asks a question of a person and he doesn't answer, so the taxi driver asks in English, and not that mocking English. The person answers, the taxi driver hears their accent and tries to say something nice about the country they think he is from. The person smiles and tells the taxi driver where he's from, the conversation ends, and not on an awkward note but on a 'you are my brother' vibe. I really love it when Africans love each other.

1 'WE ARE ALL IN THIS TOGETHER': GLOBAL CITIZEN, VIOLENCE AND ANXIETY IN JOHANNESBURG

COBUS VAN STADEN

The genesis of this book lies in the fact that there is very little writing about anxiety in the global south. While anxiety is frequently expressed *about* the south (about population growth, or people moving north), the experience of being anxious *in* global south cities receives much less attention. However, beyond facilitating the expression of this experience, it is also important to show how these two are different but not discrete. Many global south anxieties relate to specific local realities, but others overlap with preoccupations in the north, albeit in unpredictable and oblique ways. In some cases we see transnational concern about the south colliding with, and heightening, the experience of anxiety in the south.

In this chapter I will focus on one such incident: the Global Citizen Festival, a star-studded music and philanthropic event that took place in Johannesburg in December 2018. In some respects the concert was a great success. It secured more than $7 billion in funding pledges for progressive causes and transfixed a stadium of music fans. However, it also caused an eruption of public violence outside the stadium, which significantly complicated its meaning. The subsequent controversy revealed much about Johannesburg's specific anxieties, while raising wider questions about how the changing role of the state is affecting life in cities like Johannesburg. As I will argue, the Global Citizen incident was the site of a collision between the local and the global. Specifically, it reveals much about how the functionality of the state is being affected at the local and global levels simultaneously. Johannesburg becomes a useful example informing the experience of anxiety around systemic collapse and the infiltration of state structures by outside interests in cities around the world.

GLOBAL CITIZEN: WHAT WENT DOWN

On 2 December 2018, Johannesburg hosted the Global Citizen music festival. Global Citizen has become famous as an enterprise focused on galvanising volunteerism (mostly) in the global north, in order to facilitate social change (mostly) in the global south. The organisation partners with development agencies and NGOs, but its particular strength lies in instrumentalising celebrity and fandom in order to elicit funding pledges from governments and corporations. One of its key activities is arranging music festivals around the world, which become the occasion for high-profile funding announcements.

The 2018 show was the first Global Citizen event held in Africa. It featured some of South Africa's most prominent musicians, many local and international celebrities and, most notably, an appearance by Beyoncé and Jay-Z. While both are popular in South Africa, Beyoncé enjoys particularly fervent fandom among young South Africans.

The event was held in the FNB Stadium in Soweto and was timed to commemorate the centenary of the birth of Nelson Mandela. Volunteerism has been promoted by the Nelson Mandela Foundation as a key to the Mandela legacy. This focus overlaps with that of Global Citizen, and the organisations share a tendency to promote brief bouts of popular volunteerism as a measure to deal with large systemic problems in the form of hashtagged multi-partner campaigns.

This co-branding also harked back to a South Africa still touched by the Mandela halo. It glossed over the twin facts that the ruling African National Congress is struggling to realign itself with Mandela-ism[1] against perceptions that the party is riven by infighting and riddled with corruption, and that many young people blame Mandela for favouring racial reconciliation over radical economic restructuring (Burke 2019). From the vantage point of the global north, it also evoked a time when South Africa still aligned itself explicitly with Western liberal humanism, before the Zuma era with its corruption and leaning towards Russia and China.

The news that Beyoncé and Jay-Z would headline the concert caused great excitement in South Africa, which was somewhat tempered by the fact that most of the tickets had been allocated to volunteers. Those who completed a certain number of 'actions' (mostly social media-based clicktivism) were entered into a raffle. Before the concert, the South African press ran gleeful accounts of fans who hadn't got tickets deleting the Global Citizen app from their phones. One tweeted, 'Fuck being a Global Citizen. I'm South African. Don't care about famine in Yemen or some country with unsafe drinking water. I just wanted to see Beyoncé' (Zeeman 2018a).

In the build-up to the concert, South African social media eagerly circulated any glimpse of the stars or their entourages (for example, see Thakurdin 2018a). The coverage generated ever-mounting rumours, including that Beyoncé would be joined onstage by Rihanna (Zeeman 2018b). A few days before the concert, there were reports that fans hoping to get tickets were performing 1200 volunteer actions per hour (Mjo 2018a). It was clear that the event would be a major logistical undertaking. Global Citizen and the Johannesburg metropolitan administration announced that the roads around the stadium would be closed to all drivers except those with tickets. The city would provide 166 Bus Rapid Transit System buses, 166 from the metropolitan bus service, 275 park-and-ride buses that would connect to remote parking areas and 100 Gautrain buses, which would transport attendees to the nearest station of the local light rail system, which is not yet connected to Soweto (Mjo 2018b). Minibus taxis would also provide transportation. Uber announced that it would eliminate surge pricing during the day and promised an 'UberZONE – you can expect complimentary WiFi, charging stations and a supercool lounge area' (Uber South Africa 2018).

The concert started at eleven in the morning. There were soon complaints that people were stuck in queues in the summer heat trying to get into the venue. The estimated final attendance was about 65 000. The programme was made up of a mix of local and international acts, interspersed with announcements of funding pledges from transnational corporations and European governments, as well as speeches by celebrities aimed at inspiring more volunteerism. These were presented by high-level representatives of Global Citizen's NGO partners, local celebrities and several international ones, many of whom have long relationships with South Africa. They included the talk-show host Trevor Noah; Oprah Winfrey, who founded a celebrated high school for

South African girls; and Naomi Campbell, who was rapidly memefied on Twitter for mispronouncing 'amandla'.[2]

Beyoncé and Jay-Z appeared on stage at about ten that evening. By this time the concert had been going on for about nine hours. They played a full set, including several costume changes, ending around midnight. As the crowd started to file out of the stadium, the surrounding roads were soon completely blocked by traffic. The hundreds of buses that were supposed to take people to the station were late, with some only leaving for the Gautrain stations at three in the morning, long after the last train had departed (Mjo 2018b). According to some reports, the police blocked major roads to allow VIPs to leave first. This trapped the crowd in holding areas and caused massive traffic congestion. Afterwards there were also allegations that police were redeployed to provide VIP security, leaving the crowd unprotected (*The Citizen* 2018).

At the UberZONE, it soon became clear that the mobile phone network had broken down. The closest pick-up point with a cellphone signal was a service station about 3 km away. Concert-goers had no choice but to walk there in the dark. In widely circulated clips shot by CCTV cameras at the service station, one can see several hundred people waiting for rides. The crowd is agitated and groups and regroups as bands of men rush in, trying to steal bags and phones. In some cases, violent confrontations result, with concert-goers being shoved or dragged by several men at once. Shots ring out and people start fleeing. At one stage, a stampede seems imminent (the clips are embedded in several articles I cite in this chapter; see, for example, Levitt 2018a).

Eyewitness accounts posted on Twitter fleshed out the story told by the viral footage. Several mentioned women being targeted, thrown to the ground, dragged around or kicked. Some also reported seeing women with torn clothes or covered in blood. There were allegations that some women had suffered sexual assault. The eyewitnesses agree on a few points. They say groups of robbers worked together, and that they mostly grabbed phones and bags. They were armed, with many witnesses seeing people held at knife- or gunpoint and also hearing shots. While most of the witnesses described the chaos as happening outside the stadium, some also reported seeing or experiencing robberies inside. All the witnesses say there was little or no police presence either around the stadium or at the service station. Most say they saw no police at all, while one mentions seeing numerous people crowding around a single police car, begging the single officer inside to help them, even as he kept trying to leave. Eyewitnesses who saw police officers also allege that attacks happened in clear view of the police, and that appeals for help were ignored. This melee went on for a while – some witnesses described being trapped for close to five hours, while others walked an additional 2 km to get away from the violence (Selisho 2018; Kekana 2018; Mjo 2018c; 702 News 2018a; Mjo 2018d; Sithole and Dludla 2018). Meanwhile, because of the chaos, few Uber drivers were willing to enter the area, and despite earlier promises Uber activated surge pricing to attract more drivers. After braving attacks and waiting for hours, concert-goers were faced with Uber bills sometimes totalling in excess of $100. Uber later announced they would refund these charges (Levitt 2018b).

Discussions of the incident trended on Twitter for days. The stadium management blamed the South African Police Service (SAPS) and the Johannesburg Metropolitan Police Department for the lack of security at the venue, saying that police left after the last act, in contravention of a national event security plan approved by the national police commissioner (702 News 2018b; Gous 2018). Police spokespeople kept simply insisting that officers were on the scene, despite numerous eyewitness accounts to the contrary (Levitt 2018a). When that triggered another barrage of social media criticism, they countered that the onus was on citizens to lay formal charges, complaining that only one case had been brought (Selisho 2018). Two days later, the minister of police, Bheki Cele, repeated the official denial of claims that there was a lack of police personnel on the ground, and blamed the chaos on a 'total collapse' of traffic management and the breakdown of the mobile phone signal, and suggested that aggrieved fans should contact the organisers of the event. He went on to say that 50 cases had been brought and 15 people had been arrested. The charges included three of assault, two of armed robbery, one of hijacking, and 24 of mobile phone theft (Evans 2018).

Meanwhile, journalists interviewed anonymous police, who said only junior officers were on site. They had been instructed to keep circulating around the venue in order to provide 'visible policing only so people felt safe', but when they were asked for assistance, no senior officers could grant approval, so they couldn't leave their posts (Eyewitness News 2018). Two weeks later, seven suspects appeared in court – all undocumented immigrants (Sithole and Dludla 2018). None of the South African news media enquired why, of the large number of assailants, only non-South Africans were arrested.

The day after the incident, Global Citizen Africa tweeted, 'After such an inspiring evening, we are saddened to hear the challenges people had while leaving the venue.' This was followed by three more tweets, one of which encouraged victims to make statements to the police (@GblCtz, 3 December 2018).

THE CHAOS AND THE CITY

Johannesburg wasn't Global Citizen's only debacle in 2018. In September, it held a concert in New York, which featured Janelle Monáe, Janet Jackson, Cardi B and The Weeknd. During the performance a crowd-control barrier collapsed. The sound was interpreted by some as gunshots, fuelled by the fact that the event took place on the first anniversary of a mass shooting in Las Vegas, USA. The resulting stampede caused several injuries, and it took a while to calm the crowd down, after which the concert continued (Aubrey 2018).

While this event suggests the wider psychological impact of the ongoing problem with mass shootings in the United States, I would argue that the Johannesburg incident reveals more about its city than this incident does about New York. Mass shootings are a national rather than a specifically New York problem, among other reasons because of New York State's more restrictive gun laws (Reeping et al. 2019). In comparison, the aftermath of the Global Citizen Festival in Johannesburg reveals a set of factors, and correlations between those factors, that directly relate to anxiety in the city.

Firstly, much of the chaos was caused by breakdowns in the mobile phone and traffic systems linked to nested failures in management, from the event to the city to the national level. There is no way of keeping these specific failures separate from a wider national disillusionment with public institutions that has resulted from a combination of mismanagement and corruption. Electricity breakdowns resulting from failures by electricity parastatal Eskom are a notorious example.

Eskom is a vertically integrated state-owned company that generates almost all South Africa's electricity. During the Zuma administration, Eskom became the site of massive corruption, part of a process that came to be known as state capture (Mondi 2018). This culminated in the implementation of planned rolling blackouts. Labelled 'load shedding', these rotate according to neighbourhood. Depending on where Eskom is in its cycle of dysfunction, load shedding can disappear for months, only to be suddenly reimposed out of the blue.

The result in Johannesburg has been a heightened awareness of how a single systemic breakdown can reverberate through the larger system. A badly timed bout of load shedding can knock out kilometres of traffic lights, instantly snarling the city in traffic. The same bout of load shedding can disrupt whole sections of the cellphone grid and affect the pumping of water at suburban substations. There is no real way of planning for these events, which means that the difference between an uneventful commute and sitting for hours in traffic with no way to contact home, and then arriving to dry taps, feels completely random. While the middle class[3] has been particularly vocal in complaining about these breakdowns, they affect the poor in far more severe ways, compounding already egregious lapses in service delivery.

The Global Citizen incident occurred when the city was already hyperaware of the danger of massive systemic collapse. The failure of utility networks, rising traffic congestion and the absence of adequate policing are all relatively common sources of stress in Johannesburg. The events after the concert seemed to prove not only how prevalent these systemic failures are, but also how one form of failure can trigger others, in a domino effect leading to greater and greater chaos.

Secondly, the incident made clear the lack of trust between citizens and the police. It seemed to demonstrate that ensuring public safety is relatively low on the list of the police's priorities. Police representatives' dissembling, and refusal to either accept blame or suggest mitigating measures, strengthened the perception that the police can't be trusted to fulfil a relatively neutral role (Comaroff and Comaroff 2017). The official reaction to criticism was also revealing. Eyewitnesses reported that there were few police officers on the scene, a claim backed up by widely circulated video footage. Yet the official reaction was simply to insist repeatedly that the police were there. The result is a very South African rhetorical stalemate in which government figures hunker down and repeat a clear untruth until their questioners run out of time. These moments of cognitive dissonance became a key feature of public life during the Zuma administration, which undermined the value of truth and evidence (Gebrekidan and Onishi 2018).

In the same vein, the allegation that the police were redeployed to provide VIP protection, and that the traffic chaos was partly caused by roads being closed to allow convoys of VIPs to pass, chimes with perceptions that the apparatus of the state is open to use and abuse by the elite. This perception became particularly powerful during the Zuma administration, when 'blue light brigades' – speeding motorcades carrying government or party officials accompanied by police muscling commuters out of the way – became common in the city.

Thirdly, the incident played into a core assumption that underlies the wider discourse about crime in South Africa – that visuality has a direct link to violence. In other words, one of the assumptions that accompanies crime talk in Johannesburg is the idea that criminals are always watching and waiting to pounce, and that the responsibility of protecting oneself involves keeping oneself and one's valuables hidden. This underlies the often repeated instruction not to use phones in public to avoid becoming a target. It also informs the prevalence of high walls rather than fences in many suburban areas – the instinct isn't only to keep people out, but also to block any outside gaze (Murray 2011).

According to this logic, the concert-goers became victims of crime simply because they were outside in the open. In the commentary about the incident, the fact that they had to walk 3 km to the service station was repeated with more gravity than the distance warranted. That they were exposed on the street at night already doomed them, even before the criminals showed up. Together with the (realistic) assumption that there would be no police presence and no street lighting, this also assumes the presence of a permanently deployed criminal population, ever ready to pounce the moment anyone lets their guard down. It presupposes that criminality is a permanent fixture of public space, and therefore that all public space is dangerous. This has the effect of depersonalising crime into an ever-present abstract force rather than a specific problem with causes and solutions. It also puts the responsibility for crime on the victim. The problem becomes less about the nature of the encounter and more about the choice to be in public.

In the case of Global Citizen, what becomes clear is how the realistic fear of breakdowns in utility systems is linked to this perception of an inherently hostile public space. The incident seemed to prove an assumption that the moment the systems collapsed, violent crime was inevitable. This conception of violent crime as an ever-present abstract force deflects conversations about the nature of policing or the specifics of what 'crime' really means or who are labelled as 'criminals'. The fact that the only people arrested were undocumented immigrants further deflects necessary conversations about how crime functions as a structuring element in post-apartheid society (Comaroff and Comaroff 2017; also see Landau 2012).

The incident also reveals that this narrative about crime reinforces conservative gender strictures. That the concert featured Beyoncé is key to this point. The power of Beyoncé's work is not that she achieves mass identification across cultures *despite* her specific expression of black womanhood, but that she achieves it *through* her expression of black womanhood. Her work contains much meta-commentary on her own success, making an explicit connection between her personal work ethic and that of black women as they strive to overcome structural inequality (Lordi 2017). While her sheer stardom would make a Beyoncé performance in South Africa a major event by any reckoning, it was of particular importance to black women and LGBTQ+ people. Video footage of the concert revealed how big an occasion it was for them. Many had travelled from all over the country to attend.

This is where the role of visuality in public space becomes apparent. My life partner briefly attended the festival (he left early) and went dressed in a flowing kimono-like robe. Afterwards he described how he realised that this fashion choice was a mistake the moment he arrived. Already in the afternoon, crowds of men were gathered around the entrances, and as the groups of women and gay men in jewellery and party outfits passed them, the space became striated by hostile gazes. Even though no skirmishes erupted that afternoon, the play of visuality predicted the violent events to come.

The attacks on the concert-goers outside the venue can't simply be read from the perspective of class. Of course, the wealth gap between those who attended the Global Citizen concert and those who robbed them outside the stadium is significant. Keep in mind that South Africa has some of the highest mobile data prices in the world, so the constant tweeting it took to become eligible for the ticket raffle already put the concert out of the range of many South Africans (Tshwane 2019). However, the attacks on women and LGBTQ+ concert-goers by cisgender men added a second layer of meaning to the violence. The many accounts of objects being snatched away from them, the sexualised nature of some of the violence (eyewitnesses described an attempted rape in front of a crowd), clothes being torn, and weaves, braids and wigs being pulled, spoke of a form of violent policing of gender expression in public space.

The post-concert chaos was largely read by most commentators in the context of Johannesburg's history of violent crime. But it can also be read as part of a different history, one of attacks on non-traditional gender expression on the street. This runs the gamut from women being harassed in taxi ranks for wearing short skirts to murderous attacks on transgender and gender-nonconforming people and the constant scourge of so-called corrective rape of lesbians (Koraan and Geduld 2015). Beyond the violent economic exchange of robbery, this becomes the violent monopolising of public space by cisgender men, and the related suppression of other forms of gender expression in public. A report published in 2016 by a coalition of LGBTQ+ rights organisations found that during the preceding 24 months, 38 per cent of black LGBTQ+ respondents reported being verbally insulted on the street, 21 per cent physically threatened, and 19 per cent chased or followed. Forty-nine per cent knew of someone who had been murdered for being or appearing LGBTQ+ (OUT LGBT Well-Being 2016).

These incidents show the arbitrary nature of how 'crime' is delineated in relation to other violent offences. If a woman's or LGBTQ+ person's phone is stolen while they are being harassed, does that turn the interaction into a 'criminal' one rather than one aimed at reproducing patriarchal hegemony with a convenient bonus phone? Crime is usually presented as a socially disruptive force, but it also has the paradoxical effect of maintaining social hegemonies.

The Global Citizen incident forces us to think more clearly about the rhetorical role of 'crime' in the structuring of public space in South Africa. One has to ask what the term means in the context of institutionalised state capture. As Jean and John Comaroff (2017, 52) have argued:

> crime has become the discursive medium in which South Africans speak to each other about the limits and excesses of government, about citizenship and the cleavages that sunder the body politic, about material and moral economy, about their nightmares, needs, and insecurities. It is, in other words, a master signifier for the diagnosis of social division, disruption, difference, disorder.

Crime becomes an anxious lingua franca in which Johannesburgers talk about the state – both its absence (the lack of effective policing, lapses in the judicial system, even missing street lights) and its mutated over-presence (corruption, state capture). In the process, crime has ceased to be a problem with causes and solutions, instead becoming a permanent structuring element of society.

In its aftermath, the Global Citizen incident was discussed as a form of local criminality outside the stadium impinging on a noble attempt to promote philanthropy within it (most notably by Global Citizen itself; see @GblCtz, 3 December 2018). I would argue this is a misreading. Rather, while it revealed the level of dysfunction in Johannesburg, the incident can also be read as Johannesburg revealing a deeper set of realities about Global Citizen.

GLOBAL CITIZEN, SOUTH AFRICA AND THE WORLD

I have argued that visuality plays a key role in how Johannesburg understands the relation of crime to public space. Visuality structured the response to the Global Citizen incident as well. In the first place, the viral video of the attacks short-circuited the usual tendency for crime in Johannesburg to remain invisible but endlessly narrated. While these crimes were certainly narrated, the video record of the incident arguably bolstered the popular reaction against the police, as we have seen.

On a wider level, visuality played into reactions to the incident, with South Africans worrying about how it would look to the outside world. For example, in an op-ed in which he compared the incident to crocodiles picking off migrating wildebeest in the Maasai Mara, the country's former chief statistician, Pali Lehohla (2019), complained, 'On such a grand stage of the Global Citizen Concert the criminality that was displayed to the world and to potential investors was of concern.'

Anxiety about how domestic incidents look to foreign investors is a constant theme in South African discourse. These worries aren't baseless: government scandals have indeed resulted in sudden plunges in the value of the country's currency. However, they are also narratives of national abjection, with the country trying to hide its shame as ratings agencies and other god-like entities look right through it. The flip side of this narrative can perhaps be found in Gilles Deleuze's classic reading of Leopold von Sacher-Masoch, in which the masochist's abjection is also magnetic, and abjection means one is perpetually the centre of attention (Deleuze 1999).

This highly visualised oscillation between pride and abjection, between high achievement and failure at reaching even minimal standards, is a key aspect of South African identity, which needs more unpacking than I have space for here. South Africa is more than the cliché of a global south country traumatised by its past and hindered by a lack of local capacity in the global race towards development. Aspects of this narrative are certainly true of South Africa, but one of the fundamental ways in which it differs from this stereotype is its striking history of melding pride and abjection into a new source of visuality, one where the constant repetition of its many problems paradoxically lends it a kind of glamour. This isn't necessarily true for other countries in the global south – it is a result of South Africa's long history of mediation as a form of political struggle, one which dates back to the liberation forces' sophisticated wielding of international media coverage against the apartheid regime.

The entire Global Citizen experience (including, but extending far beyond, the post-concert violence) shows that Johannesburg lies at the centre of this South African strain of visuality. Global Citizen visualised a paradox where the city is at once the seat of horrors both developmental and criminal, and yet a site from which these problems can be viewed at a distance. Johannesburg is strangely glamorous, not despite its many problems, but because of them.[4] If staging the Global Citizen Festival in Johannesburg provided a frame for this oscillation of visualities, then the post-concert violence is the moment when these irreconcilable perspectives crashed into each other.

The 'what will investors think' narrative presents the country as unmasked in its abjection by the Global Citizen experience. However, one could also argue that in choosing Johannesburg as a venue, Global Citizen bit off more than it could chew, and that by attempting to shoehorn the seething city into a narrative of liberal philanthropy, Global Citizen was itself revealed. But revealed as what?

Global Citizen is an advocacy organisation founded in 2008. It is headquartered in New York, with offices in the United Kingdom, Germany, Canada and Australia. While it is a US-registered 501(c)3 non-governmental organisation, it doesn't operate like a conventional NGO. It is more accurate to describe it as a hybrid between an advocacy organisation, a media platform and an events organiser. In its own words, 'Through our mix of content and events, grassroots organising and extensive reach through our digital channels, we are building the world's largest movement for social action' (Globalcitizen. org 2019a).

What does this social action constitute? Global Citizen names the ending of global extreme poverty as its core objective. This is pursued through partnerships with large multi-cause organisations (UNICEF, the Bill and Melinda Gates Foundation, Oxfam, the World Bank Group) and single-cause NGOs (Human Rights Watch, Transparency International, the Rainforest Alliance and many others). It also has partnerships with celebrity foundations, including Beyoncé's BeyGood, Bono's ONE, the Jamie Oliver Food Foundation and FC Barcelona Foundation (Globalcitizen.org 2019d).

For Global Citizen, taking action most often means engaging on social media. One of its core activities is to forge links between partner organisations and social media users. It makes no distinction between traditional forms of engagement (volunteering, protesting) and actions like tweeting. This allows it to claim that, thanks to its campaigns between 2011 and 2017, '21,369,761 actions [were] taken' which ostensibly led to commitments of $35 billion, of which $10 billion has been disbursed (Globalcitizen.org 2019b). The sums cited here are from governments and companies rather than from small-scale donations by individual members. Instead of donating money, these volunteers donate attention, both theirs and their social media followers'.

The clearest demonstration of this system in action is a live social media feed on the organisation's website (https://www.globalcitizen.org/en/), which lists 'actions' taken by so-called global citizens in real time. Most of the posts on this rolling ribbon highlight individuals taking one of three actions: sending an email, tweeting, or signing an online petition. In each case, the materials tweeted or emailed are prepared by Global Citizen or its partners. Each of these actions earns the sender a point, which goes towards making them eligible for ticket lotteries for upcoming Global Citizen Festival events.

Celebrity forms a key link between Global Citizen, its institutional partners and its social media followers. Many of its pre-prepared materials come with a celebrity endorsement. For example, one urges recipients to 'Stand with Demi Lovato and ask world leaders to prioritise mental health in emergency settings' (Globalcitizen.org 2019c). Each action earns a follower a point, which could enable closer access to celebrity at Global Citizen events. Celebrities function as both an incentive to action and an implicit guarantor that the action has value. At the same time, these events become yet another vector for celebrity influence, lending ethical weight to star personas while expanding the platforms where celebrity is enacted (Chouliaraki 2012). This became clear in Johannesburg, with local celebrities who have become famous as TV presenters or Instagram clothes horses earnestly introducing themselves as 'activists'.

But more than a simple vector for celebrity, Global Citizen becomes a platform where elites of many stripes meet in a halo of performative righteousness in front of a transnational audience. As well as Oprah, Naomi and Beyoncé, Global Citizen Johannesburg featured at least five heads of state, several US senators, the head of the World Bank, the deputy secretary-general of the United Nations, the director-general of the World Health Organization and senior executives of transnational corporations, including Procter & Gamble, Cisco, Johnson & Johnson, and Microsoft (Shah 2018a, 2018b; Masemola 2018).

While Global Citizen portrays itself as a movement of ordinary people, its real power lies in its ability to provide a stage for elites. In the process, it also flattens the distinctions between different kinds of elites. It dissolves the gaps between entertainers, executives and bureaucrats while reinforcing an absolute barrier between elite and non-elite, even as it continuously pays lip service to the power of ordinary people to change the world.

Its dependence on the endorsement and participation of these elites inevitably makes Global Citizen party to the strategies of mediation that naturalise the massive power gap between elite and non-elite in the twenty-first century. In the context of the Johannesburg concert, this is clearly visible in two press accounts of Naomi Campbell giving a news conference at the announcement of the Global Citizen concert in July 2018. In the first (Thakurdin 2018b), Campbell (described as a 'model and philanthropist' – elite distinctions dissolved) is aligned with Nelson Mandela's humanitarian legacy. She urges South Africans to join Global Citizen's anti-poverty drive, saying, 'It is no longer possible to bury our head in the sand and pretend our brothers and sisters do not exist. We are all in this together.' In the second account, the journalist Jessica Levitt (2018c) complains that at this same conference Campbell refused to have her picture taken by anyone except her own photographer, refused to answer questions beyond her anti-poverty statement, and cancelled a series of interviews at the last moment because she had apparently overslept. In a striking foretaste of the SAPS's reaction to the violence a few months later, her publicist simply insisted that these interviews had in fact taken place.

Comparing these two articles provides a glimpse into how the rough angles of celebrity power are sanded down by mediation in order to present a persona falling in line with, and bolstering, a narrative of liberal philanthropy (a process critiqued by Chouliaraki 2012; see also Hasian 2016). It also, however, reveals that the dissolution of elite boundaries includes those between northern and southern elites. At the news conference Campbell was flanked by the South African mining mogul Patrice Motsepe and Kweku Mandela, a grandson of Nelson Mandela and the executive producer of the event. The conflation of Global Citizen's brand of social media-driven clicktivism with Nelson Mandela's legacy of democratic struggle was not imposed externally: rather, it was developed from within a southern elite sitting at the heart of the party–government nexus shaping all aspects of life in Johannesburg.

Both Motsepe and Mandela were key to bringing Global Citizen to Johannesburg, and their involvement complicates the simple critique that this form of mediated philanthropy imposes northern priorities on the global south. Rather, it raises questions about the dissolution of the boundaries between the state and transnational non-state actors. Motsepe used the concert as an occasion to commit $243 million to land reform in South Africa, without disclosing how this money will be spent or how his foundation plans to fit this into the highly contentious legal and constitutional questions surrounding land reform. More crucially, it is still unclear what the relationship is between the government, the Motsepe Foundation, the ANC and Global Citizen in relation to land reform, and where the government's stewardship of complex, potentially explosive processes like land reform ends and these other actors' begins (Davis 2018).

While it is not my intention to accuse any of these participants of wrongdoing, I have to point out that the dissolution of the institutional barriers between state, party and non-state actors also lies at the heart of the state-capture crisis that has defined life in Johannesburg for the past number of years. The funding commitments aimed at traditional government functions like development and disease prevention formed a counterpoint to findings by successive commissions into state capture that many other government functions (electricity generation, tax enforcement) have been hijacked from the inside (Thamm 2018; Smit 2019). Just as massive transnational companies were pledging money at Global Citizen, revelations were emerging that other massive transnational companies (KPMG, McKinsey) were intimately involved in irregular dealings with the South African state (Omarjee 2018).

The dissolution of the barriers between elites takes place in contrast to the strengthening of the barrier between elites and non-elites. Nothing illustrates this more starkly than the violence itself. As I mentioned above, one cause of the violence was the fact that police oversight and road access were monopolised by providing safe passage to VIPs, while thousands of attendees were held back at choke points and left without protection. Johannesburg's local problems exacerbated the effect of this use of state mechanisms to enforce elite privilege, but such enforcement is increasingly a global phenomenon.

While the hijacking of the mechanisms of state by corrupt private actors, the deadlocking of these mechanisms by powerful political parties, and the bolstering of these machinations by powerful corporations all contribute to local anxiety in the form of rolling blackouts, chaotic traffic jams and a constant economic malaise, these factors are not unique to Johannesburg. Similar issues are at play in London, Washington and Paris. Johannesburg's Global Citizen episode is a symptom of wider trends that are adding to anxiety everywhere: the growing gap between elite and non-elite, the erosion of the barriers between political and other elites, the abdication of traditional government duties to non-state actors and the unchecked power of transnational corporations.

CONCLUSION

Global Citizen becomes, then, a kind of double lens. Looking through one end, one has a wide-angle view of a shifting moment in global development. The other end reveals in miniature how a few systemic glitches can ripple through a vulnerable city, causing violence and disruption. The importance of the incident lies in the way it warps those two perspectives into one. While campaigning against extreme poverty, the concert inadvertently caused running battles with knife-wielding poor people. While activating the inspirational power of black female self-expression, it managed to plunge black women expressing themselves into danger.

However, the incident is important beyond these ironies, in ways that are closely tied to the urban anxiety it revealed in Johannesburg. In the first place, it acted as confirmation of a set of nested assumptions that lie at the heart of (some of) Johannesburg's anxieties. These include the ideas that the city is always on the verge of systemic collapse, that one failure will rapidly trigger several more, and that public space is so dangerous that any form of failure will lead to public violence.

In the second place, it seemed to confirm an assumption that if such a domino effect takes place, residents of Johannesburg can't rely on the organs of the state. It entrenched perceptions of the police as ineffectual and disengaged. It also confirmed that even pervasive evidence of dysfunction will be met with official denials and dissembling. Not only will the government not help solve the problem, but just getting them to admit that there is a problem is almost impossible.

In the third place, it raises questions about the nature of crime in Johannesburg. While complaints about 'crime' are ubiquitous, the event showed that crime isn't a purely disruptive force. It also has the role of enforcing other hierarchies, notably gendered ones. This opens a very small door into a much bigger conversation about what South Africans mean when they talk about 'crime'.

The Global Citizen incident was a moment when these local realities crashed into a global media machine weaving together governmental, intergovernmental, corporate and celebrity power. The division between upwardly mobile and middle-class Johannesburgers and the poor people robbing them was dwarfed by the line Global Citizen itself draws between elites and non-elites. While the incident made clear the brewing conflict at the heart of Johannesburg, it also showed how global trends are putting both the attackers and the attacked on the same side – crowded behind barriers protecting a powerful elite where distinctions between north and south, celebrity and politician, have become meaningless.

One of the biggest problems we faced in editing this volume was avoiding the lure of 'proving' that Johannesburgers are somehow objectively tenser than their counterparts in other big cities. The reality of systemic failure and public violence revealed by the Global Citizen incident provides a counter-methodology, by showing what some of this anxiety looks like in real life. However, it also points towards larger anxieties that underlie them: about the infiltration of state organs, the interface between corporate and governmental power, and the lack of legal jurisdiction over transnational entities. These are concerns that affect the United States under the Trump administration, the United Kingdom under Brexit, and other societies, where the extent of the infiltration of state institutions has not yet become clear. South Africans arguably know more about life under these conditions than their counterparts in other countries. In this sense, Johannesburg's anxiety might not be greater; it might just be manifesting a little earlier than elsewhere.

NOTES

1   While Nelson Mandela's legacy is complex, I define Mandela-ism as a focus on social
     justice, reconciliation and human rights, both domestically and as a basis for foreign policy.

2   'Amandla' means 'power' in Nguni languages. It was a popular rallying cry under
      apartheid. It is usually uttered by a leader, and answered with 'Awethu' or 'Ngawethu'
      ('to us') by the group. Campbell pronounced it as 'Amandala'.

3   This chapter uses terms like 'poor', 'middle class', 'elite' and 'non-elite' in order to
      approximate broad categories of lived experience. However, given apartheid's cursed
      conflation of race and class, and post-apartheid's rapid social mobility for a minority
      of black South Africans while the majority remain trapped in poverty and stagnation,
      the complexity of class in contemporary South Africa would take several books to
      unpack. The continuing legacy of white privilege adds to this complexity, in the sense
      that categories like 'middle class' and 'elite' further splinter along racial lines. Finally, the
      legacy of apartheid's vast immiseration is that the 'middle class' is hardly middle. From
      the perspective of the majority of the country, the middle class is itself an elite. However,
      while the trappings of middle-class life (a car, a security gate to protect the car) might
      seem absurdly luxurious to many poor South Africans, one needs to distinguish this way
      of life from those whose proximity to the levers of power and commerce shapes the lives
      of both the poor and the middle class. That said, categories like 'elite' and 'non-elite' are
      fundamentally approximations standing in for much more complex realities.

4   Johannesburg isn't alone in this tendency. I would argue that in staging visual spectacle
      combining glamour and horror, abjection and fashion, cities like Rio de Janeiro, Lagos
      and Mumbai occupy a similar place in the global imaginary. It is notable that these
      cities are all regional media hubs, and this arguably adds to the complexity of their
      global representation. However, the tangled north–south media economies underlying
      something like Global Citizen demand unpacking at much greater length.

REFERENCES

Aubrey, Elizabeth. 2018. "Barrier Collapse at Global Citizen Festival Leads to Mass Panic and
    Injuries amid 'Stampede'." *New Music Express*, 30 September 2018. https://www.nme.
    com/news/music/barrier-collapse-global-citizen-festival-leads-mass-panic-
    multiple-injuries-2384905.

Burke, Jason. 2019. "Struggling South Africans Lose Faith in Nelson Mandela's Legacy." *The
    Guardian*, 5 May 2019. https://www.theguardian.com/world/2019/may/05/south-africa-
    reaches-new-crossroads-25-years-after-free-elections.

Chouliaraki, Lilie. 2012. "The Theatricality of Humanitarianism: A Critique of Celebrity
    Advocacy." *Communication and Critical/Cultural Studies* 9 (1): 1–21.

Citizen, The. 2018. "Editorial: Police Arrogance over Global Citizen Criminality Bodes
    Ill for SA." *The Citizen*, 4 December 2018. https://citizen.co.za/news/opinion/

opinion-editorials/2044984/police-arrogance-over-global-citizen-concert-criminality-bodes-ill-for-sa/.

Comaroff, Jean, and John L. Comaroff. 2017. *The Truth about Crime: Sovereignty, Knowledge, Social Order*. Johannesburg: Wits University Press.

Davis, Rebecca. 2018. "Big Money Flexes Big Muscle at Global Citizen Festival." *Daily Maverick*, 4 December 2018. https://www.dailymaverick.co.za/article/2018-12-04-big-money-flexes-big-muscle-at-global-citizen-festival/.

Deleuze, Gilles. 1999. *Masochism: Coldness & Cruelty & Venus in Furs*. Boston: MIT Press.

Evans, Jenni. 2018. "15 Arrested after Global Citizen Festival Attacks, Says Cele." *News24*, 5 December 2018. https://www.news24.com/SouthAfrica/News/15-arrested-after-global-citizen-festival-violence-says-cele-20181205.

Eyewitness News. 2018. "SAPS Only Tasked with Visible Policing at Global Citizen Festival, Say Sources." *Eyewitness News*, 7 December 2018. https://ewn.co.za/2018/12/07/saps-only-tasked-with-visible-policing-at-global-citizen-festival-say-sources.

Gebrekidan, Selam, and Norimitsu Onishi. 2018. "Corruption Gutted South Africa's Tax Agency: Now the Nation Is Paying the Price." *New York Times*, 10 June 2018. https://www.nytimes.com/2018/06/10/world/africa/south-africa-corruption-taxes.html.

Globalcitizen.org. 2019a. "How We Work." https://www.globalcitizen.org/en/about/who-we-are/.

———. 2019b. "Global Citizen's Total Impact to Date." https://www.globalcitizen.org/en/content/global-citizens-total-impact-to-date/.

———. 2019c. "Join Demi Lovato: Ask World Leaders to Prioritise Mental Health in Emergencies." https://www.globalcitizen.org/en/action/mental-health-emergencies/.

———. 2019d. "Discover Our Partners." https://www.globalcitizen.org/en/partners/.

Gous, Nico. 2018. "We're Not Responsible for Global Citizen Security, Says Stadium Management." *TimesLive*, 3 December 2018. https://www.timeslive.co.za/news/south-africa/2018-12-03-we-were-not-responsible-for-global-citizen-security-says-stadium-management/.

Hasian, Marouf. 2016. *Humanitarian Aid and the Impoverished Rhetoric of Celebrity Advocacy*. New York: Peter Lang.

Kekana, Chrizelda. 2018. "Lasizwe: I Almost Died at the #GlobalCitizenFestivalSA." *TimesLive*, 3 December 2018. https://www.timeslive.co.za/tshisa-live/tshisa-live/2018-12-03-watch--lasizwe-i-almost-died-at-the-globalcitizenfestivalsa/.

Koraan, Rene, and Allison Geduld. 2015. "'Corrective Rape' of Lesbians in the Era of Transformative Constitutionalism in South Africa." *Potchefstroom Electronic Law Journal* 18 (5): 1930–52.

Landau, Loren. 2012. *Exorcising the Demons Within: Xenophobia, Violence and Statecraft in Contemporary South Africa*. Tokyo: United Nations University Press.

Lehohla, Pali. 2019. "The Criminality Displayed at the Madiba Concert Is of Concern: Op-ed." *Business Report*, 15 January 2019. https://www.iol.co.za/business-report/opinion/the-criminality-displayed-at-the-madiba-concert-is-of-concern-18814110.

Levitt, Jessica. 2018a. "Shocking! CCTV Shows Crime Chaos at Sasol Garage after Global Citizen Festival." *TimesLive*, 4 December 2018. https://www.timeslive.co.za/news/south-africa/2018-12-04-watch--shocking-cctv-shows-crime-chaos-at-sasol-garage-after-global-citizen-festival/.

———. 2018b. "Uber Offers Refunds after Admitting to Surge Pricing at Global Citizen Festival." *Business Day*, 3 December 2018. https://www.businesslive.co.za/bd/companies/2018-12-03-uber-offers-refunds-after-admitting-to-surge-pricing-at-global-citizen-festival/.

———. 2018c. "How Naomi Campbell Censored the Media: Op-ed." *Sunday Times*, 12 July 2018. https://www.timeslive.co.za/tshisa-live/tshisa-live/2018-07-12-how-naomi-campbell-censored-sa-media/.

Lordi, Emily. 2017. "Surviving the Hustle: Beyoncé's Performance of Work." *Black Camera* 9 (1): 131–45.

Masemola, Mokgethwa. 2018. "Full List of Global Citizen Speakers, Emcees, Performers and Celebrity Appearances!" *Daily Sun*, 29 November 2018. https://www.dailysun.co.za/News/Entertainment/full-list-of-global-citizen-speakers-emcees-performers-and-celebrity-appearances-20181129.

Mjo, Odwa. 2018a. "Global Citizen Build-Up: Everything You Need to Know." *TimesLive*, 29 November 2018. https://www.timeslive.co.za/tshisa-live/tshisa-live/2018-11-29-global-citizen-build-up-everything-you-need-to-know/.

———. 2018b. "Global Citizen Drama: The Plans vs the Reality." *TimesLive*, 4 December 2018. https://www.timeslive.co.za/news/south-africa/2018-12-04-global-citizen-drama-the-plans-vs-the-reality/.

———. 2018c. "Witnesses Describe How They Fought Off Muggers at the Global Citizen Festival." *TimesLive*, 3 December 2018. https://www.timeslive.co.za/news/south-africa/2018-12-03-witnesses-describe-how-they-fought-off-muggers-at-global-citizen-festival/.

———. 2018d. "My Global Citizen Festival: A Chaotic End to a Beautiful Night." *TimesLive*, 5 December 2018. https://www.timeslive.co.za/tshisa-live/tshisa-live/2018-12-05-my-global-citizen-festival-a-chaotic-end-to-a-beautiful-night/.

Mondi, Lumkile. 2018. "State, Market and Competition: Can Eskom Be Rescued?" *Viewpoints* 3 (September 2018). Centre for Development and Enterprise. https://www.africaportal.org/publications/state-market-and-competition-can-eskom-be-rescued/.

Murray, Martin J. 2011. *City of Extremes: The Spatial Politics of Johannesburg.* Durham: Duke University Press.

Omarjee, Lameez. 2018. "State Capture: 4 Companies That Owe SA Billions." *Fin24*, 10 September 2018. https://www.fin24.com/Economy/state-capture-4-companies-that-owe-sa-millions-20180910.

OUT LGBT Well-Being. 2016. "Love Not Hate: Hate Crimes against Lesbian, Gay, Bisexual and Transgender (LGBT) People in South Africa, 2016." http://out.org.za/index.php/library/reports#.

Reeping, Paul M., Magdalena Cerdá, Bindu Kalesan, Sandro Galea, and Charles Branas. 2019. "State Gun Laws, Gun Ownership, and Mass Shootings in the US: Cross Sectional Time Series." *British Medical Journal* 364. https://doi.org/10.1136/bmj.l542.

Selisho, Kaunda. 2018. "Sasol Trends at Number Two for Global Citizen Robberies." *The Citizen*, 3 December 2018. https://citizen.co.za/news/south-africa/2044857/sasol-trends-at-number-two-for-global-citizen-robberies/.

702 News. 2018a. "'I've Never Been So Scared in My Life,' Says Global Citizen Fest Fan." 702 News, 3 December 2018. http://www.702.co.za/articles/329384/listen-i-have-never-been-so-scared-in-my-life-says-global-citizen-fest-fan.

———. 2018b. "Stadium Management SA Confirms Fans' Bad Experiences after Global Citizen Fest." 702 News, 3 December 2018. http://www.702.co.za/articles/329396/stadium-management-sa-confirms-fans-bad-experiences-after-global-citizen-fest.

Shah, Neha. 2018a. "These Dignitaries Are Attending the Global Citizen Festival: Mandela 100." *Global Citizen*, 13 November 2018. https://www.globalcitizen.org/en/content/mandela-100-dignitary-announcement/.

———. 2018b. "Global Citizens Help Fulfil Mandela's Vision of Ending Extreme Poverty by Taking 5.6m Actions." *Global Citizen*, 3 December 2018. https://www.globalcitizen.org/en/content/mandela-100-impact-report-2018/.

Sithole, Sthembiso, and Siphelele Dludla. 2018. "Undocumented Foreigners to Appear in Court over Global Citizen Chaos." *The Star*, 19 December 2018. https://www.iol.co.za/the-star/news/undocumented-foreigners-to-appear-in-court-over-global-citizen-chaos-18560165.

Smit, Sara. 2019. "Zondo Commission: Eskom 'Fooled the System' to Pay the Guptas." *Mail & Guardian*, 5 March 2018. https://mg.co.za/article/2019-03-05-zondo-commission-eskom-fooled-the-system-to-pay-the-guptas.

Thakurdin, Karishma. 2018a. "Beyoncé's Band Gets into Gear for #GlobalCitizenFestivalSA." *TimesLive*, 29 November 2018. https://www.timeslive.co.za/tshisa-live/tshisa-live/2018-11-29-watch--beyoncs-band-gets-into-gear-for-globalcitizenfestivalsa/.

———. 2018b. "Naomi Campbell on Fighting Poverty: We Are All in This Together." *TimesLive*, 10 July 2018. https://www.timeslive.co.za/tshisa-live/tshisa-live/2018-07-10-naomi-campbell-on-fighting-poverty-we-are-all-in-this-together/.

Thamm, Marianne. 2018. "Nugent Commission Final Report Recommends Criminal Prosecution and Far Reaching Changes to Restore SARS." *Daily Maverick*, 14 December 2018. https://www.dailymaverick.co.za/article/2018-12-14-nugent-commission-final-report-recommends-criminal-prosecution-and-far-reaching-changes-to-restore-sars/.

Tshwane, Tebogo. 2019. "South African Data Prices Not Dropping Fast Enough." *Moneyweb*, 25 April 2019. https://www.moneyweb.co.za/news/tech/south-african-data-prices-not-dropping-fast-enough/.

Uber South Africa. 2018. "Ride with Uber to the Global Citizen Festival: Mandela 100 #DriveChange." 28 November 2018. https://www.uber.com/en-ZA/blog/global-citizen-festival-mandela-100/.

Zeeman, Kyle. 2018a. "8 Hilarious Global Citizen Meltdowns." *TimesLive*, 28 November 2018. https://www.timeslive.co.za/tshisa-live/tshisa-live/2018-11-28-8-hilarious-global-citizen-meltdowns/.

———. 2018b. "Calm Down, Fam! Rihanna ISN'T in SA for the Global Citizen Festival." *TimesLive*, 30 November 2018. https://www.timeslive.co.za/tshisa-live/tshisa-live/2018-11-30-calm-down-fam-rihanna-isnt-in-sa-for-the-global-citizen-festival/.

2 'IT'S NOT NICE TO BE POOR IN JOBURG': COMPENSATED RELATIONSHIPS AS SOCIAL SURVIVAL IN THE CITY

LEBOHANG MASANGO

I remember years ago on Twitter, Mapule, the girl from Botswana? Yes, I remember we were talking about this blessee–blesser thing. I think there was an episode of *Checkpoint* and they were talking about that.[1] I remember she tweeted, and she said something *so* interesting. She was like, 'I haven't lived in Joburg but from what I hear, it's not the best place to be poor' – which is so true! She was explaining why she sort of understood why young women would want to date older men for money – because it's not nice to be poor in Joburg … You either have the phone, or you don't. You either go on the holidays, or you don't. You either wear the clothes, or you don't. You either go to the clubs and pop bottles, or you don't – and you *want* to. It's not nice to not live a nice life in Joburg … You don't want to be poor in Joburg. It's not nice to be on the outside looking in, in Joburg.[2]

This quotation comes from an interview that I conducted for a piece of social anthropology research with 'blessees' in Johannesburg: the latest moniker for young women who date older, moneyed men and display their conspicuous consumption on their social media accounts.[3] In the study, I conducted participant observation with three middle-class, university-educated women in their twenties who are on Twitter and engage in what can be called compensated relationships. This phrase is derived from 'compensated dating', a phenomenon in Eastern Europe and Asia where adolescent girls are given money for companionship and intimacy (see Swader and Vorobeva 2015; Li 2015); here, it is applied to consenting adult women in their twenties and older. The aim of this chapter is to establish how young women in the high-pressure city of Johannesburg define and practise love and intimacy in their romantic relationships in the era of social media and the #blessed lifestyle.

Olivia, a 26-year-old candidate attorney, is in an exclusive relationship with Siyabonga, an advocate in his forties, who regularly gives her money. She lives in Johannesburg, works in Pretoria, and constantly moves between the two cities to socialise. In the interview quoted above she refers to a Twitter interaction with Mapule, a woman from Botswana, whose anecdote is evidence of Johannesburg's far-reaching notoriety.

I begin with this response from Olivia because it illustrates the connection between spatial location, romantic relationships and the anxiety that underscores them both. It indicates that Johannesburg is characterised by consumerism, as demonstrated by Olivia's lived experiences, Mapule's perceptions of the city, and the fact that *Checkpoint*, a current affairs television programme, would dedicate an episode to compensated relationships in the city. This chapter highlights space and objects in order to show how the social context of Johannesburg shapes young women's romantic subjectivities and how they use their mobile phones to navigate it. Compensated relationships are a continuation of people's strategies to navigate socio-economic inequalities and the pressures of consumerism in Johannesburg. Mobile phones, as objects of consumption, play a significant role in the safety strategies of these vulnerable young women.

JOHANNESBURG

Johannesburg is filled with young people. Braam, as Braamfontein is colloquially known, is located in the inner city and it is here that most of my research occurred. It is home to the University of the Witwatersrand (Wits), alongside other smaller tertiary institutions, with a residential population that consists of many students, including those attending the University of Johannesburg (UJ) in neighbouring Auckland Park. In addition to apartments and institutions of learning, the area is full of offices, shops, restaurants, fashion outlets and small nightclubs. It is constantly humming with activity, and the booming sounds of bass-heavy music on most weekends make it a trendy hub for students, creative people, tourists and low-income residents. Johannesburg is also home to many, like 22-year-old Bohlale, who leave smaller home towns to pursue higher education and at the same time experience a new city: 'Joburg's okay. I like the fact that there's a place for everyone here. Whatever you're into, you can find your people here. In Bloemfontein, it isn't that diverse.'

Bohlale is studying for her undergraduate degree at Wits University. As a residential student, she spends a lot of time in Braam and the upmarket suburb of Rosebank. Extending her presence to virtual spaces has not only widened her dating scope to include men from all over the world, but it has also influenced how she experiences other people in the city:

> Joburg is something else. I think if there's any city that can show you what dating is like in the modern world, then Johannesburg would be it, because particularly through online dating and sugaring[4] I've seen how, first of all, you are exposed to not just people who are different to you in culture or language, or anything like that, but literally people come from different parts of the world and have polar opposite worldviews.

As with many other major cities, Johannesburg is home to a multicultural population. Olivia has Congolese heritage and her well-travelled parents moved to South Africa before she was born. When she is not at work, she spends weekends with her friends socialising in Braam and Sandton. Like Bohlale, she is not a Johannesburg native. From this position, she has observed that the city has a unique 'hustle' about it:

> You know, this is a place you come to when you want to do better in life. You want to make more money, you want to be exposed to more opportunities … I know my parents always say that when they got here, Joburg was *that* place. *It just was*. It reminded them of New York, it reminded them of like London – very fast-paced, very expensive.

Olivia's response shows Johannesburg as having global flair and appeal, drawing in South Africans and immigrants alike with opportunities to improve their quality of life. Her mention of her parents reflects that this ideal of the city spans generations.

Sonto has had a different experience. She regularly socialises all over the city, and as someone who has lived all of her life here, she expresses a particular fatigue about its pace: 'It's a super-fast place, man … It's just a very draining space. I think if you don't have a place to recharge, you might just burn out in this space. Honestly. It's very, very demanding.'

These young women's backgrounds affect their perceptions of Johannesburg differently. For those who originate elsewhere, the city's fast-paced nature holds a positive allure that attracts them to settle and seek out opportunities. The ways in which online dating experiences have opened up Bohlale's worldview show the symbiotic relationship that exists between physical and virtual spaces.

Descriptions of Johannesburg in terms of its pace, diversity and opportunities reflect the popularity of Gauteng as a migration destination. Out of all of the South African provinces, it receives the highest number of internal migrants, with numbers calculated at 1 596 896 for the years 2016 to 2021 (Statistics SA 2018a, 15). In the same vein, the City of Johannesburg markets itself as 'a world-class African city', which has been the subject of controversy owing to its urban rejuvenation project aimed at reassimilating it 'into the civilised white world of corporate respectability' (Bremner 2000, 191) amid a declining economy. Further north of Braam, Sandton has been called the 'richest square mile in Africa' with its behemoth grey concrete and glass structures competing for the skyline (James 2018). For officials and citizens alike, the city is envisioned as accommodating a diverse population and as a lucrative commercial centre that can compete globally while remaining 'authentically African' enough to attract foreign investment and tourism.

In some indigenous languages, the descriptors 'Gauteng' and 'Egoli' (place of gold) as well as 'Maboneng' (place of lights) originated not only to mark the discovery of gold and early urban electrification: these names also speak to the enduring public imagination of Johannesburg as a faraway place of riches and modern indulgence. All these monikers reflect the aspirations and 'unrepentant commercialism' (Mbembe 2004, 373) that drive the (literal) construction and consequent perceptions of the city.

Bernard Magubane (1979) argues that there is a systemic relationship between the underdevelopment and poverty of rural areas and the development and wealth of urban areas in South Africa. His work suggests that the mining economy developed by apartheid thrived on the destruction of

African families, violence, alcoholism and disease, caused by the brutality of the forced migrant labour system. In the present day, a variety of inequalities continue to contribute to the precarity of urban life. Out of the country's total population, 41.8 per cent of those classified as 'black/African' are unemployed and there is an overall 29.2 per cent unemployment rate among the working-age population of the City of Johannesburg (Statistics SA 2018b).

As an aspirational city, Johannesburg carries the hopes and ambitions of many young people and their families, who rely on their education to secure employment. Many graduates are the first to achieve such a milestone in their families and communities, and their salaries enable them to send money back home in order to improve the conditions of the loved ones they have left behind. The landmark Fees Must Fall (FMF) student protests of 2015 and 2016 were inspired by the Rhodes Must Fall movement at the University of Cape Town and spread to Wits and other campuses. The main grievances were high university fees that exclude the poor African majority. These protests drew the world's attention to the reality that regardless of Johannesburg and Cape Town's perceived success, a great number of people are unemployed and poor and may be condemned to remain that way without access to affordable education and employment.

Thus far, I have presented two seemingly opposing realities about Johannesburg. On one hand, it is a worldly city and commercial centre that attracts many people from within and outside South Africa with aspirations of excess and access to opportunities. On the other hand, it is marred by great inequalities that include unemployment and a high cost of living – the country as a whole has a Gini coefficient of 0.62, in comparison with the United States at 0.39 and the United Kingdom at 0.35 (OECD 2019). What is commonly identified as 'fast-paced' is actually the tension between these two structural realities: its citizens respond by developing the logic that obvious scarcity ought to be overcome on an individual basis, and by any means necessary. Romantic relationships are not immune to co-optation into these repertoires of individual triumph over structural precarity. As Olivia remarked:

> Social media is the way you let everyone else know that you have money, or that you're getting money, or you're trying to get money … If it isn't documented on there, it's like, 'Did it happen? Did you really go on that holiday? Did your man really buy you that bag? Do you really have that hair?' And perhaps it brings people some sort of validation … I think that in a place

like Joburg, it probably would be important to have an Instagram … and to participate in that way as far as social media is concerned.

As Olivia demonstrates here, social media provides additional insights into the spectacle of romance.

When I first met Bohlale, she was a self-proclaimed 'sugar baby' who mainly used Tinder.[5] Her time on the online dating app began negatively in Bloemfontein but she later found it useful in curbing her boredom in Johannesburg. It exposed her to men of all ethnicities and tax brackets who were willing to compensate her for spending time on a date or on the phone. In the following response, she reveals the reality of heterosexual women competing with one another for men's desire, which requires gaining confidence over one's insecurities:

> Johannesburg forces you. In the same way people know that professionally it's really competitive, there are a lot of opportunities but it's cut-throat, it's the same with dating. There are a lot of people, a lot of opportunities, but it's cut-throat, you can't be passive … This gets to a lot of people but it shows you how you measure up against the rest because a lot of girls will say, 'Well, the girls are so pretty in Johannesburg … and I feel like I'm gonna have trouble dating here because I'm not as pretty' … But you can't let it lead to you developing a low self-esteem or whatever. You need to step your pussy game up, you need to become a more confident person, you need to put yourself out there in Johannesburg.

The fast pace and logic of competition that prevail in the city extend to dating and to personal aesthetics, especially since women vie for male attention (Weitz 2001). True to this spirit, Bohlale emphasises the importance of not being a passive romantic subject.

When I met Sonto, she was a polyamorous dater with a more stable commitment to the 'Mozambican guy', as she calls him. They are now in a mono-amorous relationship in which he gives her money and takes her on holidays. Unlike Bohlale, Sonto expresses an exasperation with being a sexually attractive young woman in the city:

> You can literally take me to the beach and I will have the best time of my life, but Joburg doesn't have a beach. So, if you're in Joburg, you need to spend

money. If you want to have a good time, you need to buy clothes, you need to put on make-up, you need to do your hair. In Mozambique, I don't do any of those things … In Joburg, it's much more of a numbers game. You know, a guy approaches a girl and the girl is like, 'No'. He'd be like, 'Okay, cool. Next!' … It's a very demanding space in terms of guys wanting sex, girls not wanting sex, and girls wanting money and guys not wanting to give that money … It's a very, very demanding space. It's actually draining.

While her observations about Mozambique are influenced by the transience of being a tourist, her remarks about Johannesburg are a reiteration of the other interlocutors' sentiments, like Olivia's comments in the introduction to this chapter. Sonto's notion of a 'numbers game' where men and women have their choice of an assortment of suitors corroborates Bohlale's statement about people having 'many options' in the city and Olivia's response about how one is 'either in or out in Joburg'.

Firstly, these responses portray the city as a place of such density that it is necessary to stand out in order to be desirable. Secondly, they indicate that consumption plays a key role in the attainment of and competition for desirability. Bohlale's reference to beauty, Sonto's talking about the effort and cost involved, and Olivia's mention of possessing the objects associated with desirability (trendy clothes, phones and places of leisure) can all be condensed into acts of consumption: people must have disposable income in order to participate. Thirdly, each participant's response, including Bohlale's 'step your pussy game up' comment, acknowledges that the competition for desirability forges a connection between money and sex. In summary, young women spend money to beautify themselves in order to attract suitors, and men spend money on romantic gestures in order to present themselves as worthy. This results in one-night stands, as shown in Sonto's response, or longer-term relationships, as shown by the lives of my interlocutors. Furthermore, Olivia's observations reflect how the phenomenon of competitiveness extends into relationships:

People who date in Joburg have a lot more going on. There's a lot more that could get in the way of their relationship because there's all these cool places to go to and so you're meeting all these different people … I feel like in Pretoria, it's just really slow … In Joburg, everything is out there and you're out there, and you have to be out there. If your relationship isn't on social media, then are you even with this person? … I feel like when you're from Pretoria, you can just get away with being boring and no one will question why your relationship is the way it is. I think in Joburg there are just so many expectations and you just have to be this really cool couple.

Olivia's argument illustrates that social media creates additional pressure for people to perform the ideal relationship. It is also an interesting reflection of how Pretoria and Johannesburg are perceived differently, although they are merely 45 kilometres apart.

'Oblique consumption', as it is termed by Illouz (1997), refers to the way consumption is inextricably tied to romance. It involves aspirational imagery of couples who are well dressed, attractive and engaged in consuming leisure activities and their associated objects. I suggest that as people's real-life social networks are reproduced on social media to a wider audience of spectators, there are dual realms in which they have to meet the expectations of a social group. In this instance, people adhere to socially acceptable norms by presenting themselves and their relationships appealingly. Consumerism makes aesthetically desirable relationships possible because, firstly, they require mobile phones and social media to make them visible and, secondly, practising romance requires money. The competition of desirability is constantly present for relationships and is evidence of the need to appear to have triumphed over the uncertainty of life in the city. My interlocutors all show that young women strive to succeed and that their main anxiety is failing to 'make it', leading to an emotional anxiety born out of their romantic choices.

ROMANCE AND VULNERABILITY

In South Africa, research on compensated relationships is rooted in responses to the HIV and AIDS pandemic. These relationships are implicated in new infection rates among young women aged between 15 and 24. Poverty, to which the high youth unemployment rate contributes, is popularly understood as being the motivation for young women to engage in such relationships (HEAIDS 2013; Zembe et al. 2013; Shisana et al. 2014; She Conquers SA 2016). Given the racialised socio-economic disparities in South Africa which have created these conditions, African women use their sexuality strategically in order to access resources (Hunter 2002; Selikow, Zulu, and Cedras 2002). But these kinds of relations have a much longer history. 'Provider love' (Hunter 2010) is a concept which chronicles South Africans' conceptions of love in the circumstances of the migrant labour system. Here love is seen to involve the traditional gender roles of male provision through labour in urban centres in the face of ever-increasing capitalist demands. In other words, money and the male provision of resources strengthen kinship and are central to how South African people actualise their romantic love for each other. However, such relationships are often negatively framed within a discourse of prostitution (Hunter 2002; Kaufman and Stavrou 2004; Selikow and Mbulaheni 2013).

It is evident from my interlocutors that their experiences of such relationships have challenged their own initial assumptions, which were undoubtedly informed by society's negative framing of compensated dating. By outlining such assumptions in relation to stereotypes, we can explore the vulnerabilities that are particular to these kinds of relationships and, more broadly in the context of the vulnerabilities endured by South African women, show that safety is a great anxiety.

The first perception is that money is these women's highest priority, to the detriment of all other considerations. However, genuine feelings are also important. Bohlale says:

> If you're irritating me, I can't pretend. That's the thing about being an SB [sugar baby], a lot of girls can pretend … That's also one thing you need to know about sugaring, where you can't allow yourself to be low-balled, or low-ball yourself, where you can see something is a bad deal but you're like, I really want the money, let me just do it. I knew how to leave a deal and say, look, I can see this isn't gonna work out for me, it's gonna make me unhappy if I hold on to it so I'm willing to let go.

According to Sonto,

> Even though I am someone who loves giving love, I do want some sort of depth, I do want some sort of connection, and I cannot have anything that is based on nothing. Even though I could have three sexual partners, I would still want to have a connection with each one of them that is dynamic, deep.

Olivia agrees: 'We definitely like each other and we care for each other. He is sometimes there for me emotionally, to the extent that a patriarchal man can be there for you.'

These women ensure that feelings, well-being and genuine emotional connections are paramount in their relationships, whether they date one or several men at a time. For Bohlale, that remains true even though money is explicitly important to sugar babies. Olivia's quip about men's lack of emotional depth reflects her gendered beliefs about men's and women's varied contributions to relationships.

The second perception is that such relationships consist of men unilaterally spending their money, even though the women do actually also spend on their partners. Olivia says:

> I buy him things. I've gotten him sneakers, gotten him books. So, I'll do that just because I would do that in any of my relationships. If I'm being honest, if someone were to ask, 'What do you do when the bill comes?' I don't do anything. I mean, just take care of it. You wanted to see me.

Sonto agrees: 'There are times when I randomly do things for him. I surprised him with a picnic because his birthday had recently passed. We had champagne and he'd been saying that he wanted strawberries so we had that in the champagne.' She adds:

> This guy, there was a point where there was a backlog in his accounts. So, I was like, 'Dude, what do you need?' He said he needs petrol money and other things. Immediately when my money from work came in, I sent him money. That's something people don't understand, that this girl can actually still send this guy money.

Both Olivia and Sonto engage reciprocally in their relationships, although Olivia maintains her belief that because of her partner's social position, he should be the main financial provider.

The third perception is that women in compensated relationships are indulged spontaneously. The interlocutors in this study show that, just as with any expectation in a relationship, receiving money requires communication. Olivia explains:

> I was saying to him that people assume that when you're with an older guy, he's just throwing money at you and all the things he's getting you is all voluntary

and you don't have to ask for it, and you kind of wake up one morning and there's money in your bank account or he's like, 'Let's go off to Cape Town'. It's not all like that; I have to ask him for money if I want it.

Bohlale's experiences are similar:

You have to go on dates and speak. You have to, literally. It's a very awkward conversation to have with someone about allowances at the beginning, and learning how to demand certain things, like, 'This is how I'm working, I have school so you can't expect me to be seeing you in the middle of the week, and this is how much I want and this is what I expect. I'm not doing this or that.'

Sonto confirms:

It's not just a conversation of 'send me money'. He also has some sort of discipline. He also tells me, 'Dude, you can't tell me that you want money now and you want a grand. No, that won't work.' It's not just a thing of, I'm with this pretty girl therefore she can just dictate my life. No, it's nothing like that. There is some sort of respect and consensus and understanding that goes into it.

The interlocutors are engaged in different kinds of compensated relationships. For Bohlale, allowances are fixed amounts that are agreed upon before the commencement of the relationship, whereas Sonto and Olivia request varying amounts of money throughout the duration of their relationships.

The final and most significant perception is that money is a means of control over the woman. Olivia says:

He's not at all controlling or a dictator. That's another thing that I thought about these relationships. I also thought, because men are just fucked up anyway, that he could be somewhat controlling and maybe even a little abusive. Someone who will tell you what to wear and where to go and where he would want you to go, like you can't go here unless I'm with you or why you wearing that?

While Bohlale explains:

I'm really strict on the consent thing and this is why I think I lose out on a lot of guys – because people think that the 'exchange' takes away the consent. 'So if I give you R3000, I can do whatever I want to you for the weekend?' No, that's not the deal. So, I'm really clear about that. If it seems like the person isn't grasping what I'm saying or I sense the entitlement, then I'm like, 'You know what? I appreciate that we've gotten this far in our conversation but I don't think you're the guy for me and it's not gonna work.'

It is a commonly held view that women who consent to compensated relationships also consent to being treated poorly, because a relationship that is regarded as 'transactional' objectifies the woman and diminishes her agency. Both Olivia and Bohlale recognise that they are especially susceptible to violence.

Dating, as the initial stage of establishing a romantic relationship, is facilitated by four main factors: means of communication; people who can exercise autonomy; money; and a society that fosters the visibility of heterosexual couples in public places. Additionally, 'everything is … expensive, and essentials, like rent, are unaffordable without a full-time salary' (Delaney and Kaspin 2011, 157, 159). On one hand, money is essential in fostering functional romantic relationships of any kind. On the other hand, the interlocutors' realities in contrast to their assumptions show how money is at the root of misperceptions about compensated relationships. As we shall see, the expectation of expenditure of money in a relationship is not extraordinary, and closer examination of compensated relationships reveals more nuance than is readily accepted by society.

VIOLENCE AND SAFETY

The prevalence of femicide and gender-based and intimate partner violence in South Africa indicates that women live with the constant possibility of violence in public and private spheres. Of all the sexual assault cases that are reported in South Africa, 68.5 per cent of victims are women (Statistics SA 2018c). Every four hours a woman is murdered by her intimate partner, defined as 'current or ex-husband or boyfriend, same-sex partner or a rejected would-be lover' (Africa Check 2017). As Sandile Mantsoe's murder of Karabo Mokoena and Oscar Pistorius's murder of Reeva Steenkamp show, it is clear that romantic relationships can be dangerous for South African women.[6]

Olivia remarks that she was initially surprised to realise that her partner is not abusive, because he is older and gives her money. Money can indeed be used as a mechanism of control and objectification. Vulnerabilities are undeniably present in compensated relationships, where power disparities leave women susceptible to overt exploitation. While my interlocutors have not experienced any physical violence as a result of their relationship choices, they are keenly aware of the dangers that surround them:

[Olivia:] I'm not doubting that these kinds of relationships can be unhealthy or abusive. I think any time you're with a heterosexual man, you need to be prepared and you can expect shit to go left. I even say to my boyfriend all the time, 'I think you're great and we have great conversations and we like each other. If you just turned on me one day, I wouldn't be surprised.'

[Bohlale:] I've never been involved in a really scary situation, but at the beginning of the year a guy that I met, he stayed at like [Hartbeespoort Dam] in Pretoria and it's really isolated. He made a joke like, 'You know I could kill you and no one would know?' and I was like, what the fuck? And we didn't see each other after that.

[Sonto:] Him and I got into a fight because his friends were sleeping over and I wanted to spend time with him. He took out his gun that he had in his apartment and I was like, 'You know what? I'm gonna leave.' But he didn't actually get physical with me, but I feel like someone taking out a gun on you is like enough for you. You need to *leave*.

The incidents involving Bohlale and Sonto having their safety threatened verbally and symbolically, and even Bohlale's and Olivia's resignation to the inevitability of male violence, demonstrate the interlocutors' reactions to living through South Africa's gender-based violence crisis. For each woman, there exists an anxiety that any moment of conflict with a man could end fatally. Therefore it is common for mobile phones to double as tools of communication and safety. For her first date with Siyabonga, Olivia ensured that she alerted her friends: 'When we eventually went out for lunch … he picked me up on campus. I was a little nervous so I let everyone know where I was going. I was texting as he was driving and I let them know where we were going.'

Sonto also texts critical information to her loved ones, especially because she dates multiple people. She was frightened after the gun incident and has since modified her practices in the following ways:

> Sending registration numbers, getting the person's last name before we actually meet but making it something that's very casual, like, 'Oh, you have such a cool name. What's your surname?' If they had their profile picture then I'd also send their picture … and maybe even possibly the current location that I'm in, like where the Uber is going to drop me, and send the pin each time. If we're at a restaurant and maybe we land up at his place, then that as well. I always try – wherever I'm going – and have some money for an Uber, just in case I feel very uncomfortable.

As both Olivia and Sonto show, mobile phones are valuable assets, and in addition, Sonto mentions the importance of money as a safety measure. Bohlale's experiences as a sugar baby have led to some significant differences in how she uses her phone, which she mentioned in a viral Twitter thread (23 August 2016) on personal safety practices, with the first tweet generating 843 retweets and 858 likes:

> I am going to do a small thread on how to screen a person that you met online before you go out w[ith] them, and general online safety hacks.[7] 1. Reverse image search pictures they send you. This is useful for catching out catfishes and general investigation … 3. When going on the date, ask him to send you an Uber. Ask the driver to give you the phone, you'll be able to see his real name there … 7. For example, I send my best friend the date location, the person's car pic and number plates, and of course their cell no. and photos. 8. NEVER, and I mean NEVER, meet a guy at the bar or restaurant of his hotel on the first date. ESPECIALLY these foreign guys. DON'T … It's easier to roofie you and take you upstairs than to get an unconscious person out of a mall restaurant, to a parking lot w/o being noticed.

The engagement that this thread garnered from her online community and beyond is evidence that there is a demand for information about safely dating online and that women yearn to be able to protect themselves from male violence in general. With 17 pieces of advice in total, her suggestions are exceptional because they are the experiential lessons of a sugar baby, going beyond the commonly known tactic of vetting strangers through Google and social media. Her knowledge is valuable because it is not readily accessible.

What Pumla Gqola calls the 'female fear factory' – the stories, depictions, images and occurrences of violence against female-bodied persons in South Africa – is a useful way to think about the symbolic and actual violence that women encounter individually and collectively, especially when opting to engage in unconventional sexual and relationship forms:

> It is exaggerated performance in front of an audience in terms that are immediately understood. It is spectacular in its reliance on visible, audible and other recognisable cues to transmit fear and control. Performed regularly in public spaces and mediated forms, it is both mythologised, sometimes through a language of respectability and other times through shame … Under capitalism work is codified as respectability … The threat of rape is an effective way to remind women that they are not safe and that their bodies are not entirely theirs. (Gqola 2015, 78–9)

While the press coverage and discourse dedicated to South Africa's violence is necessary, it also contributes to the female fear factory and the constant knowledge that women are surrounded by danger both in public and in private. In the second part of her statement, Gqola gestures towards practices such as sex work and compensated relationships in which women reject respectability in the pursuit of gaining direct compensation or forming romantic partnerships in explicitly strategic ways.

The female fear factory is revealed, firstly, in the experiences that the interlocutors share in which threats of violence are wielded to subdue and control them, and, secondly, in the events and experiences that fuel public perceptions about these relationships. It has become a norm for women to contemplate the worst possible outcomes from their interactions with men and to establish strategies to alleviate their fears of becoming statistics of violence themselves. While women who engage in compensated relationships are exercising their agency, it is important to highlight the structural context of femicide and male violence that frames their daily realities. Mobile phones are a significant intervention, with many women imagining them as 'weapons of self-defence' (Cumiskey and Brewster 2012). Indeed, women have thoroughly incorporated their phones as tools of safety in their lives. Considering that compensated relationships are not positively encouraged in society, it is clear that online communities have the potential to foster a greater sense of safety and strategy-sharing among the women involved in them.

CONCLUSION

This chapter has explored anxiety in relation to space, relationships and objects. It illuminates the ways the larger situational space of Johannesburg generates aspirational anxieties around success and influences young women's romantic decision-making accordingly. The city is burdened by the anxiety of great socio-economic inequality and electrified by a palpable sense of competition, individualism and consumerism. On the other hand, it is plagued by violence, adding another layer of anxiety for citizens to navigate. Young women are a vulnerable population and, although their ability to exercise agency is constrained by capitalism, high unemployment and a femicidal society, they are able to commune online and enact strategies of safety within their romantic lives, enabled by their mobile phones and online presences. Their choice of being in compensated relationships is a result of reckoning with the socio-economic anxieties of living in Johannesburg while desiring inclusion within aspirational lifestyles. In this way, they absorb their romantic lives into their repertoires of surviving and thriving in the big city.

ACKNOWLEDGEMENTS

I would like to acknowledge the National Institute for the Humanities and Social Sciences (NIHSS) for awarding me the scholarship 'From Digital to Sexual Revolution: Youth and Mobile Phones in India and South Africa', which has greatly aided my research endeavours. This chapter is derived from my MA research report for the University of the Witwatersrand, 2019.

NOTES

1   eNCA, 11 May 2016.

2   All interviews cited were undertaken between 2016 and 2018. All names have been anonymised.

3   Compensated relationships have been studied extensively in South Africa (Bhana 2015; Kilburn et al. 2018; Leclerc-Madlala 2003, 2008a, 2008b) and also appear in popular

texts. *The Blessed Girl* by Angela Makholwa (2017) and *Bare: The Blessers Game* by Jackie Phamotse (2017) are both works of fiction which reflect public interest in compensated relationships.

4   'Sugaring' is a phrase derived from the terms 'sugar baby' and 'sugar daddy'. It is the act of the young woman being in such a relationship.

5   A sugar baby engages in 'an equitable exchange of companionship and intimacy for financial compensation' (Daly 2017, 2).

6   Mantsoe, 27, murdered his 22-year-old ex-girlfriend Mokoena in 2017. Pistorius, the notorious Paralympian, murdered his girlfriend, Steenkamp, on St Valentine's Day 2013. Intimate partner violence is rife in South Africa regardless of age, social status and race.

7   Bohlale has set her Twitter to auto-delete every two weeks; therefore she remains anonymous even while the content is reproduced here.

REFERENCES

Africa Check. 2017. "Femicide in South Africa: 3 Numbers about the Murdering of Women Investigated." Accessed 20 January 2018. https://africacheck.org/reports/femicide-sa-3-numbers-murdering-women-investigated/.

Bhana, Deevia. 2015. "Sex, Gender and Money in African Teenage Conceptions of Love in HIV Contexts." *Journal of Youth Studies* 18 (1): 1–5.

Bremner, Lindsay. 2000. "Reinventing the Johannesburg Inner City." *Cities* 17 (3): 185–93.

Cumiskey, Kathleen M., and Kendra Brewster. 2012. "Mobile Phones or Pepper Spray?" *Feminist Media Studies* 12 (4): 590–9.

Daly, Sarah. 2017. "Sugar Babies and Sugar Daddies: An Exploration of Sugar Dating on Canadian Campuses." MA thesis, Carleton University.

Delaney, Carol, and Deborah Kaspin. 2011. *Investigating Culture: An Experiential Introduction to Anthropology*. Oxford: Wiley-Blackwell.

eNCA. 2016. *Checkpoint: Blessed Part 1*, 11 May 2016. https://www.youtube.com/watch?v=QiT_TVOHZjw.

Gqola, Pumla Dineo. 2015. *Rape: A South African Nightmare*. Auckland Park: MF Books.

HEAIDS (Higher Education and Training HIV/AIDS Programme). 2013. "Zazi: Know Your Strength." Pretoria: Centre for Communication Impact (formerly, Johns Hopkins Health and Education South Africa).

Hunter, Mark. 2002. "The Materiality of Everyday Sex: Thinking beyond 'Prostitution'." *African Studies* 61 (1): 99–120.

———. 2010. *Love in the Time of AIDS: Inequality, Gender and Rights in South Africa*. Bloomington: Indiana University Press.

Illouz, Eva. 1997. *Consuming the Romantic Utopia: Love and the Cultural Contradictions of Capitalism*. Berkeley: University of California Press.

James, G. 2018. "Releasing Higher Education from Its Elitist Captivity: The Change Agency of Unisa's Chance 2 Advance Programme." *HTS: Theological Studies* 74 (3): 1–10.

Kaufman, Carol E., and Stavros Stavrou. 2004. "'Bus Fare Please': The Economics of Sex and Gifts among Young People in Urban South Africa." *Culture, Health and Sexuality* 6 (5): 377–91.

Kilburn, Kelly, Meghna Ranganathan, Marie Stoner, James Hughes, Catherine MacPhail, Yaw Agyei, Xavier Gómez-Olivé, Kathleen Kahn, and Audrey Pettifor. 2018. "Transactional Sex and Incident HIV Infection in a Cohort of Young Women from Rural South Africa." *AIDS* 32 (12): 1669–77.

Leclerc-Madlala, Suzanne. 2003. "Transactional Sex and the Pursuit of Modernity." *Social Dynamics* 29 (2): 213–33.

———. 2008a. "Age-Disparate and Intergenerational Sex in Southern Africa: The Dynamics of Hypervulnerability." *AIDS* 22 (4): 17–25.

———. 2008b. "Intergenerational/Age-Disparate Sex: Policy and Programme Action Brief." Paper presented at the Technical Meeting on Young Women in HIV Hyper-Endemic Countries of Southern Africa. Accessed 20 March 2017. http://www.unicef.org.mz/cpd/references/84-womenGirls_AgeDisparate.pdf.

Li, Jessica. 2015. "Adolescent Compensated Dating in Hong Kong: Choice, Script, and Dynamics." *International Journal of Offender Therapy and Comparative Criminology* 59 (5): 588–610.

Magubane, Bernard. 1979. *The Political Economy of Race and Class in South Africa*. New York: Monthly Review Press.

Makholwa, Angela. 2017. *The Blessed Girl.* Johannesburg: Pan Macmillan.

Mbembe, Achille. 2004. "Aesthetics of Superfluity." *Public Culture* 16 (3): 373–405.

OECD (Organisation for Economic Co-operation and Development). 2019. *Income Inequality Indicator*. Accessed 8 March 2019. https://data.oecd.org/inequality/income-inequality.htm.

Phamotse, Jackie. 2017. *Bare: The Blessers Game*. Pinegowrie: Porcupine Press.

Selikow, Terry-Ann, and Tola Mbulaheni. 2013. "'I Do Love Him But at the Same Time I Can't Eat Love': Sugar Daddy Relationships for Conspicuous Consumption amongst Urban University Students in South Africa." *Agenda* 27 (2): 86–98.

Selikow, Terry-Ann, Bheki Zulu, and Eugene Cedras. 2002. "The Ingagara, the Regte and the Cherry: HIV/AIDS and Youth Culture in Contemporary Urban Townships." *Agenda* 53: 22–32.

She Conquers SA. 2016. "Careers and Jobs: Building Your Future." Accessed 28 November 2019. http://sheconquerssa.co.za/careers-and-jobs/.

Shisana, Olive, Thomas Rehle, L.C. Simbayi, Khangelani Zuma, Sean Jooste, Nompumelelo Zungu, Demetre Labadarios, and D. Onoya. 2014. "South African National HIV Prevalence, Incidence and Behaviour Survey, 2012." Pretoria: Human Sciences Research Council.

Statistics SA. 2018a. "Statistical Release P0302: Mid-Year Population Estimates." Pretoria: Statistics South Africa. http://www.statssa.gov.za/publications/P0302/P03022018.pdf.

———. 2018b. "Statistical Release P0211: Quarterly Labour Force Survey." Pretoria: Statistics South Africa. http://www.statssa.gov.za/publications/P0211/P02113rdQuarter2018.pdf.

———. 2018c. "Crime Statistics Series Volume V. Crime against Women in South Africa: An In-Depth Analysis of the Victims of Crime Survey Data 2018." Report No. 03-40-05. Pretoria: Statistics South Africa. http://www.statssa.gov.za/publications/Report-03-40-05/Report-03-40-05June2018.pdf.

Swader, Christopher, and Irina Vorobeva. 2015. "Receiving Gifts for Sex in Moscow, Kyiv, and Minsk: A Compensated Dating Survey." *Sexuality and Culture* 19 (2): 321–48.

Weitz, Rose. 2001. "Women and Their Hair: Seeking Power through Resistance and Accommodation." *Gender and Society* 15 (5): 667–86.

Zembe, Yanga Z., Loraine Townsend, Anna Thorson, and Anna Mia Ekstrom. 2013. "'Money Talks, Bullshit Walks': Interrogating Notions of Consumption and Survival Sex among Young Women Engaging in Transactional Sex in Post-Apartheid South Africa: A Qualitative Enquiry." *Globalization and Health* 9 (28): 1–16.

3 DRIVING, CYCLING AND IDENTITY IN JOHANNESBURG

NJOGU MORGAN

Mobility in Johannesburg plays an outsize role in the everyday practices and imaginaries of residents. Every aspect of movement invites scrutiny, rendering it a social activity that commands the attention of all residents – albeit in ways that are shaped by demographic differences. For instance, people living in informal settlements and townships located on the outskirts of the city have a 'higher percentage of trips taking longer than one hour' to reach their destinations. In contrast, data suggest 'that residents of suburban locations are most "time-advantaged"' (Venter and Badenhorst 2014, 47). Like travel times, experiences and perceptions of mobility are varied. Yet public narratives are often suffused with, to use Meshack Khosa's (1998) expression, 'the travail of travelling'. This is, for example, manifest in traffic reports delivered by radio stations. Such reporting is more often than not concerned with difficulties in movement, discussing traffic congestion and traffic light outages. This way of representing mobility dovetails with other public narratives which evoke themes of anxiety. In such portrayals, the social world as well as the technologies and infrastructures of mobility is framed in terms of risk: users are depicted as encountering road rage, crime, potholed roads, poorly maintained buses and trains, errant minibus taxi drivers and more. Whether these and other anxieties about mobility in

Johannesburg correspond precisely to objective reality is uncertain. The concern of this chapter is to explore how these anxieties shape transport behaviour and shed light on social dynamics in the city.

There have been numerous studies on this subject. Along with other rational-instrumental categories such as cost and time, anxieties over the risks of road safety and crime have been shown to shape transport behaviour. One travel survey showed that 6.8 per cent and 3.6 per cent of households within the Johannesburg municipality cited fear of accidents and crime respectively as the most important factors shaping their travel modes. In the same survey, 44.4 per cent of respondents who had not used a minibus taxi in the previous month reported that this had to with service attributes, a broad category that includes concerns about crime, driver behaviour and road safety (Statistics SA 2015, 78, 82).

Anxieties over transportation present differently according to socio-economic background. In another survey, people in high-income brackets indicated that concerns over personal safety were their main reason for not using public transport. Those in low-income brackets, however, reported it was the unavailability of public transport that was their reason for not using it (Venter and Badenhorst 2014). Intersecting with these concerns, research has found that fears over sexual harassment and other forms of violence shape choice of mode and spatial-temporal mobility patterns among women (Makan 2015; Seedat, MacKenzie, and Mohan 2006). Female fears of insecurity in public spaces are also found with respect to the mobility of children (Kruger and Chawla 2002). Parents who can afford to do so cushion their children by chauffeuring them in their own vehicles, organising car-pooling arrangements or hiring private commercial transport services. In contrast, schoolchildren from lower-income homes 'who use buses, public taxis or trains or who walk spend more time in insecure public spaces . . . [experience] higher levels of fear, uncertainty and anxiety in their commutes' (Lancaster 2011, 62).

These type of anxieties over road safety, crime and other insecurities are well rehearsed in public narratives and in the literature. This chapter explores another concern related to transport in Johannesburg that receives less attention: status anxiety. Status anxiety has been defined as 'a broad syndrome comprising status-related worries and status-related negative experiences' (Delhey, Schneickert, and Steckermeier 2017, 216). As the case of bicycles and cars in Johannesburg shows, worries about what it means to be cycling or driving, and in particular whether doing so suggests superiority or inferiority along intersections of race and class, echo across the city's psychosocial landscape and shape mobility patterns. While research has discussed this phenomenon, there has been insufficient attention given to its historical nature. Not only does it have a long history, but contemporary worries originate partly in the past. Such worries are a response to inequality – a feature that developed from the earliest days of Johannesburg. Since the founding of the city, struggles over identity – in terms of race and social class – have been waged through transport behaviour, as can be seen in the dynamics of cycling and driving. This has been a contest through which changing claims about identity have been made. New studies of transport behaviour can provide insights into emergent notions of how contemporary Johannesburg residents think about themselves and others.

IDENTITY, STATUS ANXIETY AND TRANSPORT

In thinking about transport behaviour, Dave Skinner and Paul Rosen have argued that 'identity [should be considered] as intrinsic to people's transport choices'. Here, identity is understood as '[encompassing] both people's sense of who they are (what might be termed personal identity) and their sense of who they are like and who they are different from (what might be termed social location)' (Skinner and Rosen 2007, 86, 83). One of the models that they offer in thinking about the relationship between transport and identity works on the premise that pre-existing notions of self, which are influenced by social backgrounds, in turn influence transport choices. In this vein, the current chapter considers the directional relationship between identity and transport. In doing so it follows a social constructive perspective where elements of identity are seen as being produced in 'specific sociohistorical or social interactional processes' (Weinberg 2009, 283). While this conceptual orientation is key to the analysis offered here, it also explains the use of racial terms such as 'black' and 'white' and derogatory terms such as 'native' and 'kaffir' used to describe social groups: I retain these as they are used in particular historical periods in order to underline the nature of relations between social groups. Further, while elaborate racial and ethnic constructs evolved through colonialism and apartheid, and still shape social interactions in the post-apartheid era, an overall dynamic on which this chapter reflects is the dominant role of 'white' groups vis-à-vis others. While these racial constructs were and are heterogeneous, for the sake of readability and to reflect the overall structures of dominance and subordination, I refer to two groups: 'whites' and 'blacks'.[1]

A key question is why worries about the 'self' and what others think about that 'self' should influence choice of transport mode. These types of worries, which have to do with evaluations or appraisals by others, have been conceptualised as status anxieties (Delhey, Schneickert, and Steckermeier 2017). Within the broad field of consumption studies, 'A primary assertion . . . is that objects have the ability to signify things – or establish social meanings – on behalf of people, or to do "social work"' (Woodward 2007, 4). Objects can be status symbols. For Erving Goffman, a status symbol 'carries *categorical* significance, that is, it serves to identify the social status of the person who makes it . . . [and] it may also carry *expressive* significance, that is, it may express the point of view, the style of life, and the cultural values of the person who makes it, or may satisfy needs created by the imbalance of activity in his particular social position' (1951, 295; italics in original).

As scholars have shown, the symbolic meanings attached to material objects are shaped by societal structure. In unequal societies (such as those having uneven access to material goods) characterised by what Wilkinson and Pickett (2018, 120) call 'dominance hierarchies', possession of material goods allows individuals to show their rank and 'value' in the social hierarchy. Here, possessing goods, particularly more expensive ones, 'becomes honorific; and conversely, the failure to consume in due quantity and quality becomes a mark of inferiority and demerit' (Veblen 2009, 53). An important concept here is that status is relational. It 'derives from the judgements that other members of society make of an individual's position in society [and therefore] for this position to be established there must be a display of wealth' (Trigg 2001, 99–101). This is Thorstein Veblen's famous concept of conspicuous consumption.

However, it is important to note that status competition and related anxieties affect people differently. Evidence shows that impacts vary according to one's position in the social hierarchy. Empirical studies based on very large data sets have found a heightened relationship between status anxieties and inequality – the higher the levels of inequality, the worse the negative feelings individuals experience (Layte and Whelan 2014; Delhey and Dragolov 2014; Delhey, Schneickert, and Steckermeier 2017). Since South Africa has historically high and persistent levels of income inequality, heightened status anxieties can be expected (Piketty 2014; Sulla and Zikhali 2018).

NO, YOU CANNOT CYCLE!

One of the earliest cases involving worries over identity and transport appeared forcefully about twenty years after Johannesburg's founding, in 1905. After lobbying from an organisation representing elite white society called the Rand Pioneers, the municipal council proposed a special law to regulate the use of bicycles among the subordinate social group referred to as 'natives'. The proposed by-law stated that 'every native who rides a bicycle shall obtain a special permit, and shall wear, while actually riding, a numbered badge on his left arm, so that he be readily identified'. Furthermore, the law 'proposed to restrict the riding of bicycles by natives to the hours of daylight on ordinary days, and to prohibit on Sundays and holidays except when a native is sent out on a message by his master' (City of Johannesburg 1905, 130). The proposed law went further to specify that on occasions when a 'native' had been given special authorisation by his 'master' to ride outside the allowed hours, if he did not ride in the most direct route to the destination he would fall foul of the law.

The purported intention of the law was 'to check cycle thefts, and [to control the] nuisance caused in the streets by the reckless riding of native cyclists' (City of Johannesburg 1905, 130). With regard to the claim that 'natives' were riding stolen bicycles, the Rand Pioneers argued that 'the possession of bicycles by many natives [was not] compatible with their apparent means' (Rand Pioneers 1905, 13). There were widespread narratives in colonial newspapers alleging that 'natives' rode bicycles dangerously and these were likely to be stolen machines (*Indian Opinion* 1905; *Sunday Times* 1907; *Star* 1908; *Daily Mail* 1910). The by-law was adopted by the town council on 8 March 1905 and sent for approval from the government. The Transvaal government, however, refused to accept the law on the grounds that it was beyond the powers that municipalities were allowed to exercise (Bourne 1905). The Rand Pioneers Association, which had lobbied hard for the by-law, was disappointed (Rand Pioneers 1905, 112, 13).

What was behind these moves? Paul Maylam (1995) has argued that the overriding logic of colonial and, later, apartheid systems of domination aimed to exert control over every aspect of the lives of black people. These moves to regulate the use of bicycles are a good illustration of the control imperative. According to Cotten Seiler (2007) in his study of the relationship between race and transport in the United States before African Americans were granted equal rights under the law, independent forms of mobility can play a special role in the construction of racial identity. This is because 'self-directed mobility signifies freedom and self-transformation'. Consequently, 'regimes of white supremacy have sought to police the movement of racial Others both to preserve physical racial separation and to guard the integrity of racial identity itself' (Seiler 2007, 308). In this light, it would have been irksome for 'white' people concerned with establishing separate identities to see black people cycling, and thus they would have sought to govern such practices. Within the overall ambit of control, Deborah Posel (2010) argues that regulating consumption practices was a way of constructing identities in colonial and apartheid South Africa.

In the early colonial political economy of Johannesburg, wealth born out of the gold-mining industry was in white hands (Beavon 2004), as were bicycles, which were then expensive commodities (Learmont 1990), requiring the municipality to offer subsidies to white workers so they could purchase them (Morgan 2019). The ubiquity of bicycles among the white population came to be associated with membership of that social group. This can be seen from a public meeting in 1904 consisting of white residents of working-class suburbs west of the city centre, who protested against plans by the municipal council to relocate black African, Indian and coloured people next to them (Phillips 2014). In illustrating the need for separation, one person in the audience argued that 'kaffirs [sic] were now riding bicycles; the next thing they would have would be the motor-car' (*Indian Opinion* 1904).[2] This speaker feared that similarities in practices between the white and black populations were increasingly blurring distinctions in identity. The notion was crystallised in a remark by a leading supporter of the by-law in the municipal council, who argued, 'It was absolutely necessary to distinguish the native from the white men' (*Indian Opinion* 1905, 69). In the late nineteenth century in the United States, African Americans were also subject to ridicule in media narratives that effectively questioned their right to cycle. In a watershed decision, in 1897 a national bicycling association, the League of American Wheelmen, voted to bar African Americans from membership, overriding objections even from white members (Friss 2015, 58–61; Longhurst 2015, 60–2). Evan Friss (2015) suggests that such prejudice was especially rife in the American South, in tandem with growing racial segregation enshrined in law.

Figure 3.1
Members of a cycling club in late-nineteenth-century Johannesburg pose with their machines. Courtesy of Museum Africa Picture Archives

The failure to limit bicycle use among the black population through legal means diminished the ability of bicycles to signal 'whiteness' as it allowed greater ownership among the subordinated. Subsequent decreases in bicycle prices accelerated such ownership (Morgan 2019). However, to the relief of those determined to express racial difference through consumption, another means of asserting distinction was already emerging – the motor car. Following technological developments, cars appeared in Johannesburg, as they did worldwide, after bicycles. The first car exhibited at the Wanderers sports and recreational club in 1897 could hardly bear any loads and reportedly struggled to carry a single person up some of the town's hills. It would

take some time for cars to mature technically before their use would grow
(Morgan 2019) and spark debate about who their legitimate users were.

NO, YOU CANNOT DRIVE!

In the early history of automobility in Johannesburg, fears appeared in public
narratives about the fact that black people were driving cars. Given the disparity in income and wealth in colonial Johannesburg, car ownership grew
principally among the white population. When people of colour got behind
a steering wheel, it was more often as hired drivers for commercial operations
or as private chauffeurs. It was thus that an early controversy surrounding
these practices emerged.

In 1919, organisations representing various actors in the motoring industry
met to discuss proposed regulations governing motoring. At this meeting, an
association representing white commercial automobile operators called the
Witwatersrand Taxi Owners' and Drivers' Association put forward a resolution that 'native' people should not be given driving licences (Jay 1919, 53).
However, other economic arguments won the day. The South African Motor
Traders' Association, representing 'the interests of manufacturers, whole-
salers, retailers and users of motor goods and of others having commercial
relationships with the motor industry' (RAC 1919, 19), did not 'consider
the driving of cars skilled labour' (Jay 1919, 31). If driving was regarded as
a 'skilled' practice, then it would have fallen within broader regulations that
reserved certain jobs for the white population that were understood to require
'skilled' workers (De Zwart 2011). However, for the South African Motor
Traders' Association, it did not make economic sense to limit driving to the
white population. Doing so would restrict the growth of the sector. Were such
restrictions to be put in place, the Association argued that they should instead
pertain to car repair and maintenance (Jay 1919).

However, anxieties about black people driving did not disappear. They
would re-emerge in overtly racial terms. In 1921 the Johannesburg municipal council suspended the issuing of driving licences to 'coloured drivers'.
This was provoked by a tragic accident 'in which a native driver was
involved' (RAC 1921, 11) but was also allegedly justified by the 'many
complaints [received]', as a council official reported. The official argued, 'I
am advised that these coloured people are not temperamentally qualified

to drive cars. They have no idea of judging speed' (*Daily Mail* 1921). In 1926 the *Sunday Times* argued that black people should be prohibited from car driving altogether on the grounds that they were responsible for the traffic accidents besetting Johannesburg. In the view of the paper, 'the safety of the community is at stake [therefore] the advisability of prohibiting natives from driving altogether should be seriously considered' (*Sunday Times* 1926, 14). According to these arguments, black people were somehow mentally incapable of handling motor cars. The assertion that they constituted a danger behind a steering wheel was similar to claims about their bicycle-riding practices made by the Rand Pioneers in 1905. To be sure, these claims were not unique to Johannesburg. Seiler writes that in the 1910s and 1920s the presence of African Americans behind steering wheels was continuously challenged in 'racist laws, social codes, and commercial practices' (2006, 1094).

Economic arguments and straightforward racial prejudice came together crisply in 1934. In that year South Africa's prime minister, General Hertzog, supported a motion that 'natives' should not be allowed to drive cars as chauffeurs for 'Europeans'. This move was regarded by an organisation that opposed it as a thinly veiled attempt to protect the trade of driving for white workers (Schreiner 1934), as had been attempted before. General Hertzog was quoted as saying, 'I have always felt that natives lack the psychology required to manage a dangerous machine like a motor car' (*Rand Daily Mail* 1934, 9). The call for an outright ban failed. Instead, 'an alternative proposal was adopted whereby driving tests would be so strict that few, if any, Blacks would qualify' (Johnston 1976, 180).

These regulations meant that driving would remain a predominantly white preserve, unlike cycling, which had become a form of transport mainly used by black males (Morgan 2019). Thus, notions of racial distinction linked to asymmetries in the ownership patterns of cars could be maintained. This was aided by continuing economic deprivation among black people, which ensured car ownership remained primarily restricted to the white population. Underlining this disparity in wealth across South Africa, Mark Lamont and Rebekah Lee note that 'of the 1.1 million registered motor vehicles on record in 1960, only 100 000 were owned by non-whites' (2015, 473). By the late twentieth century, as South Africa was on the verge of a transition to democracy, these patterns continued.

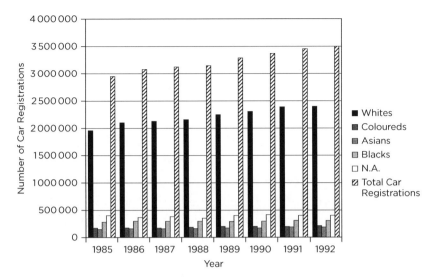

Figure 3.2
Car ownership according to the racial categories which were employed by the apartheid and transitional governments. Graph constructed by author from data available from Central Statistical Service (1992)

WE HAVE TO DRIVE!

In post-apartheid Johannesburg cars have become a means of expressing social status (Laqui 2009). Writing on Johannesburg as well as other South African cities, Megan Jones (2011, 379) argues: 'In a social landscape increasingly defined by aspirational consumption, the car has powerful purchase in the South African imaginary as a site for the enactment of status, wealth and choice.' Similarly, André Czeglédy (2004, 78) observes that 'in South Africa, the car is second only to the home as a mode of material expression and aspiration'. Market trends in the consumption of luxury cars in Johannesburg and the rest of South Africa have shown exceptionally high demand (Frost & Sullivan 2016; Fioriti 2013). A frequently cited study conducted by a market research firm among the emerging black middle class a few years after the end of apartheid found that 'the product which was seen as conferring the highest status on people was the car – with men preferring BMWs or Mercedes, whilst women favoured VW Golfs or Jettas' (Seekings and Nattrass 2002, 14). Abraham McLaughlin (2005) reported in 2005 that 'more BMWs are sold in South Africa, as a percentage of new-car sales, than anywhere else in the world except Germany, the brand's home country'. Reporting on the booming sales of expensive cars, Anthony Lefifi (2013) wrote that 'South Africa has been thriving as an unlikely market for luxury cars', where the very rich did not blink at buying luxury models while 'poorer consumers [were] struggling to keep their heads above water'.

The argument that cars should be considered the most important objects in signalling social status is consistent with consumption theory. Material objects that are portable acquire more salience and are more useful since they can be more readily seen by others (Charles, Hurst, and Roussanov 2009). Yet it is also the case that while cars are a means of offering social status, they are also a 'compelled' mode of transport, given the poor public transport, the enduring legacies of car-centric transport planning, and a sprawling and segregated urban form (Morgan 2019).

If the use of cars, and especially luxury models, to display social status is not exceptional, what is unusual is the cultural overtone and intensity of the phenomenon. While the use of cars in the 'arms race' to display status affects all demographic groups, according to the nature of status competition under inequality (Wilkinson and Pickett 2018), for the black population who had been oppressed under colonialism and apartheid cars have a special meaning. In this my argument is similar to Paul Gilroy's, who, on reflecting on the relationship between African Americans and motor cars, argued, 'Their distinctive history of propertylessness and material deprivation has inclined them towards a *disproportionate investment in particular forms of property that are publicly visible and the status that corresponds to them*' (2001, 84; emphasis mine). In a study of consumption patterns across South Africa, Wolfhard Kaus found that 'Black and Coloured households spend relatively more on visible consumption than comparable White households'. He suggested this difference was between 30 and 50 per cent (Kaus 2013, 63, 70; see also Burger et al. 2015). Such consumption goods also have their own discursive registers. For example, the luxury car brand BMW is reportedly known as Black Man's Wish (Calvert 2005). Reflecting and even accentuating these practices, Bandile Leopeng and Malose Langa (2018, 2) show how, in a popular men's magazine, 'middle-class black South African masculinity is [depicted as in part] based on the acquisition of material goods' such as luxury cars. Irikidzayi Manase (2016) suggests that such depictions in the media are widespread and are found in a range of literary texts and broader media narratives across South Africa.

In post-apartheid Johannesburg, the socio-economic, spatial and cultural landscapes issue, as it were, a command to drive. For previously subordinated groups, this command has its own qualitative force: it is a way of claiming previously denied respectability and thereby constructing a dignified identity.

NO, WE CANNOT CYCLE!

If cars, and especially luxury models, are objects of desire, bicycles can ill compete. Surveys reliably indicate that the share of cycling as a mode of transport across the municipal area is below one per cent and that those who cycle to work are predominantly the poor (City of Johannesburg 2013; Statistics SA 2015). A 2014 study showed that within the Johannesburg municipality, the proportion of those who walked to work (10.6 per cent) was higher than those who cycled (0.5 per cent) (Statistics SA 2015, 36). Higher-earning income groups do not use bicycles even for short travel distances (Valjarevic and Beer 2015), relying instead on private motor cars (Mokonyama and Mubiwa 2014; Venter and Badenhorst 2014). Their use of bicycles is for leisure and sporting purposes (Bechstein 2010), involving expensive bicycles, some with similar commercial values to motor cars (Barry 2014; Branquinho 2018). Here one can deduce that such expensive machines offer prestige to their users.

The relationship between class, attitudes and utility cycling in Johannesburg is generally representative of the patterns across the country. A national household travel survey found a clear relationship between monthly income and travel mode. The majority (65.4 per cent) of people earning more than R3000 a month travelled by car, with only 8.4 per cent of this income bracket walking or cycling. In contrast, the majority (57.9 per cent) of those earning less than R500 a month walked or cycled, and only a small fraction (4.4 per cent) took a car (DOT 2005, 18). A study of travel patterns in 2011 within Gauteng province, where Johannesburg is located, concluded that 'the analysis of trip purpose, employment and household income highlights that those people who are able to afford any mode of transport . . . tend to choose to use private transport' (Culwick 2014, 140), where the 'private' category referred to cars. Underlining historical evolution in the relationship between transport and race, the same analysis found that only two per cent of the white population identified walking or cycling as their main mode of transport, instead reporting driving or motorcycling as the major mode (94 per cent).

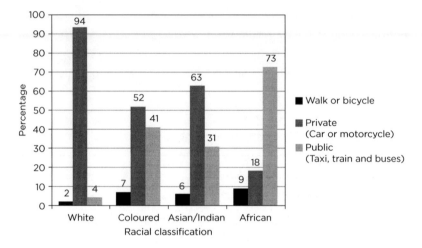

Figure 3.3

Main mode of transport by racial classification. Graph constructed by author from data available in Culwick (2014, 139)

While the more prevalent use of bicycles among the poor can be put down to a lack of choice, the popular image of cycling also figures as a deterrent to other groups (City of Johannesburg 2009; Venter et al. 2013). Reporting on public attitudes, a municipal strategy document argued that 'cycling and walking are generally associated with activities for recreation or with poverty' (City of Johannesburg 2009, 7). It was against this background that anxieties about the symbolic meanings of commuter cycling came to the fore when various actors tried to encourage the practice in the early 2000s.

Given rising concerns about traffic congestion, inequity in access to transport, and air pollution, the post-apartheid municipality sought to promote alternatives to the private car. In this search, officials turned to bicycles. Students at the University of the Witwatersrand and the University of Johannesburg were thought to be a group more amenable to commuter cycling, given the cost advantages (City of Johannesburg 2009). In an attempt to encourage students to cycle within and around the campuses, the municipal council offered various incentives. A key incentive was the introduction of cycle lanes as a road-safety solution. However, the lanes were poorly used. In part to understand the reasons behind this, researchers undertook various studies. They were surprised to find that one of the barriers to use pertained to what they called the 'stigma of being a cyclist'. In this study, respondents reported

Figure 3.4
A bicycle lane situated near the University of the Witwatersrand.
Author's collection

that cycling was viewed as a practice conducted by the working class and was not 'cool', unlike car driving (Crowhurst et al. 2015, 11–12). A newspaper columnist illustrated these concerns vividly when he complained about the municipality's pro-cycling agenda:

> An ordinary South African has big dreams. He dreams of driving the same 'black Mercedes-Benz' you drive every day yourself, and then you ask him or her to ride a bicycle? What an insult! Do you cycle to your office? Do you cycle over the weekend to do your shopping? Do you cycle yourself to check out your buddies over the weekend? Who is supposed to cycle? A poor South African! (Siso 2016, 8)

For some Johannesburg residents, then, utility cycling is shunned because of the types of identity it may connote. This is a common barrier that other researchers have found across the country. Gail Jennings writes of 'the low esteem in which bicycle transport is held by certain of the political elite'. This appraisal is shared by working-class South Africans who shake their heads at the cycling practices of a Malawian citizen, who reported to Jennings: '[Locals] don't ride bicycles . . . They feel sorry for us [foreigners]: it's like we are suffering and that we don't have money to pay for a taxi' (Jennings 2016, 63). Without an understanding of the socio-cultural legacy within which bicycles have been ensnared, it would be difficult to understand why working-class South Africans do not cycle despite the economic rationale.

If cycling for transport suggests something negative about identity, proponents aim to engineer a different desire. Some have tried to do this by launching interventions that associate cycling with urban cool. Organisers have arranged group social rides where participants are encouraged to appear in fashionable clothes (Sleepless in Soweto 2015; Waddington 2015; Tyesi 2015). Local manufacturers have also taken aesthetics into consideration, designing bicycles that are supposed to be visually appealing. In doing so they enrol bicycle owners in the design process to give an accent to individualised consumption (Whippet Cycling Co. 2013; Fixin Diaries 2016).

In a related intervention, an international organisation in collaboration with local partners designed a bicycle that was 'bright yellow and styled deliberately to be different to the conventional roadster which has almost exclusively dominated the African bicycle market for the past century'. Called the California Bike, it was supposed to vastly improve the image of 'the black, upright roadster' not only in aesthetics but also in quality and use potential, since it was, unlike the black bicycle, an 'all-terrain style' (Cox 2010, 149, 148). As an advocate of the project recalls, 'This bicycle would need to be two words – cool and functional' (Schroeder 2007, 18–19). The project reportedly 'proved successful . . . [growing] beyond the initial start-up' (Cox 2010, 149). However, the fact that the yellow bicycles and other styles designed by local companies have not become ubiquitous in Johannesburg complicates assumptions about the extent to which aesthetics can encourage cycling in the face of other constraints as well as the continuing attractions of cars. Some users remain reluctant to associate their sense of themselves with cycling.

CONCLUSIONS

This chapter has demonstrated that status anxieties over the use of bicycles and cars have been a key factor shaping their use since the founding of

Johannesburg. Struggles over identity and what it means to be a member of one social group or another have been waged through transport behaviour since 1886. In the first two historical cases cited above, we witnessed some of the work that was required to maintain notions of whiteness in colonial and apartheid South Africa: the use of legal, rhetorical and economic restrictions to restrain black people from cycling or driving. In the second two cases, I described efforts by previously dominated black people to claim respectability or dignity by acquiring luxury car models that signal wealth. This is a consequence of high post-apartheid levels of inequality and of the historically symbolic power of cars.

In all of the cases, we see a dynamic relationship between transport and identity. The initial formulation of Skinner and Rosen's notion of pre-existing identities shaping transport behaviour gives way more to their final, more fluid and complex understanding. In this, the relationship between 'identity and mobility . . . is . . . multi-faceted and contingent . . . a process rather than a fixed, finished state . . . informed by wider representations of transport users' attitudes and practices, but founded upon a far messier reality' (Skinner and Rosen 2007, 94). Instead of identities such as 'white' or 'black' existing and then informing transport behaviour, identities are constructed *through* transport behaviour. Studying mobility practices, discourses and representations will thus continue to offer new insights into how Johannesburg residents are producing their identities.

NOTES

1   The former refers to people of European descent and the latter to all subordinated people under colonialism and apartheid such as black African people, people of mixed-descent (called 'coloured'), and Indian people.

2   The newspaper *Indian Opinion* was created by Mohandas Gandhi in 1903 when he lived in South Africa. It monitored and reported on political developments in South Africa as they affected the newly immigrant Indian population. The plight of the Indian population frequently intersected with that of other subordinated groups, so it also reported on those issues.

REFERENCES

Barry, Hanna. 2014. "Cycling Is the New Golf." *Moneyweb*, 17 January 2014. http://www. moneyweb.co.za/archive/cycling-is-the-new-golf/.

Beavon, Keith. 2004. *Johannesburg: The Making and Shaping of the City*. Pretoria: Unisa Press.

Bechstein, Eva. 2010. "Cycling as a Supplementary Mode to Public Transport: A Case Study of Low Income Commuters in South Africa." Paper presented to the 29th Annual Southern African Transport Conference, South Africa, 16–19 August 2010.

Bourne, H.R.H. 1905. TAB, LTG, 115, 103/36, 22 March 1905. National Archives of South Africa, Pretoria.

Branquinho, Lance. 2018. "You Can Buy Two Brand-New Cars for the Price of SA's Most Expensive Bicycle." *Business Insider South Africa*, 26 February 2018. https://www.businessinsider.co.za/most-expensive-bicycles-in-sa-2018-2.

Burger, Ronelle, Megan Louw, Brigitte Barbara Isabel de Oliveira Pegado, and Servaas van der Berg. 2015. "Understanding Consumption Patterns of the Established and Emerging South African Black Middle Class." *Development Southern Africa* 32 (1): 41–56.

Calvert, Scott. 2005. "Black South Africans Prize Luxury Cars as Status Symbols." *Knight Ridder Tribune Business News* (Washington), 26 October 2005.

Central Statistical Service. 1992. "Report: 71-11-01: New Vehicles Registered, South Africa." Pretoria: Central Statistical Service.

Charles, Kerwin Kofi, Erik Hurst, and Nikolai Roussanov. 2009. "Conspicuous Consumption and Race." *Quarterly Journal of Economics* 124 (2): 425–67.

City of Johannesburg. 1905. Council Minutes. Johannesburg: City of Johannesburg.

———. 2009. "Framework for Non-Motorised Transport." Johannesburg: City of Johannesburg.

———. 2013. "Draft Strategic Integrated Transport Plan Framework for the City of Joburg." Johannesburg: City of Johannesburg. http://issuu.com/cojdocuments/docs/sitpf_jhb_2013.

Cox, Peter. 2010. *Moving People: Sustainable Transport Development: Challenging Expectations*. London: Zed Books.

Crowhurst, Rhiannon, Anastasia Kalantzis, Babitsanang Lekhuleng, Koketso Rakgokong, and Zaakira Raymond. 2015. "Users' and Potential Users' Perceptions of the Cycle Lanes and Their Intentions to Utilise Them." Johannesburg: University of the Witwatersrand.

Culwick, Christina. 2014. "Transitions to Non-Motorised Transport in Gauteng." In *Mobility in the Gauteng City-Region*, edited by Chris Wray and Graeme Gotz. Johannesburg: Gauteng City-Region Observatory.

Czeglédy, André P. 2004. "Getting around Town: Transportation and the Built Environment in Post-Apartheid South Africa." *City and Society* 16 (2): 63–92.

Daily Mail. 1910. "Cycle Snatching." *Daily Mail*, 31 August 1910.

———. 1921. "Coloured Men Need Not Apply." *Daily Mail*, 27 July 1921.

Delhey, Jan, and Georgi Dragolov. 2014. "Why Inequality Makes Europeans Less Happy: The Role of Distrust, Status Anxiety, and Perceived Conflict." *European Sociological Review* 30 (2): 151–65.

Delhey, Jan, Christian Schneickert, and Leonie C. Steckermeier. 2017. "Sociocultural Inequalities and Status Anxiety: Redirecting the Spirit Level Theory." *International Journal of Comparative Sociology* 58 (3): 215–40.

De Zwart, Pim. 2011. "South African Living Standards in Global Perspective, 1835–1910." *Economic History of Developing Regions* 26 (1): 49–74.

DOT (Department of Transport). 2005. "Key Results of the National Household Travel Survey: The First South African National Household Travel Survey 2003." Pretoria: Department of Transport.

Fioriti, Joris. 2013. "The New El Dorado for Luxury Cars." *IOL*, 29 December 2013. https://www.iol.co.za/business-report/international/the-new-el-dorado-for-luxury-cars-1627232.

Fixin Diaries. 2016. "About." 2016. http://fixindiaries.co.za/about.

Friss, Evan. 2015. *The Cycling City: Bicycles and Urban America in the 1890s*. Chicago: University of Chicago Press.

Frost & Sullivan. 2016. "Demand Analysis for Luxury Cars in Africa." 27 October 2016. https://www.researchandmarkets.com/reports/3979160/demand-analysis-for-luxury-cars-in-africa.

Gilroy, Paul. 2001. "Driving while Black." In *Car Cultures*, edited by Daniel Miller, 81–104. Oxford and New York: Berg.

Goffman, Erving. 1951. "Symbols of Class Status." *British Journal of Sociology* 2 (4): 294–304. https://doi.org/10.2307/588083.

Indian Opinion. 1904. "Transvaal Locations: The Western Suburbs Object to Locations." *Indian Opinion*, 17 March 1904.

———. 1905. "Does a Kaffir Feel?" *Indian Opinion*, 4 February 1905.

Jay, Ell. 1919. "News from the Rand." In *Motoring in South Africa: The Official Organ of the Royal Automobile Club of South Africa*. Cape Town: Royal Automobile Club of South Africa.

Jennings, Gail. 2016. "Freedom of Movement/Freedom of Choice: An Enquiry into Utility Cycling and Social Justice in Post-Apartheid Cape Town, 1994–2015." In *Bicycle Justice and Urban Transformation: Biking for All?* edited by Aaron Golub, L. Melody Hoffman, Adonia E. Lugo, and F. Gerardo Sandoval, 53–69. Abingdon and New York: Taylor and Francis.

Johnston, R.H. 1976. *Early Motoring in South Africa: A Pictorial History*. Worthing: Littlehampton Book Services.

Jones, Megan. 2011. "Cars, Capital and Disorder in Ivan Vladislavić's The Exploded View and Portrait with Keys." *Social Dynamics* 37 (3): 379–93.

Kaus, Wolfhard. 2013. "Conspicuous Consumption and 'Race': Evidence from South Africa." *Journal of Development Economics* 100 (1): 63–73.

Khosa, Meshack M. 1998. "'The Travail of Travelling': Urban Transport in South Africa, 1930–1996." *Transport Reviews* 18 (1): 17–33.

Kruger, Jill Swart, and Louise Chawla. 2002. "'We Know Something Someone Doesn't Know': Children Speak Out on Local Conditions in Johannesburg." *Environment and Urbanization* 14 (2): 85–96.

Lamont, Mark, and Rebekah Lee. 2015. "Arrive Alive: Road Safety in Kenya and South Africa." *Technology and Culture* 56 (2): 464–88.

Lancaster, Illana. 2011. "Modalities of Mobility: Johannesburg Learners' Daily Negotiations of the Uneven Terrain of the City." *Southern African Review of Education with Education with Production* 17 (1): 49–63.

Laqui, Laura. 2009. "Reorganizations of Space and Culture in a Car-Oriented Society: The Case of Johannesburg." Master's dissertation, University of Cape Town. https://open.uct.ac.za/handle/11427/12504.

Layte, Richard, and Christopher T. Whelan. 2014. "Who Feels Inferior? A Test of the Status Anxiety Hypothesis of Social Inequalities in Health." *European Sociological Review* 30 (4): 525–35.

Learmont, Tom. 1990. *Cycling in South Africa*. Sandton: Media House.

Lefifi, Anthony Tekiso. 2013. "SA Thrives as an Unlikely Market for Luxury Cars." *TimesLive*, 8 September 2013. https://www.timeslive.co.za/sunday-times/lifestyle/2013-09-08-sa-thrives-as-an-unlikely-market-for-luxury-cars/.

Leopeng, Bandile, and Malose Langa. 2018. "Black Middle-Class Masculinities in Postapartheid South Africa: Consumerism, Fashion and the Portrayal of Masculine Identities in Destiny Man Magazine." *Fashion Theory* 23 (1): 1–27.

Longhurst, James. 2015. *Bike Battles: A History of Sharing the American Road*. Seattle: University of Washington Press.

Makan, Darshika. 2015. "Navigating the City: Female Students' Experiences of Movement in Johannesburg." Johannesburg: University of the Witwatersrand. http://wiredspace.wits.ac.za/handle/10539/20966.

Manase, Irikidzayi. 2016. "Black Diamonds and Excess in the Fictional and Lived South African City of the Early 2000s." *English Academy Review* 33 (1): 87–96.

Maylam, Paul. 1995. "Explaining the Apartheid City: 20 Years of South African Urban
    Historiography." *Journal of Southern African Studies* 21 (1): 19–38.

McLaughlin, Abraham. 2005. "South Africa's Rising BMW Class: 6.9 Percent of New Cars
    Bought in the Country Last Year Were BMWs, Compared with 1.5 Percent in the US."
    Christian Science Monitor, 6 October 2005.

Mokonyama, Mathetha, and Brian Mubiwa. 2014. "Transport in the Shaping of Space." In
    Changing Space, Changing City: Johannesburg after Apartheid, edited by Philip Harrison,
    Graeme Gotz, Alison Todes, and Chris Wray, 194–214. Johannesburg: Wits University Press.

Morgan, Njogu. 2019. *Cycling Cities: The Johannesburg Experience*. Eindhoven: Foundation
    for the History of Technology.

Phillips, Howard. 2014. "Locating the Location of a South African Location: The Paradoxical
    Pre-History of Soweto." *Urban History* 41 (2): 311–32.

Piketty, Thomas. 2014. *Capital in the Twenty-First Century*. Translated by Arthur
    Goldhammer. Cambridge, MA: Belknap Press.

Posel, Deborah. 2010. "Races to Consume: Revisiting South Africa's History of Race,
    Consumption and the Struggle for Freedom." *Ethnic and Racial Studies* 33 (2): 157–75.

RAC (Royal Automobile Club of South Africa). 1919. "The Motor Trader's Association." In
    *Motoring in South Africa: The Official Organ of the Royal Automobile Club of South
    Africa*. Cape Town: Royal Automobile Club of South Africa.

———. 1921. "Johannesburg Driving Licences." In *Motoring in South Africa: The Official Organ
    of the Royal Automobile Club of South Africa*. Cape Town: Royal Automobile Club of
    South Africa.

Rand Daily Mail. 1934. "Ban on the Car-Driving Native: Legislation Proposed." *Rand Daily
    Mail*, 4 August 1934. www.readex.com.

Rand Pioneers. 1905. *Second Annual Report with Appendices of the Rand Pioneers*.
    Johannesburg: The Rand Pioneers Association.

Schreiner, O.D. 1934. "Native Motor Drivers: A Prohibitive Law Unthinkable." *Rand Daily Mail*,
    6 August 1934.

Schroeder, Bradley. 2007. "Doing Business in Africa: The California Bike Coalition Comes of
    Age." *Sustainable Transport* (Fall): 18–31.

Seedat, Mohamed, Sarah MacKenzie, and Dinesh Mohan. 2006. "The Phenomenology of
    Being a Female Pedestrian in an African and an Asian City: A Qualitative Investigation."
    Transportation Research Part F: Traffic Psychology and Behaviour 9 (2): 139–53.

Seekings, Jeremy, and Nicoli Nattrass. 2002. "Class, Distribution and Redistribution in
    Post-Apartheid South Africa." *Transformation: Critical Perspectives on Southern Africa*
    50 (1): 1–30.

Seiler, Cotten. 2006. "'So That We as a Race Might Have Something Authentic to Travel By':
African American Automobility and Cold-War Liberalism." *American Quarterly* 58 (4):
1091–1117.

———. 2007. "The Significance of Race to Transport History." *Journal of Transport History*
28 (2): 307–11.

Siso, Sipho. 2016. "Tau's 'Braaivleis' Lanes." *Rosebank Killarney Gazette* (blog).
22 September 2016. http://rosebankkillarneygazette.co.za/199640/
taus-braaivleis-lanes/.

Skinner, Dave, and Paul Rosen. 2007. "Hell Is Other Cyclists: Rethinking Transport and
Identity." In *Cycling and Society*, edited by Dave Horton, Paul Rosen, and Peter Cox,
83–96. Aldershot: Ashgate.

Sleepless in Soweto. 2015. "Cycle Chic: Ladies Join Johannesburg's Fixie Movement and
Tips for Joining a Ride." *Tastemakers Africa*, 2 April 2015. http://tastemakersafrica.com/
tstmkrs2015/cycle-chic-ladies-join-johannesburgs-fixie-movement-tips-
for-joining-a-ride/.

Star, The. 1908. "Bicycle Thefts: Transvaal Cyclists' Union Proposal." *The Star*,
20 November 1908.

Statistics SA. 2015. "National Household Travel Survey: Gauteng Profile. 03-20-10."
Pretoria: Statistics South Africa. www.statssa.gov.za/publications/Report-03-20-10/
Report-03-20-102014.pdf.

Sulla, Victor, and Precious Zikhali. 2018. "Overcoming Poverty and Inequality in South
Africa: An Assessment of Drivers, Constraints and Opportunities." World Bank. http://
documents.worldbank.org/curated/en/530481521735906534/Overcoming-Poverty-
and-Inequality-in-South-Africa-An-Assessment-of-Drivers-Constraints-and-
Opportunities.

Sunday Times. 1907. "Cycle Thieving." *Sunday Times*, 17 November 1907.

———. 1926. "All Drivers Must Be Licensed." *Sunday Times*, 18 July 1926.

Trigg, Andrew B. 2001. "Veblen, Bourdieu, and Conspicuous Consumption." *Journal of
Economic Issues* 35 (1): 99–115.

Tyesi, Thobeka. 2015. "Fixin Diaries: A Lifestyle Brand That Creates Custom Bikes."
Represent, 24 April 2015. https://represent.co.za/fixin-diaries-a-lifestyle-brand-
that-creates-custom-bikes/.

Valjarevic, D., and L. de Beer. 2015. "Bike Sharing in Johannesburg: Trendy Idea but Is It
Financially Feasible?" Paper presented at the 34th Annual Southern African Transport
Conference. http://www.satc.org.za/.

Veblen, Thorstein. 2009. *The Theory of the Leisure Class*. Edited by Martha Banta. Oxford: Oxford University Press.

Venter, Christo, and Willem Badenhorst. 2014. "2011 GCRO Quality of Life Survey: Analysis of Transport Data." In *Mobility in the Gauteng City-Region*, edited by Chris Wray and Graeme Gotz. Johannesburg: Gauteng City-Region Observatory.

Venter, K., M. Mokonyana, M. Letebele, S. Dube, and N. Masondo. 2013. "Analysis of Modal Shift in South Africa: A Qualitative Investigation." Paper presented at the 32nd Annual Southern African Transport Conference, 8–11 July, CSIR International Convention Centre, Pretoria.

Waddington, Jaime. 2015. "Cycling in Soweto." *Elle South Africa*, 27 March 2015.

Weinberg, Darin. 2009. "Social Constructionism." In *The New Blackwell Companion to Social Theory*, edited by Bryan S. Turner, 281–99. Hoboken: Wiley-Blackwell.

Whippet Cycling Co. 2013. "About." The Whippet Cycling Co., 29 January 2013. http://whippetcyclingco.com/about/.

Wilkinson, Richard, and Kate Pickett. 2018. *The Inner Level: How More Equal Societies Reduce Stress, Restore Sanity and Improve Everyone's Wellbeing*. London: Allen Lane.

Woodward, Ian. 2007. *Understanding Material Culture*. Newbury Park: Sage Publications.

TAXI DIARIES II: TRAVELLING WHILE FEMALE

BAELETSI TSATSI

ONE

There are certain clothes I can't wear when I get into some taxis. I had a job interview at the SABC and I wore my beautiful silk wraparound skirt and that day I learnt, 'Don't wear soft clothes in a taxi headed towards Auckland Park, they will tear'. I can't wear certain dresses or pants if I'm going on particular routes because they just worsen the taxi rank abuse I'm already prone to. The night before, I think long and hard about the outfit that will make me disappear or make me less enticing to the queue marshals and the taxi drivers. An outfit that will make it easy to sit in front with the driver should that be the only seat left. But it is not about sex, it is about power. And the taxi driver's power doesn't really care what I'm wearing, it only cares that I'm female.

TWO

The taxi driver and the queue marshal are cruel to us young women, but when a person with a disability comes, their hearts soften. The men who called you names, from fat to bitch, all drop their ego and plot to make the trip comfortable for the person with a disability. They help get the person in the taxi, ask during the trip if the person is OK, and help them get off at their destination. They are soft, gentle and caring, but with the same mouth they abuse you for being present in this world. These men know right from wrong, they choose who deserves their kindness.

THREE

The driver talks with his hands. He does what Shakespeare calls 'sows the air with his hands'. Next to him sits a beautiful woman, the kind you feel compelled to talk to, and as a result the taxi is driving itself.

FOUR

The taxi driver hands the woman his phone for her to enter her number. She looks at the phone and waves her hand to say no: 'Huuuu, my boyfriend, every day checking, checking my phone,' the woman says. 'Mhhmmm, checking your phone?' the driver says, suggesting that he does the very same thing to his girlfriend, and puts away his phone.

FIVE

It is a Friday night and I'm catching the last taxi to Phumula. There are a lot of drunk men in the taxi, talking loud and boldly enjoying the spirit of month-end. There are two more women. One is in front, chatting with the driver and therefore safe and protected from harm. Another is travelling with a colleague and they're spewing xenophobic talk: the company they work for is retrenching South Africans because foreign nationals are willing to work for less. And then there is me. I come from a performance. I stood in front of a paying audience and showcased my skill and talent. For an hour, I had power and led the audience on a journey through ancient Africa and all its magic and wonder, but now I'm here, in a taxi, powerless and saying a prayer, 'Don't let any of these men get off where I'm getting off. Please God.' Men can cause harm. Drunk men can cause even more harm. Drunk men at night can be deadly. Please God. Amen.

SIX

It's a winter evening. My cousin is travelling from Mafikeng to Joburg to accompany my aunt on a trip. We, my aunt, my other cousin and I, are waiting for him with excitement. My aunt calls to check on him and he asks that my cousin meets him in town, Park Station, where the taxi from Mafikeng will drop him. He is unsure about which taxi to take to come to where we stay, but I know even he, a man of over 30 years, is scared to walk alone in town at night. A few hours later, my two cousins walk through the kitchen door into the lounge and with deep sighs sink into the couch. My aunt and I need not ask what happened, so we listen intently as the story pours out bit by bit, each cousin taking a turn to tell a moment of the incident. A father and daughter are travelling together, the seats are filled so father and daughter are separated, and daughter ends up sitting next to a drunk paedophile, who takes the opportunity to fondle the girl child repeatedly until her whimpers are attended to. Seats are swapped and the paedophile sits comfortably in the dark, having satisfied his need, even if only for a bit. Honestly, what stops us from killing people?

4 'THE WHITE CENTRELINE VANISHES': FRAGILITY AND ANXIETY IN THE ELUSIVE METROPOLIS

DEREK HOOK

'IMAGINE THERE ARE NO WHITES'

In March 2016, a young white academic and colleague of mine, Terblanche Delport, sparked outrage at a Johannesburg conference at the University of the Witwatersrand. As part of an imagined demise of structures of white privilege, Delport called on white people in South Africa 'to commit suicide as an ethical act'. Or, as was reported by the PRAAG (Pro-Afrikaans Action Group) website, 'A lecturer in philosophy yesterday said at a radical anti-white, anti-Afrikaner conference at the University of the Witwatersrand that "whites should die".' Here is perhaps the most controversial part of his written paper:

> The reality [in South Africa] is that most white people spend their whole lives only engaging black people in subservient positions – cleaners, gardeners, etc. My question is then how can a person not be racist if that's the way they live their lives? The only way then for white people to become part of Africa is to not exist as white people anymore. If the goal is to dismantle white supremacy, and white supremacy is white culture and vice versa, then the goal has to be to dismantle white culture and ultimately white people themselves. The total integration into Africa by white people will also automatically then mean

the death of white people as white as a concept would not exist anymore. (Delport, pers. comm., 16 March 2016)

Provocative as Delport's statements were, it seems clear from reading this extract that his primary target was white privilege, that is, white culture within South Africa as a structure of domination – what many critics today refer to as 'whiteness' (Ahmed 2007; Ngo 2017; Yancy 2012). Delport was, of course, not alone in offering such a speculative picturing of white demise, as the titles of two recent books – Ferial Haffajee's *What If There Were No Whites in South Africa?* (2015) and Nicky Falkof's *The End of Whiteness* (2016) – make clear. Nonetheless, as quickly became apparent, his remarks touched a nerve. SA-News.com announced that Delport had 'publicly called for the genocide of White South Africans' and lamented how unfortunate it was that he had 'not been accused of hate speech'. The Bondstaat Facebook page alleged that Delport had claimed that 'White South Africans should commit suicide and die out without having children', before adding, 'The genocidal hatemonger's details are below if you would like to "discuss" his very public opinion with him' (Bondstaat n.d.).

There seemed to be a degree of wilful misunderstanding at work in such reactions. Delport emphasised that his was a provocation, a rhetorical act, an ethical gesture rather than – as one would imagine was quite obvious – a literal suggestion. Ultimately, Delport's point was made more in the responses to his provocation than in that provocation itself. This is where I want to pick up the thread: by arguing that there was something genuinely ethical in these statements. Delport took his white audience to a space of contemplated racial demise, to the threshold of a type of symbolic extinction, to a proposed 'end of whiteness'. It is precisely this site of anxiety as it has occurred in recent post-apartheid culture that concerns me in this chapter. Such examples of white anxiety are, I argue, omnipresent, found in both dramatic and mundane instances, underlying both intellectual discourse and everyday dilemmas of identity.

As an example of anxiety at the level of racial identity, we might take the case of an exasperated white caller who phoned in to Eusebius McKaiser's popular radio talk-show. Responding to McKaiser's thoughts on the ingrained entitlement of many white South Africans, the man meekly protested, 'But I've even learned Xhosa.' McKaiser (2012) responded by pointing out that, significant as this was, it was by no means an adequate measure of redress. The caller's following question, with its clear undertone of desperation, 'So what must I do?', carried the connotation of an even more pronounced crisis: 'What must I be?', or more appropriately yet perhaps: 'What must I become?'

WHITE FRAGILITY IN THE ELUSIVE METROPOLIS

In 2011, American scholar Robin DiAngelo coined the concept of 'white fragility', which she defined as

> a state in which even a minimum of racial stress becomes intolerable, triggering a range of defensive moves. These moves include the outward display of emotions such as anger, fear, and guilt, and behaviours such as argumentation, silence, and leaving the stress-inducing situation. These behaviours, in turn, function to reinstate white racial equilibrium. (2011, 54)

DiAngelo is indebted to a series of influential theorists of whiteness (Dyer 1997; Fine 1997; Frankenberg 1993), who, she tells us, have used the notion to signify a set of locations that are historically, socially, politically and culturally constructed and that are intrinsically linked to dynamic relations of domination. Whiteness is thus 'a constellation of processes and practices rather than a discrete entity' (2011, 56).

Like several recent theorists of whiteness (Bonilla-Silva 2017; Ngo 2017), DiAngelo draws inspiration from Bourdieu's influential notion of the habitus, which helps us understand how whiteness 'produces and reproduces thoughts, perceptions, expressions and actions. Strategies of response to "disequilibrium" in the habitus are not based on conscious intentionality but rather result from unconscious dispositions towards practice and depend on the power position the agent occupies in the social structure' (1993, 58).

The idea of white fragility highlights a mode of experience that comes to the fore when white subjects feel themselves to be out of place. White fragility is in many ways a theory precisely of dislocation. There is, in DiAngelo's account, a recurring emphasis on whiteness as situated, as a located and thereby also symbolic and historically grounded set of habits, responses and dispositions. The concept also evokes a sense of whiteness as vulnerable, as something that can be fragmented, broken, even destroyed. It stresses how whiteness is itself a nervous condition (see also Falkof 2014; Steyn 2004). This underlines what

I would call the narcissism of whiteness: its apparent inability *not* to experience a type of racial anxiety once forced out of its habitual bounds. The factor of dislocation, of literally being out of one's place, clearly also possesses a concrete spatial and indeed geographical dimension.

It is no coincidence, then, that the examples I draw on in this chapter are all centred on Johannesburg. Johannesburg is not only the most densely populated, racially diverse and rapidly changing city in South Africa – bearing out Achille Mbembe and Sarah Nuttall's (2008) description of the city as both 'the elusive metropolis' and a globalised African megacity (indeed, an 'Afropolis') – it is also the country's cultural and economic hub, characterised by a high rate of 'border crossings' between different and often geographically proximate yet sharply divergent socio-economic and racial zones. While Johannesburg is certainly not alone in this, it does feature – on a larger scale than anywhere else in the country – jarring juxtapositions between the near-adjacent spaces of white suburban affluence and township life, as the disparities between Sandton and Alexandra, Fourways and Diepsloot, and, to a somewhat lesser extent, Johannesburg South and Soweto make clear (Harber 2011). Of all South African cities – and the influx of African immigration into the city over the last decade plays a key role here – Johannesburg retains the greatest prospect of destabilising 'racial encounters' (Durrheim and Dixon 2014), the greatest possibility of whiteness being dislocated, experiencing itself as visible, vulnerable and anxious.

'SOWETO DOES NOT EXIST'

Johannesburg is also a city which contains ghosts. In the opening pages of Mark Gevisser's autobiographical *Lost and Found in Johannesburg*, the author reflects on a childhood game in which he impersonated the role of a taxi dispatcher. With the aid of his much-loved Holmden's map book of Johannesburg he would play at plotting routes between various far-flung locations and addresses. Although he became increasingly adept at such challenges, there was a series of anomalous empty spaces in the book, areas that had not been mapped, which seemed thus to contain no inhabitants but impeded his route-making activities. These apparently non-existent, or indeed ghostly, areas – although integral to the greater Johannesburg metropolitan area – were, of course, townships, principally Soweto. After the events of the Soweto uprising in 1976, when this area could no longer be easily repressed from the everyday thoughts of white South Africans, the young Gevisser came to realise that

> *Soweto wasn't there!* The huge, sprawling agglomeration of townships was a phantom in that bottom left-hand corner, in the white space below Riverlea … where I had insouciantly plotted so many of my own fantasy suburbs; unmarked, unheeded, home to hundreds of thousands of people who commuted to the rest of the city to make it to work each day … even though the area constituted a huge part of Johannesburg, both in population and physical size, it did not feature at all on any road maps to the city … In some brazen example … cartographers actually had the audacity to mark out Soweto, albeit in a solid bluish block … before obscuring it with the inset of the downtown area. Thus does it appear, a leering dark underside to the city, its evening shadow. (2014, 15–16)

In retrospect Gevisser recalled as a child having heard of Alexandra ('it was that thing called a "township", that place where the black people who worked for us would go'), even though, to all intents and purposes, 'It was on another planet' (2014, 12). (Tellingly, he uses this phrase twice in two pages in speaking about Alexandra.) As well as the prospect of whiteness made highly visible, Johannesburg also contains a powerful tradition of 'non-whiteness' denied. Both these features – Soweto and, by extension, blackness being denied and whiteness being made unnerving, self-conscious, vulnerable – give us reason to characterise Johannesburg as a place haunted by anxiety, indeed, as *the* anxious metropolis in contemporary South Africa.

FEAR AND LOATHING OUTSIDE LUTHULI HOUSE

In an earlier study of post-apartheid whiteness, one of my interviewees told me about his experience of inner-city Johannesburg. Walking near Luthuli House, the headquarters of the governing African National Congress, he became aware of some black men watching him. (A point of context: this event occurred in 2011, around the time that Julius Malema, who was then the rowdy president of the ANC's Youth League and who had become something of a 'folk devil for whiteness' [Falkof 2014], was appearing at a disciplinary hearing for, among other things, the dressing-down of a white BBC journalist.)

Respondent: I went to Luthuli House, during the Julius Malema [disciplinary] hearing ... I actually went to have a look ... There I am standing ... and there is this group of six guys wearing yellow T-shirts with Malema's face on it, [holding] knobkerries and sticks. They walked past and looked at me and one ... said, 'We hate all you fucking whites in South Africa.' I was with four Indian guys and one said, 'It's time for us to get out of here' and so we bolted.

Interviewer: What did you make of that? You felt ... nervous, put under threat?

Respondent: Nervous? *Jeeslike*. I felt like a complete idiot walking down there. I couldn't feel comfortable standing on the street. They came right past me ... and I felt seriously under threat. They were armed. They could have done anything. There were two cops standing across the road and they probably wouldn't stop these guys.

Interviewer: You think this was said in the heat of the moment, or do you think this is how they really felt?

Respondent: I think it is how they feel.

Interviewer: What do you think white people think about that ... do they take [such comments] seriously?

Respondent: I constantly hear people talking about leaving the country. Then someone in the government will say, 'Well, pack your bags, we don't need you here.'

FEAR OF A BLACK PLANET

A strikingly similar anecdote – even if separated by twenty or so years – is supplied by journalist and author Rian Malan in *My Traitor's Heart*. This is how Malan recalls a drunken night with his black colleague Mike, which ended up in Soweto:

> At night in Soweto, you fear what you can't see; you fear the *tsotsis*, the knifemen ... It struck me that I was possibly the only white man in this vast black city and I started getting edgy ... On our way into one shebeen, a disembodied black face suspended in that weird yellow light muttered something to Mike in a tribal tongue. 'He wants to know,' Mike chuckled, 'if this whitey is ripe for the picking.' Inside that shebeen, the black drinkers scowled darkly at the sight of white skin, and even Mike thought it prudent to go elsewhere ...

> Ancient, animal unease started eating at my viscera. I slipped outside myself, and started watching Malan go through the motions … fumbling the black power handshake, saying 'Hey' bra,' 'How you,' bra' – and, 'Tell me,' bra, is my paranoia showing?' (1990, 287–8)

A little past midnight, Malan and his colleague find themselves at 'someone's Formica kitchen table, having one for the road', when

> A black stranger appeared in the doorway, looked me up and down, and muttered something to Mike … in a language I did not understand … I started thinking about murder and robbery, about sharpened bicycle spokes in the heart, a favourite means of dispatch in Soweto … I surged to my feet … and walked out into the menacing yellow night. A lone white man on foot in Soweto in the middle of the night … I kept my eyes down and moved fast. I passed a group of youths loitering in the surreal yellow glow; their mouths opened, and they spoke to me but no sound registered. One disembodied foot followed another … The night was as silent as outer space. I was walking on the moon … I was out of my mind with terror. (1990, 289)

Interestingly, at several points in his account Malan draws on the tropes of science fiction. He is the last (white) man in a foreign world (illuminated with a 'surreal yellow glow'); the experience of being out of (racial) place is tantamount to being on another planet; he is surrounded by others whose speech is unintelligible and whose motives are darkly opaque. This veering into a different genre is crucial: racial difference – and, indeed, racial threat (or white fragility) – is so acutely experienced that it cannot be conveyed within the terms of conventional journalism.

The anecdotes described above mark very different moments in the history of the city. The reference to bicycle-spoke killings in the Malan extract is a marker of late-1980s apartheid Johannesburg, when large-scale public violence featured daily in the news and the country seemed on the verge of civil war. The Luthuli House example occurred around thirty years later in post-apartheid South Africa, a historical situation which, while still characterised by particularly criminal violence, was not a period of large-scale civil unrest and political violence. That being said, there are also fascinating parallels between them. In both accounts a white man enters a black majority space ('the black city', in Malan's terms); is made the object of the gaze of black men; battles to fathom the intentions of those around him; and subsequently undergoes a vertigo of unease, experiencing the dread not merely of racial isolation but of whiteness alone.

While it seems evident that DiAngelo's notion of white fragility is relevant to the above examples, it needs to be amended if it is to be applied to a post-apartheid South African context. Moreover, it does not go far enough. Anxiety, I will argue, is a better concept with which we might explore such fraught, defensive and vulnerable experiences of whiteness in the post-apartheid context (in this respect see also Crapanzano 1985; Hook 2015).

I make this claim for three reasons. Firstly, although DiAngelo is certainly right to highlight the factor of unconscious dispositions, she could go further to explore the imaginaries of white fragility, to attend to the narratives and, more pertinently, the fantasies that attach to such experience of whiteness dislocated. Secondly, the moments of threatened and defensive whiteness that I have come across in the post-apartheid context (see also Steyn 2004; Steyn and Foster 2008) are more pronounced than those discussed by DiAngelo. 'Fragility' doesn't quite do justice to the affective intensity, to the virulence of the threat or the aggressiveness of response typically elicited in such situations. A broader and more multidimensional sense of ontological insecurity is involved. Thirdly, fragility is static (to be fragile is to remain fragile; there is little scope to adapt, to become robust). It does not lend itself to an understanding of transformation, and is therefore of limited value if political theorisation prioritises precisely the possibilities of change.

CONFRONTING THE INSECT: A PARADIGM OF ANXIETY

Time for theory. I draw inspiration in this chapter from a Lacanian conceptualisation of anxiety (Harari 2001; Lacan 2014; Soler 2016). Let me say why. A Lacanian model is profoundly linked to issues of symbolic location, to positionality. As such it offers us a viable means of extending the notion of white fragility precisely as experience of *dis*location. A Lacanian psychoanalytic conceptualisation, moreover, is highly attuned to the realm of unconscious fantasy, to the multiple dimensionality of vulnerability, to ontological insecurity beyond the merely subjective, and to the prospects of change. A caveat immediately follows: although I will draw on a psychoanalytic conceptualisation of anxiety in what follows, this is not a call for a more explicitly *psychological* engagement. My suggestion is that we might treat anxiety as a conceptual frame which reaches beyond the remit of the psychological, indeed as a framework with which to read a variety of literary references, fieldwork observations and experiences within post-apartheid culture.

Jacques Lacan (2014) offers a brief vignette at the beginning of his Seminar X which draws together many of the constituent elements of anxiety. This 'apologue', as he calls it, serves as a bridge between Seminar X (Anxiety) and his previous Seminar IX (Identification), a fact which stresses how crucial the latter topic is for Lacan in phenomena of anxiety. He invokes a scenario in which a dazed person awakens to find themselves in a dreadful situation. They can feel that they are wearing a mask, although they have no idea what the features of the mask might be; in short, they don't know what they look like. Before them towers the inscrutable figure of a giant praying mantis, whose intentions are difficult to gauge, but which seems less than friendly. The Kafkaesque quality of this fable should not distract us from its expository value. What the subject experiences for Lacan is an anxiety – or, indeed, an anguish, to follow more recent translations of his work (see Soler 2016) – of multiple intersecting levels.

There is, firstly, what Freud (1926) would have understood as anxiety due to a real danger (*Realangst*), that is, a 'realistic' anxiety at the prospect of grievous bodily injury. (In both the above examples this factor is present, even if it is not clear how realistic the bodily threat is.) There is also, secondly, anxiety at the level of personal identity, the anxiety of the ego or, differently put, the anxiety arising from the subject's inability to summon up a familiar or self-sustaining image of themselves. It helps to recall here that in Lacan's example the subject does not know what they look like; their self-image – their sense of who they are – cannot be relied upon. (It is interesting in this respect that Malan's description entails a dissociative moment in which, as he puts it, 'I slipped outside myself'. It seems significant also that both Malan and my interviewee felt themselves to be the only white man present.) Then there is, thirdly, anxiety at the level of symbolic intersubjectivity, the anxiety of not knowing quite what one represents relative to the opaque desire of the Other. It is black men in both the above examples – potentially aggressive or unduly agitated – who assume the place of this vexing Other.

Anxiety thus entails the subject's difficulty of reassessment, the dilemma of trying to redefine themselves, of trying to be sure of their own desires and those of the Other. Importantly, then, anxiety here is not a passing emotion or psychological experience. Anxiety, thus understood, cannot be limited to a circumstantial or simply intrasubjective affect; it entails an intersubjective dimension (with the Other) and it speaks as such to the underpinnings of the subject's most crucial identifications.

In practice, of course, the above schematisation appears to break down: anxiety is difficult to confine to any one of these areas (realistic anxiety, anxiety related to a failing self-image, anxiety of symbolic intersubjectivity). Conceptually, however, it remains useful, highlighting that anxiety can be engendered in a wide variety of experiences, rational and imaginary, and that the characteristically human experience of anxiety spills across the above conjoined registers of experience.[1] Anxiety can, as such, be thought of as a reverberation of lacks – lack being coextensive with excess in Lacanian theory. (A pronounced lack of physical or ontological security gives rise, for example, to a surplus of anxious excitation.) The Lacanian conceptualisation is particularly helpful in this respect: it enables us to appreciate the reverberating and, thereby, escalating quality of anxiety.

Taking account of this multidimensionality perhaps helps us appreciate why, in the Luthuli House example, the research participant's sense of agitation moved so rapidly across types of anxiety. The issue of (perceived) physical danger ('I felt seriously under threat') shifted quickly to anxieties of identity and self-definition ('I felt like a complete idiot'), to the question of the desire of the Other, embodied in this situation by the imagined figure of Malema, to the broader societal dilemma of what the role of whites might be in a future South Africa. There is a similar multidimensionality in Malan's case: a concern about bodily security ('bicycle spokes in the heart') is linked to a sense of ego dissociation ('I slipped outside myself') and to a pronounced distance from the familiar symbolic world ('walking on the moon', 'silent as outer space'). This is characteristic, I argue, of white anxiety in the post-apartheid context, experienced as it is on the associated levels of physical security, a compromised ego (in other words, the failure of one's self-image) and symbolic identity (the threat to one's historical, societal set of values). It is on account of this multidimensionality, this multifaceted sense of ontological insecurity, that the notion of white fragility proves inadequate.

None of this is to make excuses for – or justify – white anxiety. To adopt an apologetic or defensive stance would be to imply that anxiety is necessarily a negative or detrimental phenomenon. Clinically, this is certainly not the case. If anything, we could argue that there is a need for *more* white anxiety in the post-apartheid context. Why? Well, we might ask a related question: why should the notion of anxiety benefit us at all, analytically? One answer is to be found in psychoanalyst Bruce Fink's thoughts on the value of anxiety in clinical treatments:

> Anxiety plays a role in clinical work in that when it manifests itself it signals to the clinician that he or she is getting close to something, and that interpretation could really have a truly significant effect at that moment. It indicates something about *object a* [i.e. that which causes desire] … that it is operating at that point, that there's a concern with loss, a question of castration. A treatment in which anxiety doesn't present itself is almost unthinkable; if you never arouse any anxiety in your patients, you probably will never get anywhere … Anxiety always appears at the moment where there's something repressed – the repressed is about to appear in some way or is in play, being touched upon in some way. (2014, 247)

We might say then, speaking figuratively, that there is some value in confronting the insect.

THE UNWANTED FUTURE

Having discussed the multidimensionality of white anxiety and having pointed very briefly to how the notion of anxiety might alert us to the possibilities of change at least in the clinical domain, let us move now to explore the fantasmatic dimension of such anxieties.

Anxiety is always a temporal relation, certainly inasmuch as it entails a future-oriented sense of anticipation or dread. Anxiety is, as Freud (1926) insists, in part a signal, a warning; it is not itself a traumatic experience, but rather the nervous expectation of such an experience (hence Crapanzano's [1985] equation of anxiety in the white South African context with the state of *waiting for something to happen*). Such a future-oriented temporality lends itself to the production of fantasmatic narratives. Hence also the importance of the state of anticipation for Lacanian psychoanalysis: what cannot be known with any degree of certainty is fertile ground for the ruminations of the unconscious.

One of Lacan's favoured means of illustrating the temporality of fantasy is the example of cinema. A cinematic narrative can be halted at a given moment, the frame fixed, meaning that we are stuck apprehending a given scene so as to prevent the depiction of something catastrophic or traumatic, namely (to use the psychoanalytic jargon) the scene of castration. However, not only does anxiety necessitate the dimension of futurity, but futurity itself necessitates fantasy. Why so? The nervous energies of anticipation call for attempts at narrative domestication, to be given the coherence of a scenario, a storyline – even if that storyline is a nightmarish one. It is for this reason also that fantasy in a Lacanian framework always involves two facets: the unconscious deployment of a nightmarish potentiality (the psychoanalytic name for which is castration) and the narcissistically satisfying and typically utopian scene of reassurance – oft revisited – that holds this catastrophic eventuality at bay.

The dimension of fantasy enables us to respond to a foreseeable objection. Given the staggering rate of murders and criminal violence occurring each year in South Africa, surely the above anxieties are justified, even reasonable? A brief look at South Africa's crime statistics would seemingly confirm that such anxieties are neither neurotic nor irrational. That being said, two considerations emerge which suggest that this seemingly 'realistic' anxiety nonetheless entails a thoroughly fantasmatic component. The first requires a brief digression.

In *A Time to Kill* (1996) – a film adaptation of a John Grisham novel set in the southern US state of Mississippi – Matthew McConaughey plays Jake Brigance, a young attorney with the difficult task of defending a black man accused of murdering two white men who had raped his 10-year-old daughter. Aware that the case is slipping away from him, Brigance asks the jury, as part of his closing argument, to imagine in as much detail as possible the scene of the rape: a little black girl being raped by two white men. After leading the jury through a gruesome description of the various injuries and traumas perpetrated against the girl, Brigance says: 'Now imagine she is white.' The effect of this switching of racial identity is, of course, to evoke a racist double standard. We should attempt a similar thought experiment in reference to our two key examples. Would Malan have been quite so agitated if he found himself in an analogous situation (drunk, alone after midnight, in an unfamiliar place) in a 'poor white' location of Johannesburg? Similarly, would my interview respondent have experienced quite the same surge of dread if he had received threatening comments from, say, white Afrikaners in a different part of the city? (Citing Brigance's line, we could have challenged my respondent: 'Now imagine they are white.') Presumably in these alternative contexts both Malan and my interview respondent would have still felt some degree of apprehension and anxiety. If, however, they felt greater anxiety precisely due to the factor of race, due indeed to the perceived blackness of their situation or antagonists, then racial – indeed, racist – fantasy surely did play its part.

There is also another factor to consider here, one which is especially significant in Malan's account, and that is the form of the description. There is a shrillness to Malan's Soweto anecdote, an otherworldliness to the anxiety – apparent also in Gevisser's description cited earlier – which involves recourse to an altogether different scene, indeed to another world, another planet. As hinted above, recourse to such figurative language ('the moon', 'outer space', 'another planet') indexes the experience of extreme otherness and thereby also the dimension of fantasy.

PORTRAIT OF AN ANXIOUS CITY

In the case of Johannesburg, then, we have not only a site of racial anxiety, but a city that induces fantasy. Any postcolonial city characterised by ever-present racialised social asymmetries will produce fantasies, a situation of which Frantz Fanon was all too well aware. In an unsurpassed description in *The Wretched of the Earth* – one which applies with uncanny aptness to Johannesburg's racialised divides of privilege and impoverishment – Fanon describes how fantasmatic values and anxieties accrue within spaces of colonial racialisation:

> The settler's town is a strongly built town, all made of stone and steel. It is a brightly lit town; the streets are covered with asphalt, and the garbage cans swallow all the leavings, unseen, unknown and hardly thought about … The streets … are clean and even, with no holes or stones. The settler's town is a well-fed town, an easygoing town; its belly is always full of good things. The settler's town is a town of white people, of foreigners. The town belonging to the colonised people, or at least the native town, the Negro village … is peopled by men of evil repute … It is a world without spaciousness; men live there on top of each other, and their huts are built one on top of the other. The

native town is a hungry town, starved of bread, of meat, of shoes ... a town on its knees, a town wallowing in the mire ... The look that the native turns on the settler's town is a look of lust, a look of envy; it expresses his dreams of possession ... to sit at the settler's table, to sleep in the settler's bed, with his wife if possible. The colonised man is an envious man. And this the settler knows very well; when their glances meet he ascertains bitterly, always on the defensive, 'They want to take our place.' (1963, 38)

Ivan Vladislavić's *Portrait with Keys* corroborates my reading of Johannesburg as a city of anxious fantasy. Vladislavić's anecdotes add empirical and historical flesh to the skeleton of Fanon's analysis of the psychogeography of the colonial city. Vladislavić reflects on the obsession with security and security devices ('when a house is alarmed, it becomes explosive' [2006, 1]); on white flight from the inner city (his brother Branko comments that the downtown area is 'too dangerous ... unpleasant with the empty shops ... and the smell of piss' [32]); on vandalism and theft ('In Joburg now ... the hunter-gatherer is in the ascendancy ... people steal the wheels off our cars at night ... and make off with the garden furniture' [39]); on transforming racial demographics (remarking on an Ndebele mural on a neighbour's wall, he says, 'Africa was coming to the suburbs in the nicest possible way' [28]); on white unease at the spread of black services and businesses ('Pan-African Financial Systems, Siyathuthuka Tavern Ngubane ... White eyes appraise these declarations on flaking facades ... and put the premises and proprietors in inverted commas: "Herbalist", "Moneylender", "Eating house"' [64]).

ARMAGEDDON TIME

Let us return to two principal themes of anxiety as introduced above. These two themes, the future-directed temporality of anxiety and its relation to fantasies of extinction or erasure, feature regularly in the empirical field. Indeed, they make for a virtual subgenre in contemporary South African literature. In his discussion of autobiographical South African writing, Martin J. Murray identifies alarmist narratives of 'the future unwanted' as one of the basic categories of stories that white post-apartheid South Africans tell about themselves. Such narratives are 'futurist, eschatological tales that warn of impending doom. They exemplify a dystopian, apocalyptic discourse of fear, anxiety, and disavowal. They operate as powerful vehicles for the politics of negation – a dismissive repudiation of the transformative, progressive consequences of the transition to democracy' (2013, 175).

Such accounts vary in tone from self-aggrandising to self-deprecating, and in affective range from cautionary tale to full-blown apocalyptic vision. Clinically, the imperative here is clear: we should remain particularly attentive if a patient wishes to dwell on reveries concerning the aftermath of their life. From a psychoanalytic perspective, such speculative thoughts – once encouraged and further articulated – make for rich material indeed. Such imaginaries of demise have much to tell us about the fantasmatic preoccupations of a particular individual or community, about their narcissistic myths, their entrenched fears, their wishful utopias and ideals, their most intense libidinal investments. Each of these considerations has, in turn, much to tell us about their identifications – conscious and unconscious – and about the prospects of changing such identifications.

Back then to Malan. His journalism after *My Traitor's Heart* (1990) has – unsurprisingly perhaps – been characterised by a pessimistic vision of South Africa's future and a deep anxiety about the role, if any, of whites and Afrikaners in the country. There is an 'end times' quality to many of the scenes and situations that Malan describes, as two of the chapter titles in his recent collection, *Resident Alien*, make abundantly clear: 'The last Afrikaner' and 'Houses going cheap in doomed country'. An effective but more obviously parodic counterpart to Malan's imagery is that of visual artist Anton Kannemeyer, who uses a comic-book style to depict scenes of 'apartheid apocalypse', where we bear witness to the mortification of various norms and ideals of white apartheid South Africa, such as a black domestic worker serving up the head of his dead white former master in an image entitled 'N is for Nightmare'. (For more, see his *Alphabet of Democracy* [2010].) The anxiety Malan expresses – and this holds true also of *My Traitor's Heart* – concerns not only a desperate sense of non-relevance, but a suspicion that the broader significance of white South African history might itself be altogether erased.

In the postscript to *Resident Alien*, which is largely centred on his experiences of Johannesburg, Malan likens South Africa's post-apartheid future to a period in the history of ancient Britain. After the Romans abandoned the country, the roads, villas and systems of social organisation that they had

Figures 4.1 and 4.2
'N is for Nightmare', Anton Kannemeyer (2007). Courtesy of the artist

put in place were plunged into the Dark Ages by the savage Celts. In much the same way, Malan laments, 'Johannesburg as we know it will vanish'. He continues: 'Many centuries hence … Africans [will struggle] to decipher the crumbling texts of a race that once lived there, planting cornfields … splitting atoms, and making the trains run on time … Afrikaans will be the ghost that rattles its chains in the depths of some new African tongue … The good that white men did will be acknowledged, the evil forgotten' (2011, 338). The cultural and racial narcissism here, like the self-pitying image of white (Afrikaner) extinction, seems obvious enough. Here the difference between Kannemeyer and Malan is writ large: Kannemeyer's portrayals of white anxiety occur from the remove of ironic distance; no such irony exists in Malan. It could be argued – if unconvincingly – that Malan is attempting to build narrative tension by a deliberate conjuring of historical images of Africa as the de-civilising Heart of Darkness. For many readers, interest in Malan's work stops here, when the racism of the text and its colonial-era associations become unavoidable. However, rather than abandoning the text at this point or treating it simply as symptomatic of the racism of its context, we should, I think, persist. Indeed, Malan's images of racial apocalypse are more ambivalent than they at first appear. We should treat this description in the same way one treats fantasies in the clinical context – that is, not only as illusory (and racist) flights of fancy, but as indications of a broader process within psychical reality.

A lengthy section of *My Traitor's Heart* entitled 'A root in arid ground' is devoted to the story of Neil and Creina Alcock, two white South Africans who turned their backs on apartheid privilege and attempted to make a success of farming in the unforgiving conditions of Msinga.[2] Here Malan once again deploys the tropes of the Dark Continent in ways which arguably both animate and agitate racist stereotypes. In the opening pages of this essay, Malan enjoins his reader to join him on an expedition to Msinga, using thus the narrative device of the imagined journey to evoke unease and dread. 'Some ten miles beyond the last white town, you cross the border between the First and Third Worlds, between white South Africa and black KwaZulu … You know you are coming into a different country, a different world. The white centreline vanishes, and the road itself starts rearing and plunging, like a turbulent river rushing toward a waterfall' (1990, 339).

While this perspective, that of the well-intentioned explorer in the non-white world, cannot but imply a colonial standpoint, there is more to be discovered here.[3] The Alcocks, he informs us,

> spent two decades living among Africans, like Africans, trying to undo some of the harm done by apartheid. They lived in mud huts and shat in holes in the ground. They washed their clothes and bodies in the Tugela River … [They] were always dusty and dishevelled. They endured fire ants in their armpits and rats in their beds, unbearable heat in summer and biting cold in winter. They were as ragged as the black peasants among whom they worked. (1990, 342–3)

I intimated above that an attentive psychoanalytic consideration of fantasies of demise can be fruitful in revealing identifications. It can be particularly important in exploring latent identifications, identifications of the 'unthought known' variety which have not yet been consciously accepted or spoken. Anxiety here might be conceptualised as a barrier that keeps the subject from exploring prospective identifications or, perhaps more importantly, identifications that – in a partial and perhaps unconscious sense – a subject may not yet realise they have already made.

If the abiding concern of much of Malan's writing is with the question of what will become of whites and, more particularly, white Afrikaners in a future South Africa, then his work also offers – despite the dystopian fatalism he seems so prone to – an answer: something Other. This is a something that cannot yet be imagined, although it requires that prior constituent identifications be left behind, laid to rest in a way not too dissimilar to the notion of a suicide of symbolic values.

So, if anxiety for Freud and Lacan is often a signal, a signal moreover that (unlike other affects) does not lie, then one particular value of the concept is that it signals the prospective end of an ego, the end of a set of identifications. This, to be sure, is a frightening situation and the reason that the conjoined imaginaries of castration, of subjective and racial extinction, seem so apt. And yet the potentiality of anxiety must be kept in mind; white anxiety – unlike white fragility – entails the prospect of radical transformation. We might reiterate this point by noting that to speak of the end of an ego (or the end of a set of identifications) is not to speak simply of death, but of an event in which something new may emerge via a given imaginary or symbolic demise. Even within the context of heightened anxiety, many of the above examples also contain a concession – even if frequently fearful or reactionary – that a new form of identification is the subject of unconscious rumination.

ANOTHER SCENE, ANOTHER DISTRICT

The scene is thus set for the most riveting text of post-apartheid dystopian science fiction: Neill Blomkamp's *District 9*. One of the most memorable features of the film was its setting in Johannesburg. While it would not have been particularly resonant for an international audience, for South Africans the title cannot but invoke District Six, the historically cosmopolitan, racially diverse, working-class area of Cape Town with a large immigrant population that was subjected to forced removals by the apartheid government. These removals followed depictions of the area as a crime-ridden, dangerous slum whose interracial interaction necessarily bred conflict. *District 9* recasts many of these historical features, projecting them from South Africa's apartheid past to the megacity context of contemporary Johannesburg, where the above characterisations (crime-ridden, dangerous, etc.) are present in hugely amplified proportions. While in the film District 9 is a district of Johannesburg, one could argue that it is itself a metonymic extension of the city. At once foreign (or indeed alien) to many US viewers – a glaring contrast to the gleaming-then-crumbling skyscrapers of most generic disaster films – Blomkamp's Johannesburg is perfectly suited to the abjection of the situation it depicts.

Much has been written on the film emphasising its relationship to apartheid-era race relations and highlighting the abject quality of the insectoid alien others. Let us consider a fairly representative sympathetic engagement with the film:

> *District 9* … was subversive, intelligent, amusing and felt authentic … By transplanting the apartheid logic and culture in a speculative future Joburg populated by giant … prawns … who operated as the perennial 'other', Blomkamp found a way for South Africans to meditate on their history from a distance and, paradoxically, through the lens of the future. This distance proved ideologically useful to us; it was like a mirror that allowed us to see how the culture of a prejudice based on difference had been passed from generation to generation, like a cursed heirloom. (Corrigall 2014)

While I agree with much of what Mary Corrigall maintains here, her comments focus more on the past than on the future of whiteness in South Africa. It seems to me that in view of the film's genre we should equally consider how it anticipates a future and, more particularly, future forms of whiteness.

We can read the film as responding to the political-existential dilemmas running through all the forms of post-apartheid white anxiety mentioned above. Namely: what must I, the white South African, do – or become – in this post-apartheid era? What, furthermore, is to become of us whites (and white Afrikaners) in this 'strange place' where we can no longer rely on the defining values and symbolic identities from which we benefited in the era of apartheid? Wikus, the unfortunate hero of *District 9*, who of course begins to change into one of the alien 'prawns' so reviled and feared by the humans in the film, seems at first to offer little hope. In fact, his fate seems simply to replay, at an exaggerated intergalactic level, one of the great fears of colonial anxiety – that of miscegenation.

Here I think we should exercise caution before reading the film merely as recycling the racist tropes and figures of apartheid and deploying them in a future context. Or, to put things somewhat differently, what occurs if we approach Blomkamp not merely as revisiting apartheid, but as a reader of Franz Kafka? The literary reference to Kafka's famous story *The Metamorphosis*, about a man who becomes an insect, is difficult to deny ('When Gregor Samsa woke one morning from uneasy dreams, he found himself transformed into some kind of monstrous vermin' [Kafka 2009, 26].) Similarly, it is curious that the emblem Lacan uses in his paradigmatic example of anxiety – the human-sized praying mantis – is so close to the scenario envisaged by Blomkamp, in which Wikus is suddenly tasked with the role of negotiating with the inscrutable and dangerous insectoid aliens.

I mentioned above that in Lacan's estimation anxiety and questions of subjective and social identification are inextricably linked. Anxiety arises most acutely not simply as an isolated issue of physical security or impending death, but when the coordinates of personal, subjective (imaginary) identification and sociological and historical (symbolic) identification are simultaneously threatened with erasure. The precariousness of existence experienced at these multiple levels characterises the angst, dread or nausea described by existential thinkers as varied as Kierkegaard, Camus and Sartre. This is why Kafka's parable is so disturbing: the experience of becoming an insect is not merely that of death or psychological or symbolic transformation; it is that of existing at a wholly different ontological level, of completely unbecoming one's (physical, psychological, symbolic) self.

The exaggerated otherness of Blomkamp's aliens seems to affirm the point: these insectoid figures – so far from the 'human' aliens of Steven Spielberg's

E.T. and *Close Encounters of the Third Kind* – are impossible to identify with. To become one of the prawns is to sever all links with one's previous existence. Wikus-as-prawn will be changed in his very species-being; he will have completed the process of fully unbecoming what he once was.

And this is why one might read the film as offering us an important ethical opportunity, one which unexpectedly mirrors the controversial gesture of white racial suicide suggested by Terblanche Delport (2016). Delport's rhetorical and deliberately provocative suggestion, pronounced in South Africa's most anxious city, is perhaps not as counter-intuitive or crazy as it at first sounds. Delport took his white audience to the threshold of symbolic extinction, to a proposed 'end of whiteness'. In psychoanalytic terms, Delport offered his audience the opportunity to contemplate the castration of whiteness. This is, admittedly, a risky strategy – but perhaps a necessary one.

Arguably, the gesture of giving up what one is – the shedding of narcissistic investments, symbolic and fantasmatic identities – proves a necessary first step to becoming what one is not but might become. This is the transformative potential of anxiety that clinicians work so hard to facilitate, and that I think can also be discerned – however fleetingly – in the instances of white anxiety discussed above, the potentiality that a new and hitherto unthinkable form of identification is being unconsciously processed and negotiated.

CONCLUSION

For some, the above excursion into the fantasy terrain of white anxiety will have proved too much by virtue of the racism it forces one to confront. To explore this realm of fantasy is to find one's self neck-deep in many of the most persistent historical tropes of white racism. And yet there is a sense in which this trawling through racist fantasy remains an important political task.

Here we might again pause to draw some inspiration from the psychoanalytic clinic. Isn't this, after all, what psychoanalysis aims at: to elicit fantasy, to guide the slow and careful process of 'unrepressing' distressing material that cannot normally be spoken by the subject? By working through this material, hearing it out and thus exhausting it, we might decrease its hold on the patient so that they are less controlled by it. One outcome of such a process is that what had previously been considered unthinkable, tantamount to extinction, fundamentally unassimilable ('from another planet') might, in due course, become manageable, even banal. Here we need to return to Malan's fretting about a post-whiteness Johannesburg of the future. 'Johannesburg as we know it will vanish,' he remarks, before adding: 'visitors to this New Jerusalem will encounter something presently inconceivable – Africans … struggling to decipher the crumbling texts of a race that once lived here' (2011, 338). While this fantasmatic rendering certainly does not escape white hubris, it does present us with a view of post-whiteness Johannesburg, about which Malan remarks: 'I scheme it will be quite lekker' (2011, 338). Likewise, *District 9* certainly has not shaken off colonial themes (of subhuman otherness, of miscegenation), and yet it stages a type of white extirpation that is surely a precondition for forgoing subjective investments in whiteness. Perhaps one political task ahead concerns thinking of how we might move beyond merely the attempt to censor racist fantasy and instead use various of its narrative components, intervening within them as a means of rerouting the subject of whiteness, facilitating in this way its unbecoming.

ACKNOWLEDGEMENTS

Many thanks to Nicky Falkof and Cobus van Staden, whose editorial comments, encouragement and thoughtful input regarding various qualifications and historical contextualisation have very greatly improved this chapter. Thanks also to Anton Kannemeyer for his kind permission to reproduce two of his 'N is for Nightmare' images.

NOTES

1   Or, to make much the same point in the philosophical terms of Kierkegaard and
    Heidegger respectively – both of whom inform Lacan's conceptualisations in
    Seminar X – anxiety pertains to one's existence, to *being* as such.

2   While this section of Malan's book seemingly represents a digression from my
    Johannesburg focus, it is a crucial addition, not only because it reverses the fantasy
    of escaping from Johannesburg to the rural areas (the split between Johannesburg
    and 'the farm' is a repeated theme in Afrikaans literature), but also because it plays to
    another source of anxiety in Johannesburg: how it is stranded in a sea of rurality, that
    rural underdevelopment is always encroaching.

3   While race and whiteness are my primary concerns, there is also a clear element of
    class erasure evident in this example. Simply put, living in the city forces the awareness
    that not all middle-class people are white. While this is truer today than when *My
    Traitor's Heart* was first published, the fact remains: this erasure of class complexity

aids Malan in claiming all middle-class values (trains running on time, etc.) for a white minority. I owe this point to Cobus van Staden.

REFERENCES

Ahmed, Sara. 2007. "A Phenomenology of Whiteness." *Feminist Theory* 8 (2): 149–68.

Blomkamp, Neill, director. 2009. *District 9*. Wingnut Pictures/Tristar.

Bondstaat. n.d. Facebook page. Accessed 28 April 2019. https://www.facebook.com/bondstaat/posts/white-south-africans-should-commit-suicide-and-die-out-without-having-children-t/1054435757981307/.

Bonilla-Silva, Eduardo. 2017. *Racism without Racists: Colorblind Racism and the Persistence of Racial Inequality in America*. Lanham: Rowman and Littlefield.

Bourdieu, Pierre. 1993. *The Field of Cultural Production*. New York: Columbia University Press.

Corrigall, Mary. 2014. "SA's Forward-Looking Neill Blomkamp Is Stuck in the Past." *Sunday Independent*, 6 April 2012.

Crapanzano, Vincent. 1985. *Waiting: The Whites of South Africa*. London and New York: Granada.

DiAngelo, Robin. 2011. "White Fragility." *International Journal of Critical Pedagogy* 3 (3): 54–70.

Durrheim, Kevin, and John Dixon. 2014. *Racial Encounter: The Social Psychology of Contact and Desegregation*. London and New York: Routledge.

Dyer, Richard. 1997. *White*. New York: Routledge.

Falkof, Nicky. 2014. "Talking the (White) Talk; Walking the (White) Walk." *Daily Maverick*, 19 June 2014.

———. 2016. *The End of Whiteness: Satanism and Family Murder in Late Apartheid South Africa*. Johannesburg: Jacana Media.

Fanon, Frantz. 1968. *The Wretched of the Earth*. New York: Grove Press.

Fine, M. 1997. "Witnessing Whiteness." In *Off White: Readings on Race, Power and Society*, edited by M. Fine, L. Weiss, C. Powell, and L. Wong, vii–xii. New York: Routledge.

Fink, Bruce. 2014. *Against Understanding, vol. 2: Cases and Commentary in a Lacanian Critique*. New York: Routledge.

Frankenberg, Ruth. 1993. *The Social Construction of Whiteness: White Women, Race Matters*. Minneapolis: University of Minnesota Press.

Freud, Sigmund. 1926. "Inhibition, Symptoms and Anxiety." In *The Standard Edition of the Complete Psychological Works of Sigmund Freud*, vol. 20, 75–174.

Gevisser, Mark. 2014. *Lost and Found in Johannesburg*. Johannesburg: Jonathan Ball.

Haffajee, Ferial. 2015. *What If There Were No Whites in South Africa?* Johannesburg: Pan Macmillan.

Harari, Roberto. 2001. *Lacan's Seminar on 'Anxiety'.* New York: Other Press.

Harber, Anton. 2011. *Diepsloot.* Johannesburg: Jonathan Ball.

Hook, Derek. 2015. "Petrified Life." *Social Dynamics: A Journal of African Studies* 41 (3): 438–60.

Kafka, Franz. 2009. "The Metamorphosis." In *The Metamorphosis and Other Stories.* Oxford: Oxford University Press.

Kannemeyer, Anton. 2010. *Alphabet of Democracy.* Johannesburg: Jacana Media.

Lacan, Jacques. 2014. *Anxiety: The Seminar of Jacques Lacan, Book X.* Edited by Jacques-Alain Miller, translated by A.R. Price. Cambridge: Polity Press.

Malan, Rian. 1990. *My Traitor's Heart.* New York: Atlantic Monthly Press.

———. 2011. *Resident Alien.* Johannesburg: Jonathan Ball.

Mbembe, Achille, and Sarah Nuttall. 2008. "Introduction: Afropolis." In *Johannesburg: The Elusive Metropolis,* edited by Sarah Nuttall and Achille Mbembe, 1–33. Johannesburg: Wits University Press.

McKaiser, Eusebius. 2012. *A Bantu in My Bathroom.* Johannesburg: Macmillan.

Murray, Martin J. 2013. *Commemorating and Forgetting: Challenges for the New South Africa.* Minneapolis: University of Minnesota Press.

Ngo, Helen. 2017. *The Habits of Racism: A Phenomenology of Racism and Racialization.* Lanham: Lexington Books.

Schumacher, Joel, director. 1996. *A Time to Kill.* Regency Enterprises/Warner Bros.

Soler, Colette. 2016. *Lacanian Affects: The Function of Affect in Lacan's Work.* Translated by B. Fink. New York: Routledge.

Steyn, Melissa E. 2004. "Rehabilitating a Whiteness Disgraced: Afrikaner White Talk in Post-Apartheid South Africa." *Communications Quarterly* 52 (2): 143–69.

Steyn, Melissa E., and Don Foster. 2008. "Repertoires for Talking White: Resistant Whiteness in Post-Apartheid South Africa." *Ethnic and Racial Studies* 31 (1): 25–51.

Vladislavić, Ivan. 2006. *Portrait with Keys: The City of Johannesburg Unlocked.* London: Portobello Books.

Yancy, George. 2012. *Look, a White! Philosophical Essays on Whiteness.* Philadelphia: Temple University Press.

5 UGLY NOO-NOOS AND SUBURBAN NIGHTMARES

NICKY FALKOF

> While our language about cities generalises them, makes them comparable with other cities, able to circulate as part of urban (or sociological or cultural) discourse, cities themselves are unique. They are unparaphrasable … They have more in common with poetic than literal language, with literature than information. – Lindsay Bremner, *Writing the City into Being* (2010, 44)

When I think about my childhood in suburban Johannesburg in the 1980s, I encounter a discomfortingly nostalgic mishmash of pastel colours and swimming pools, long summers of men braaiing and women in kitchens, the ubiquitous presence of my family's domestic worker and her children, who felt like cousins except that they lived in a room outside the back of our house. I remember the parks where white children played on swings and black women chatted and fanned themselves on benches. I remember television: crowding around to watch a blonde Afrikaans contestant take the Miss World competition or trying to sync up the radio simulcast so that we could watch *Dallas* in English. I remember the vague sense of apprehension and the shuttered awareness that I lived in a place where violence happened but only 'over there', somewhere else that was never specified but was lurking in the quiet conversations of adults and the news reports that

I wasn't allowed to watch. I remember the warnings we were given at school about being vigilant and the looming awareness that the world – or rather our world – was fragile in ways that I could not understand.

But overall, my childhood was haunted by a far more potent and visible foe than the liberation fighters who stalked the nightmares of white voters. The monster of my youth was not the ANC terrorist or Angolan communist whom we were warned about. I did not fear stories of the murderous urges of 'maids' and 'garden boys'. Rather, I was haunted by a more tangible demon: *Libanasidus vittatus*, the African king cricket, tusked king cricket or, to give it its most common South African designation, the Parktown prawn.

The Parktown prawn, its colloquial name derived from a suburb of Johannesburg, is an astonishing creature. It is one of the largest naturally occurring invertebrates in the region and can grow up to six or seven centimetres. It ranges in colour from pale yellow and white-flesh pink to brown to glossy red. Its head is dark brown, sometimes edged in yellow, with large, black and teardrop-shaped eyes. In males its large mandibles bear tusks that can grow to impressive sizes. The thorax and abdomen are paler, often with bands of black around the body. The legs are extremely powerful and covered in spines (Brettschneider et al. 2007, 111–13). Indeed, its appearance is so unusual that in the 1960s students at the University of the Witwatersrand 'spread a rumour … that these large and intimidating insects were the result of genetic engineering gone wrong' (Byrne 2015).

Libanasidus vittatus exhibits a range of defensive behaviours including hissing, 'kicking, jumping, biting, stridulation, defecation and feigning death' (Wolf, Bateman, and Brettschneider 2006, 76). It is known among humans for expelling a noxious black substance composed of stored faecal matter, thought to be more closely related to sexual communication than to predator defence. It is a nocturnal and opportunistic omnivore that often eats carrion and even live snails, as well as feasting on the pet food and faeces that are common to many suburban homes in Johannesburg. It is a sexually dimorphic and solitary insect, dormant during the winter, that has been known to grow in captivity for at least three years (Brettschneider and Bateman 2005, 382). Once extremely common in suburban homes and gardens in Johannesburg, it has undergone a dramatic population decline in recent years, although it continues to exist in the city in smaller numbers.

Parktown prawns are also notoriously difficult to kill. Johannesburg lore is awash with tales of prawns trapped under rubbish bins and sprayed with insecticide that refuse to die for days. They jump, often in the direction of threatening humans or predators, in a way that can seem to be an attack. Their spiky legs appear weapon-like. They spray their foul-smelling faecal matter at people and, as we have seen, they have the capacity to hiss, kick, bite and scratch (Byrne 2015). They like warm and dark places such as those found scattered around homes and in gardens.

For humans, who are often (and often violently) unwilling to cohabit with any other species barring those we have domesticated, the Parktown prawn presents a pressing set of problems. It is larger and more solid than most insects and its dense materiality can sometimes appear more akin to a mammalian or vertebrate than an invertebrate, insect species. This shifting between categories can lend it a quality of the uncanny (Freud 1990), something that is both frightening and familiar, a thing that is not what it 'should' be and not what it 'is' but rather hovers somewhere in between, suggesting the thinness of both positions. Its size, colouring, nocturnal behaviour and appearance place it into an aesthetic category that many of us align with monstrousness. Completely harmless to humans, it is nonetheless easy to anthropomorphise as an aggressive interloper into the controlled environment of the suburban home.[1] Indeed, until undertaking the research for this chapter I had never questioned the common notion that the Parktown prawn was a mutant cockroach rather than a perfectly normal and, in fact, rather impressive species of cricket.

My childhood memories are peppered with instances of being chased around the garden by a prawn-wielding older brother, of prawns lurking menacingly in the corners of bedrooms, of shrieking groups of children abandoning swimming pools that had been infested by exploratory prawns. They loom large in my own and others' imaginary landscapes of the city; and it is this affective force, this quality of seeming both metaphorically and physically larger than life, that lends them their peculiar power as a symbol of some of suburban Johannesburg's pressing communal anxieties.

In this chapter I draw on popular culture, personal narrative, and urban and environmental histories to consider the prawn as both a living creature and a powerful, if obscure, metaphor for the shifting neuroses of Johannesburg's most privileged residents.

THE CULTURAL CRICKET

Parktown prawns play a small but significant role in popular culture in and about Joburg, performing various functions in the collective imagining of the city. In many of these they are related to experiences of otherness, particularly race, and more specifically to expressions of white anxiety.

In 1988 the actor Andrew Buckland first performed his comic satire *The Ugly Noo Noo*, an award-winning piece of physical theatre in which the primary character was a Parktown prawn. According to one critic, 'Buckland confronts and exposes the fear and the violence of the particular period by displacing the events and political issues onto a series of comic skits, replete with scatological references and expletives' (Blumberg 1997, 86). The play used mime, comedy, physical performance and voice to bring alive the 'noo noo', the 'ugly yet harmless creature, who terrifies the inhabitants of the wealthy Johannesburg suburbs' (Blumberg 1997, 85), and thus to satirise white South African fears in the last years of apartheid.[2] Buckland's play was enormously popular in South Africa, performed both at the Market Theatre in Johannesburg and at the Baxter in Cape Town. *The Ugly Noo Noo* inaugurated the portrayal of Parktown prawn as metaphor, firmly linking the frightening insect to the frightened white suburbanite.

Parktown prawns also make an appearance in Neill Blomkamp's 2009 science fiction film *District 9*, which has been celebrated for its arch urban satire. Scholars have commented on its multilayered critiques of South Africa's apartheid past, of current explosions of xenophobia, and of contemporary neoliberalism, globalisation and corporatisation (Heller-Nicholas 2011). Many have also pointed out the irony in its casual portrayal of Nigerians as violent, voodoo-obsessed gangsters, in line with the darkest stereotypes of xenophobic and Afrophobic South African hypernationalism (see, for example, Heller-Nicholas 2011; Janks and Adegoke 2011). The film is set in a near-future Joburg above which hangs a menacing alien spacecraft. The inhabitants of this craft, marooned far from their home planet, are confined to makeshift refugee camps in the city's less salubrious areas, where they live in shacks and squabble over trash. They are despised by 'legitimate' residents, experimented on by shady medical corporations, and stalked by a Nigerian warlord who wants access to their advanced weaponry. The aliens have been nicknamed prawns owing to their shiny carapaces, powerful legs and insectoid appearance, all of which recall Joburg's favourite monstrous invertebrate.

Comparing the film's refugee aliens to Giorgio Agamben's notion of *homo sacer* (1998), the figure of 'bare life' who is subject to but not protected by law and can thus be killed without consequence, Greg Bourke writes that the word prawn is 'a prejudiced and derogatory term that implies that the aliens are bottom feeders who scavenge for left-overs. Clearly, the term is not one of affection or endearment, but rather reflects the xenophobic turn of the polity.' The alien prawns 'inhabit a space where they are treated with impunity and never afforded any of the protections we, as citizens, take for granted' (Bourke 2012, 443, 455). The film's main character, Wikus, is a white Afrikaner man who works for a multinational corporation that is studying the aliens. On one of his journeys through their shantytown, Wikus ingests a mysterious substance that leads to him slowly transmuting from human to prawn, in the process becoming both an object of corporate greed and an abject example of miscegenation, a cause of horror and disgust for his community, forced to flee to the prawn 'township'. In *District 9*, then, the Parktown prawn connotes a despised otherness or outsiderness.

Parktown prawns also appear in the music video for 'Fatty Boom Boom', a 2012 single by the South African band Die Antwoord. Die Antwoord have been heavily critiqued for cultural appropriation and commercial exploitation of black art and music (Haupt 2013, 471). Despite its claims to 'apparently [poke] fun at stereotypical Western perceptions of Africa' (472), this particular video received a large amount of negative coverage because it presents an 'obvious instance of contemporary blackface', alongside 'Die Antwoord's notorious use of hypermasculine imagery with misogynist and homophobic overtones' (Schmidt 2014, 133).

The video features a male impersonator of American pop star Lady Gaga moving through a chaotic, stylised, hyper-bright version of contemporary Joburg, in what seems meant to present the fears of a white foreign tourist adrift in the concrete jungle. In a scene referencing both *District 9* and a drawing by the South African artist Anton Kannemeyer, whose work appears in this book, the caricature Gaga finds herself in the office of a gynaecologist, complaining that there is something 'really funny going on down there'. In response the doctor removes a Parktown prawn from her vagina, an image which is 'loaded', according to Talia Meer, in a 'global culture that vilifies women's bodies and sexuality and portrays vaginas as requiring douching, perfuming and bejewelling … this music video is yet another depiction of women's bodies as sexualised, violated and diseased' (quoted in Haupt 2013,

472). In this context the Parktown prawn connotes dirt, decay and the disgusting. In emerging quite literally from within the woman, it depicts her as rotting from the inside.

Parktown prawns appear elsewhere in popular and personal texts, usually in hyperbolic terms that are primarily concerned with the emotions they inspire. In February 2018 the US musician Amanda Palmer crowd-sourced, wrote and performed 'The Parktown Prawn song' at a gig in Johannesburg, to much audience enthusiasm.[3] They are the subject of posts on popular blogs and websites like JHBLive (Rivers 2012) and 2Summers, whose author calls them 'Joburg's most legendary insect … Part cricket-on-steroids, part giant cockroach, park prehistoric monster' (Mason 2013). Local journalists define them as one of the five 'ugliest, creepiest insects on planet earth' (Horn 2017) and as 'crickets from hell' (Saks 2009).

In the preparation for writing this chapter, I discussed them with a number of people. Friends, colleagues and students responded with a litany of alarming tales of their interactions with these insects. Stories abound of Parktown prawns hiding in shoes, clothing and other warm dark places. One acquaintance told me:

> Everyone in my family is terrified of Parktown prawns. I think it's epigenetics or something. My mom, in the seventies, pulled on tight pants and laced up knee-high boots before realising she had something in her knickers. And my gran once had one attach itself to her bum when she was making a wee.

Another said:

> I was in Grade 3 at school and pulling on my white tackies to go play tennis … and felt a sharp prick in the front of my shoe. I ignored it and ran down to the school courts but it got worse. I took my shoe off to see what the issue was (maybe a blackjack on my sock?) and a half-smushed and very angry Parktown prawn clawed its way out. I screamed, the loudest scream ever in my entire life, dropped the shoe and bolted to the other side of the court.

A friend from Europe related the following tale:

> It was the second month after I arrived to Joburg. I was packing at two in the morning to go somewhere in Mpumalanga for fieldwork. Everybody had told

me about crime in Joburg but not about the local entomology fauna of this city. Suddenly, among my sandals I noticed something moving. It was the biggest cucaracha that I have seen in my life … I was not going to sleep in that room with such a beast. Suddenly, the thing throws ink, I have no words to express my feelings of horror. I gathered a lot of strength to take my sandal and kill the massive cucaracha. I was traumatised by the act. It was like if I killed a mammal.

Stories like this are told with a mix of hilarity and horror at the incongruity of the prawn's appearance and behaviour and the excessive, often unintentional reaction it produces.

INSECTS OUTSIDE, INSECTS INSIDE

The visceral horror and physical disgust that Parktown prawns inspire in many humans lead me to think about Julia Kristeva's conception of the abject (1982). Kristeva writes about the intense and bodily experiences that we have when viewing a corpse, also occurring in more common reactions to shit, sewage, even the skin that forms on milk, as instances of the possible breakdown of meaning which occurs when the differentiation between the self and the object, or the self and the other, becomes unstable. I do not want to suggest that coming across a Parktown prawn is necessarily an equivalent experience, or that it requires diagnosis in psychoanalytic terms; rather, I am employing Kristeva's notion rhetorically to consider what the Parktown prawn's confusing body and boundary-breaching behaviour may suggest within the narrative and mythological landscape of the city.

For suburban, usually white Johannesburgers, the distinction between self and other is powerfully manifested in the distinction between inside and outside the city, the suburb and the home. Apartheid brought in a pernicious set of laws that were designed to facilitate so-called influx control, limiting black people's access to cities and the potential social and economic mobility promised by urbanisation. Influx control 'was seen as a regional version of much wider efforts to engineer and restrict cross-oceanic and cross-border migration' (Nightingale 2015, 253). Certain areas, including the 'leafy green forest of Johannesburg's affluent northern suburbs' (Gevisser 2008, 318), were legally zoned for whites-only residence. In these ways whites attempted to maintain the always spurious distinction between inside and outside: the city was presented as a whites-only space and black people were imaginatively discarded outside its limits.

Of course, these curbs on mobility were always flawed, not least because of white reliance on the physical labour of black bodies. In particular, black working women unsettled the idea that suburbs were for whites only: they 'occupied literally all corners of Johannesburg's residential neighbourhoods and as a result they knew the suburbs intimately and distinctly' (Ginsburg 2011, 2). Perhaps more importantly, as Rebecca Ginsburg shows, they used their 'back room' accommodation as an illicit landing station for friends, family and acquaintances arriving in the city. Nonetheless, black women were 'careful not to draw attention to themselves through their dress or their bearing, [so] their ubiquity made them invisible to whites; their positions as family servants made them appear innocuous' (Ginsburg 2011, 53). Familiarity and invisibility allowed whites to maintain the fiction that their homes and neighbourhoods were free of 'outsiders', and that the 'inside' was safe and controlled. Incursions from the outside, such as workers' husbands or children, were often considered illegitimate and even frightening. Overall, barring domestic and garden workers in their comforting uniforms, white South African suburban residents seldom saw black people in their neighbourhoods, allowing them to maintain the collective fiction that the boundary between inside and outside remained solid.

In the years since formal apartheid ended, South Africa has replaced looming civil war with a high rate of often violent crime, responses to which draw on existing apprehensions about outsiders. Lindsay Bremner writes that 'old notions of race and the contemporary malignant, though blurry, figure of the criminal have combined, very quickly in the South African imaginary' (2010, 92). As in other major South African cities (Durington 2009; Lemanski 2004), suburban Joburgers invest heavily in what Martin J. Murray, among others, calls 'siege architecture' (2011, 222). Private houses in 'Fortress Johannesburg' (Lipman and Harris 1999) are surrounded by high walls and automated gates. They are festooned with security gates and bars, warning signs, spikes, barbed wire, electric fences and beams that trigger alarms linked to armed private security companies. Meanwhile, 'neighbourhood associations have blocked off streets, erected boom gates, and built checkpoints and sentry posts staffed with private security operatives' (Murray 2011, 273; see also Comaroff and Comaroff 2017). The external architecture of suburban

Johannesburg and the security industry that serves it are designed to keep the outside from accessing the inside.

But despite our best attempts, such boundaries are difficult to apply to other species or to the natural world as a whole. Things have a way of creeping in. Kristeva writes that the abject is that which 'disturbs identity, system, order. What does not respect borders, positions, rules' (1982, 4). The appearance of a frightening Parktown prawn within an otherwise fortified home can mirror the experience of abjection, of the sudden instability of meaning, precisely because it reveals that the home – and, by extension, the self for which it stands – is permanently vulnerable; the borders do not hold. With their disturbing colouring, their fleshy materiality, their impossible leaping, their foul smells and their refusal to die, Parktown prawns make an easily available monster. They are an instance par excellence of the debased outside forcing its way into the sanctified inside and in the process revealing the fiction of the division between them. The qualities that make them intimidating are comparable to our worst stereotyped fears about intruders of our own species. They are solitary, and thus untrustworthy; they are predators and bottom feeders, so are both dangerous and without morality; they are outsized creatures that appear too large and solid to be 'normal' insects, and thus seem exceptional and monstrous; they 'attack' in a way that can be experienced as unprovoked and even violent; they spray foul-smelling faecal matter and are thus dirty pollutants impacting on the hygiene of the suburban home. They reveal the porousness of arbitrarily constructed divisions between inside and outside in a way that suggests greater anxieties: about crime, about safety, about others.

It is somewhat ironic, given how closely they are associated, that Parktown prawns should not in fact exist in Johannesburg. *Libanasidus vittatus* is native to the small mining town of Barberton, east of Joburg (Byrne 2015). It made its first appearance in the city in the 1960s and may have been carried there by migrant workers who moved between mining sites. It was colloquially named for Parktown, which was in the early twentieth century the city's 'quintessential white suburb' (Nightingale 2015, 267), a 'remote but highly fashionable' area that 'became the residential neighbourhood of choice for the wealthiest families of Johannesburg' (Murray 2011, 43).[4] Parktown was developed as a place where the rich could escape the foul smells, poverty and moral decay that came along with the mining boom, and where they could build a neighbourhood that matched the sensory expectations of a newly minted upper class. To this end, Parktown and other areas became the focus of enthusiastic landscape architecture designed to distance them from the surrounding bleakness of the Witwatersrand ridges. Murray (2011, 43) writes that

> the large-scale importation of exotic saplings, shrubs, and other plants from coastal nurseries fundamentally transformed the ecological landscape of the 'villa neighbourhoods' of Doornfontein, Belgravia, Hospital Hill, and Parktown, creating in almost an instant tree-lined streets and lush suburbs on the once wind-swept and treeless land plateau.

As well as inaugurating Johannesburg's famous 'man-made forest', the greening of Parktown also created the perfect set of environmental conditions for *Libanasidus vittatus*, which thrives in moist forested areas. When combined with a lower number of natural predators and with suburban gardening and leisure practices (plentiful pet food and animal faeces to scavenge, water-heavy plants and grass), this ideal climate and environment led to a population explosion and consequently to Johannesburg's 'plague' of Parktown prawns.

The presence of these creatures is a symptom of both the city's wealth and its improbability. Located for mineral extraction rather than for proximity to water or other practical elements of human survival, Johannesburg is the largest city in Africa not situated near a coast, significant lake or river.[5] It is at base a deeply exploitative and hubristic endeavour, built on the criss-crossing shafts of gold mines and, consequently, the bodies of those who dug and worked in them. According to Nuttall and Mbembe, 'There is no metropolis without a necropolis. Just as the metropolis is closely linked to monuments, artefacts, technological novelty, an architecture of light and advertising, the phantasmagoria of selling, and a cornucopia of commodities, so is it produced by what lies below the surface' (2008, 21). In Johannesburg what lies beneath the surface is a complex and longstanding extractive economy that depends on both human and mineral capital, that spurred the city's establishment and led to its formalisation as a financial centre and consequently to its ongoing existence as an African megacity. Geographically, Johannesburg should not exist. Economically, though, it is a regional and even continental powerhouse.

During the colonial and apartheid eras the greening of the northern suburbs allowed privileged white Johannesburgers to avoid knowledge of the
human costs of where they lived – the sweat, the blood, the sewage, the broken bones and broken families – in favour of a sanitised and 'civilised' vision
of a modern and aesthetically pleasing city. Landscape was an ideological
tool in the creation of the suburbs (Cane 2019). The natural-unnatural forest
(Johannesburg's famous purple jacarandas are in fact an invasive imported
species) smoothed over traces of the city's underbelly so that white suburbanites could look away from the necropolis beneath their feet. The suburban
forest helped to conceal both the geographical unlikelihood of building a
major city on this high, arid and rocky plateau and the distasteful complications of migration, forced urbanisation, poverty and segregation that were a
consequence of the mining industry's rapacious hunger for disposable black
labour.

Wealth and improbability thus go hand in hand. The first is required to
create the second, and both helped build a city where no city should be.
In this reading of the physicality of Johannesburg, Parktown prawns are a
reminder of unpleasant realities that some of us prefer not to think about.
They suggest what Stuart Hall calls the 'constitutive outside': 'the radically
disturbing recognition that it is only through the relation to the Other, the
relation to what it is not … that the "positive" meaning of any term – and
thus its "identity" – can be constructed' (1996, 4). Their fleshy corporeality,
brought to the city by the same strategies that made it pleasantly liveable for
certain categories of humans, reminds suburban dwellers that the city is not
'natural'. If Parktown prawns suggest the entry of the abject outside into the
managed inside, and consequently the unsettling of borders and boundaries
that shifts the stability of meaning, they do this precisely *because of* the way in
which white racial capitalism attempted to formalise boundaries and to build
a white city in its own image.

Like Johannesburg, *Libanasidus vittatus* should not exist on this Highveld
plateau, and, like Johannesburg, it owes its unnatural prosperity to the mineral wealth that was brought up from underground and used to establish a
suburban paradise. The monstrousness that so many humans perceive in it
is emblematic of the monstrousness of the violent and unnatural city that
suburban boundaries can never fully keep out.

ERASABLE MEMORIES

In contemporary Johannesburg, Parktown prawns are more of a curiosity than a plague. Long-time residents comment on how they seem to have vanished in recent years, while thrill-seeking newcomers bemoan the fact that they have never managed to catch a glimpse of this famous local creature. One of the most popular theories surrounding their demise claims that it is due to the increase in numbers of hadedas, the prehensile ibis, or *Bostrychia hagedash*, known for its onomatopoeic call and fondness for feasting on crickets. Hadedas were also introduced to Johannesburg by natural range expansion, drawn by the city's favourable climate, multiple gardens and constructed wetlands. It is more likely, however, that the drop in the city's Parktown prawn population is due to a combination of human and environmental factors. Drought, unpredictable rainfall and small shifts in climate mean that the moist forest environment favoured by *Libanasidus vittatus* is no longer as common. Changes in the way in which people live in suburban Johannesburg may also be responsible. Patterns of labour, employment, ownership and space have changed as the city has become increasingly linked into global flows of capital, culture and people. Contemporary suburbanites often renovate domestic workers' quarters to create so-called garden cottages (see Falkof 2015) for income-producing rental. This is part of the comparative densification of Joburg's suburbs from large individual stands with extensive gardens to cluster homes, gated communities and golf estates (Murray 2011). For many, professional outdoor services have replaced the 'garden boys' of yore (Cane 2019), and gardening trends have changed, meaning that outdoor spaces are tidier and more manicured with fewer compost heaps and areas of moist decomposition. Increased use of pesticides has lessened the availability of food sources like snails. As a cursory search for sensationalist YouTube videos reveals, Parktown prawns persist in Joburg. However, their population has undergone a steep decline, to the point where they are now considered a rare phenomenon rather than a persistent problem.

I have suggested that Parktown prawns have a symbolic meaning that outweighs the realities of their physical existence, and that leads humans to misrecognise them as a source of legitimate threat when in fact common reactions to their presence are a manifestation of collective anxieties that characterise suburban life in the 'elusive metropolis' (Nuttall and Mbembe 2008). By getting in everywhere they can, Parktown prawns show the paucity of the myth that the suburbs can be kept separate from the city. They suggest the panic with which suburban dwellers approach the idea of outsiders being inside, as well as the pollution that this mixing anticipates. Perhaps most importantly, they act as a small reminder of Johannesburg's underpinnings: that this is not just a 'normal' city in a 'normal' place (as though such a thing could exist) but is rather a city in which the beauty of the constructed land-scape was designed to distance the privileged from the scars of colonial and apartheid practices of labour and segregation. The Parktown prawn is thus a creature of both excess and remainder. The outsized reactions it inspires reveal its symbolic weight as a signifier of the gross, uncanny and abject outsider; but at the same it drags with it unsettling traces of what the suburbs wish to forget about the city.

What happens, then, to a city whose constitutive outsides begin to dis-appear? I have written elsewhere (Falkof 2012) about the slow vanishing of other visual reminders of Johannesburg's extractive histories, 'the city's sec-ond mountain range, the artificial one, [which] rose slowly throughout the twentieth century in the form of enormous, bright-yellow piles of waste-earth known as the "mine dumps"' (Nightingale 2015, 230). Gerald Garner calls these the 'remnants of besmirched mine dumps that are symbols of disinte-gration … and resemble an uninhabitable and polluted moonscape' (quoted in Iqani and Baro 2017, 113). As time progresses, these fake hills – tinted innards scraped from deep beneath the surface, piled up haphazardly and decorated with weak attempts at plant life – have begun to crumble and frag-ment. Eventually they will slide back into the ground, taking with them a by-blow of the violence of Joburg's birth. The same applies to the collapse in the population of Parktown prawns. In vanishing from sight and from the city's collective imagination, these creatures remove a certain awareness of what Johannesburg was. Their disappearance is part of its 'sociohistorical amnesia' (Murray 2011, 329), an urban tendency to demolish and build over the remnants of the past, to insist that the 'world-class African city', as its current marketing slogan presents it, is a hypermodern and global place or product 'in which tradition and the past have become stylised constructions forged out of the present' (Murray 2011, 329).

If we consider the Parktown prawn as a metaphor for the anxieties of apart-heid and post-apartheid suburban life, then we must also consider what its vanishing means for the urban imaginaries of the most fortunate – and often most separate – denizens of this 'new' Johannesburg, a city that is 'porous, indefinite and open-ended' (Bremner 2010, 34), built on the bones of the old one but refusing to recognise its situation as part necropolis, part charnel house. Those who are not affected by them on a daily basis can, even more blithely than before, forget the legacies of migrant and domestic labour, influx control, spatial engineering, xenophobia, Randlord rapacity, even the mines themselves. Without the lurking potential of the insect-monster-outsider-other, the hermetic frame of cloistered suburban self-imagery remains sealed. No liminal creatures burst in to reveal the weakness of the fictions supporting suburban Johannesburg life. The particular uncanniness of the extractive city is exchanged for more general forms of urban anxiety, in which Johannesburg is just another big, frightening and crime-ridden southern city whose threats can be managed (although never exterminated) by wealth, taste and private security.

For its middle classes, then, the vanishing of reminders of certain aspects of the past has allowed Johannesburg to become truly 'global'. Generic urban fears about crime, immigration, environmental problems, political instability and other concerns have papered over more existential anxieties that once haunted the imaginations of many suburban whites. As the Parktown prawns have vanished, so too has their capacity to imaginatively undermine spurious claims about the city's meritocracy and post-racial transformation. This 'new' Johannesburg is not simply shorn of memory, a claim that can be made about its many incarnations, from mining town to modernist experiment to edge city sprawl (Murray 2011). Rather, it is shorn of *symbols*, barring those that are approved (and often paid for) by the heralds of the new globalism.

The ubiquitous *Libanasidus vittatus* of my childhood has devolved from a constant token of the weirdness lurking under Johannesburg's glitzy skin to a minor curiosity of local urban mythology. With it has gone one of the many necessary reminders of the city's violent origins and histories of racial exclusion.

ACKNOWLEDGEMENTS

Many thanks to James Harrison, the zoological curator of the Wits Life Sciences Museum (WLSM) based at the School of Animal, Plant and Environmental Sciences (APES) at Wits University, for generously sharing his insect knowledge; to Sara Orning, for her insightful comments and skill at reining in melodrama; and to Greg Falkof, for spending much of the 1980s terrorising me with Parktown prawns.

NOTES

1   Although my focus here is on what Parktown prawns meant and mean within suburban anxieties, they are by no means confined to the suburbs. Township and inner-city residents are equally likely to share personal and apocryphal stories of their interactions with these creatures. The forested and gardened conditions of the suburbs provide their most appropriate environment, but they do often spread further afield within the greater city area.

2   Between 1989 and 1991 *The Ugly Noo Noo* was nominated for multiple international awards. It won eight, for acting, production, script and comedy, in South Africa and at the Edinburgh Festival in the UK. A version of its script appears in the book *More Market Plays* (Kani 1994), although this cannot do justice to the physicality of the piece.

3   I am grateful to Lauren Beukes for this point.

4   Despite its many heritage sites, twenty-first-century Parktown is neither remote nor particularly fashionable. It is extremely close to Hillbrow, discussed in the chapter by Aidan Mosselson, one of the densest and most crime-ridden parts of central Joburg. Its sprawling homes and gracious apartment blocks are surrounded by barbed wire and patrolled by security. Parktown has become a liminal suburb: the architecture of the rich in uncomfortable proximity to the poor.

5   Research suggests that, along with Birmingham in the UK (also at one time a heavily industrial city), Johannesburg is one of only two major cities in the world not built on a water source (Kings 2016).

REFERENCES

Agamben, Giorgio. 1998. *Homo Sacer: Sovereign Power and Bare Life*. Stanford CA: Stanford University Press.

Blumberg, Marcia. 1997. "More Market Plays, and: Mooi Street and Other Moves (review)." *Theatre Journal* 49: 85–7.

Bourke, G. 2012. "Bare Life's Bare Essentials: When All You've Got Is Hope – The State of Exception in The Road, District 9 and Blindness." *Law, Culture and the Humanities* 10: 440–63.

Bremner, Lindsay. 2010. *Writing the City into Being*. Johannesburg: Fourthwall Books.

Brettschneider, H., and P.W. Bateman. 2005. "Differential Shelter Selection in Response to Predator Chemical Cues by Two Orthopterans: Libanasidus vittatus (Anostostomatidae) and Platygryllus primiformis (Gryllidae)." *Journal of Insect Behavior* 18: 381–7.

Brettschneider, H., C.T. Chimimba, C.H. Scholtz, and P.W. Bateman. 2007. "Review of Southern African Anostostomatidae (Orthoptera: Ensifera), with a Key to Genera." *African Entomology* 15: 103–20.

Byrne, Marcus. 2015. "Scary King Cricket Is a Beautiful Example of Evolution at Its Best." *The Conversation*. http://theconversation.com/scary-king-cricket-is-a-beautiful-example-of-evolution-at-its-best-43674.

Cane, Jonathan. 2019. *Civilising Grass: The Art of the Lawn on the South African Highveld*. Johannesburg: Wits University Press.

Comaroff, Jean, and John L. Comaroff. 2017. *The Truth about Crime: Sovereignty, Knowledge, Social Order*. Johannesburg: Wits University Press.

Durington, M. 2009. "Suburban Fear, Media and Gated Communities in Durban, South Africa." *Home Cultures* 6: 71–88.

Falkof, Nicky. 2012. "Mining the Dumps." Johannesburg Workshop in Theory and Criticism. http://jhbwtc.blogspot.com/2012/07/mining-dumps.html.

———. 2015. "Out the Back: Race and Reinvention in Johannesburg's Garden Cottages." *International Journal of Cultural Studies* 19 (6): 627–42.

Freud, Sigmund. 1990. "The Uncanny." In *Penguin Freud Library, vol. 14: Art and Literature*. London: Penguin Books.

Gevisser, Mark. 2008. "From the Ruins." In *Johannesburg: The Elusive Metropolis*, edited by S. Nuttall and A. Mbembe, 317–36. Durham: Duke University Press.

Ginsburg, Rebecca. 2011. *At Home with Apartheid: The Hidden Landscapes of Domestic Service in Johannesburg*. Charlottesville: University of Virginia Press.

Hall, Stuart. 1996. "Who Needs 'Identity'?" In *Questions of Cultural Identity*, edited by Stuart Hall and Paul du Gay, 1–17. London: Sage.

Haupt, Adam. 2013. "Citizenship without Representation? Blackface, Misogyny and Parody in Die Antwoord, Lupé Fiasco and Angel Haze." *Communicatio* 39: 466–82.

Heller-Nicholas, Alexandra. 2011. "From District 6 to District 9: Apartheid, Spectacle and the Real." *Screen Education* 61: 137–42.

Horn, G. 2017. "5 Ugliest, Creepiest Insects on Planet Earth." *SA Country Life*. https://www.countrylife.co.za/wild-earth/36607.

Iqani, Mehita, and Gilles Baro. 2017. "The Branded Skyline? A Socio-Semiotic Critique of Johannesburg's Architectural Adverts." *African Studies* 76: 102–20.

Janks, Hilary, and R. Adegoke. 2011. "District Nine and Constructions of the Other: Implications for Heterogeneous Classrooms." *English Teaching: Practice and Critique* 10: 39–48.

Kani, John, ed. 1994. *More Market Plays*. Johannesburg: Ad Donker.

Kings, Sipho. 2016. "Johannesburg Water Implements Heavy Water Restrictions, Urges Residents to Be Frugal." *M&G Online*. https://mg.co.za/article/2016-09-05-breaking-johannesburg-water-has-serious-implemented-level-3-water-restrictions/.

Kristeva, Julia. 1982. *Powers of Horror.* New York: Columbia University Press.

Lemanski, Charlotte. 2004. "A New Apartheid? The Spatial Implications of Fear of Crime in Cape Town, South Africa." *Environment and Urbanization* 16: 101–12.

Lipman, Alan, and Howard Harris. 1999. "Fortress Johannesburg." *Environment and Planning B: Urban Analytics and City Science* 26: 727–40.

Mason, Heather. 2013. "Close Encounter with a Parktown Prawn." *2Summers*. https://2summers.net/2013/04/22/close-encounter-with-a-parktown-prawn/.

Mbembe, Achille, and Sarah Nuttall. 2008. "Afropolis." In *Johannesburg: The Elusive Metropolis*, edited by Sarah Nuttall and Achille Mbembe, 1–33. Durham: Duke University Press.

Murray, Martin J. 2011. *City of Extremes: The Spatial Politics of Johannesburg*. Durham: Duke University Press.

Nightingale, Carl H. 2015. *Segregation: A Global History of Divided Cities*. Chicago: University of Chicago Press.

Nuttall, Sarah, and Achille Mbembe, eds. 2008. *Johannesburg: The Elusive Metropolis*. Durham: Duke University Press.

Rivers, Billy. 2012. "War of the Parktown Prawn." *JHBLive*. http://www.jhblive.com/Stories-in-Johannesburg/article/war-of-the-parktown-prawn/5949.

Saks, David. 2009. "Crickets from Hell: Encounters with Parktown Prawns." *Thought Leader*. https://thoughtleader.co.za/davidsaks/2009/11/08/crickets-from-hell-%E2%80%93-encounters-with-parktown-prawns/.

Schmidt, Brian. 2014. "Fatty Boom Boom and the Transnationality of Blackface in Die Antwoord's Racial Project." *TDR/The Drama Review* 58: 132–48.

Wolf, S., P.W. Bateman, and H. Brettschneider. 2006. "The Predator Defence System of an African King Cricket (Orthoptera: Anostostomatidae): Does It Help to Stink?" *African Zoology* 41: 75–81.

6 THE UNRULY IN THE ANODYNE: NATURE IN GATED COMMUNITIES

RENUGAN RAIDOO

'The dawn breaks across the Serengeti landscape. The dew glistens on the pristine greens and the air is crisp. The early morning sunlight catches the faint mist rising once more ... Another beautiful day unfolds at The Whistling Thorns.' These words appear in white text on an image of rolling fields of grass punctuated by sparse tree cover. A few of the trees are reflected in a small body of water in the middle ground of the image. The grass is well manicured, and in the foreground a section of the grass is slightly lighter than the rest. This section offers a clue to what is meant by 'pristine greens': it is part of the golf course on the Serengeti Golf and Wildlife Estate, a decade-old gated community in Kempton Park, near Johannesburg's O.R. Tambo International Airport. The image appears in an advertisement for a new sectional title scheme called Whistling Thorns being developed on the estate. Allusion to the celebrated Serengeti National Park in Tanzania illuminates the developers' attempt at marketing to its residents a kind of African ur-landscape – despite the obvious human interventions that go into creating a golf course, and despite the fact that references to an unadulterated landscape are paradoxically being used to market forms of human habitation.

At a conference of gated estate managers that was held on the estate, I had a chance to learn exactly what *is* whistling through the thorns. I and about twenty other delegates sat at three large round tables covered in white cloth on a portion of grass just outside the clubhouse. While others played a golf tournament, we non-golfers were gathered for a wine tasting that served as an alternative welcome activity. Halfway through introducing the first wine, and just as he was describing its bouquet of 'strawberry with strong floral notes', the representative from the wine estate paused. Perhaps prompted by the attention he was drawing to aroma, he crinkled his nose, frowned and switched from English to Afrikaans: 'Dit ruik hier soos 'n plaas' [It smells like a farm here]. The other delegates sniffed, noting the distinct stench of manure that saturated the air.

Kempton Park, like the rest of the Highveld, is dry and dusty at the end of winter. One could easily forget that one was in this part of South Africa once passing through the gates of the estate, where suddenly – as in the advertisement quoted above – the landscape gives way to dense greenery framing luxurious homes around the verdant expanse of the golf course. Or, rather, one could easily forget where one is until the illusion of splendour is betrayed by the intrusion of traces of the labours that underlie this feat of elite world-building. The estate managers tell me that the smell wafts in from neighbouring farms, attesting to an agricultural history no longer visible on the tract that has since become Serengeti.

In this chapter, I theorise the material world as a source of anxiety that threatens not only the enjoyment of gated communities, but also the capital interests that residents and developers have invested and the budding regimes of property ownership claimed by (predominantly white) elite South Africans at a time when older idioms of ownership seem under threat. This serves as an attempt to get beyond efforts to account for the proliferation of gated communities that foreground fear and insecurity, trying instead to describe the forms of anxiety and affective attachment that emerge in gated communities, forms that also characterise the uneasy kinds of postcolonial and post-apartheid belonging that elites foster. In particular, I focus on the use of heritage and natural environment in efforts to create affective worlds that make life liveable in twenty-first-century South Africa. At a time of heightened global attention to climate and environment, which is coincidental with an apparent upsurge in nationalist demands to reify borders and with the proliferation of gated communities around metropoles throughout the world, this study considers a set of phenomena just as relevant outside South Africa's borders as within them.

THE CASE FOR ANXIETY IN THE STUDY
OF GATED COMMUNITIES

According to most urban planning researchers, respondents cite fear of crime as the primary reason for moving into gated communities (see Landman and Schönteich 2002). This is despite highly publicised crimes within gated communities in South Africa, including robberies, intimate crimes as in the Oscar Pistorius case, and family murders like the brutal Van Breda case. (Both cases, tellingly, featured legal defences hinging on imagined black intruders: Oscar Pistorius asked us to believe that he shot his girlfriend, Reeva, through the bathroom door because he thought there was a black burglar on the other side; Henri van Breda blamed on a laughing black axeman or two the murders he had perpetrated involving his mother, father and brother, and the non-fatal injuries caused to his sister.) And this despite studies that may indicate increased crime around gated communities (Breetzke, Landman, and Cohn 2014) and that note how the *fear of crime* varies independently of the *incidence of crime* (Comaroff and Comaroff 2016; Durington 2009).

But there is another, more philosophical objection to be made to the focus on 'fear' in attempts to understand South Africa's gated communities, one that I think justifies a turn to anxiety. The classic distinction made between fear and anxiety – often used interchangeably in everyday parlance – is, simply put, that fear has an object whereas anxiety has none. The object of anxiety is deferred from the here and now to some dreaded future possibility or some calamity emerging seemingly from nowhere. In a way, anxiety is a sense that one should be afraid, although one doesn't yet know of what.

Indeed, it is perhaps *only* these affects deferring objects of attachment that allow us to probe the relationship between affect, on the one hand, and the hard edges of political economy, on the other, for 'the present is perceived, first, affectively: the present is what makes itself present to us before it becomes anything else, such as an orchestrated collective event or an epoch on which we can look back' (Berlant 2011, 4). Raymond Williams calls such complexes of affect and political economy 'structures of feeling'. Despite the fixity suggested by the word 'structure', these are ways of feeling that are constantly emerging and that never (or rarely) achieve the kind of solidity often attributed to similar formulations, such as 'ideology' or 'worldview'. They are structural in the sense that the constitutive elements form 'a set, with specific internal relations, at once interlocking and in tension' (Williams 1977, 132).

However inchoate, structures of feeling serve to constrain or make possible different forms of action, thought and affect. But once an epoch solidifies as something that can be labelled as such, it is a sign that it has already passed, that the affective orientations peculiar to it have fossilised.

Hence my focus on anxiety: the feeling captured by something like 'fear of crime' – so often, and understandably, referred to in the study of gated communities – signals a mode of attention that has already found a fixed object and whose study thus forecloses discovering the aspired-to, but as yet unignited, senses of futurity and world-making that dwell in more inchoate affective states such as anxiety. In what follows, I argue that attachments to nature in gated communities can be understood as anxious in so far as they exhibit a menacing fragility: they are crucial to projects of elite world-making, but they persistently threaten to sour.

NATURE, HERITAGE AND BELONGING

'Nature,' writes Raymond Williams, 'is perhaps the most complex word in the language' (1976, 164). It has referenced, variously and sometimes at once, essential (even divine) character, the given order and progression of things, and parts of the material world not included in humanity. While a full exploration of the many valences of the word is beyond the scope of the present discussion, its complexity gives it both descriptive and normative force. What counts as nature has political and epistemological consequences.

The political consequences arise out of the management of the boundary delimiting nature from its other (whether cultural, artificial, synthetic, alien or something else). In the name of nature people have not only been inspired to leave the landscape alone (itself a particular intervention that involves barricading), but they have also sought to intervene on its behalf. Although a review of the global literature on the politics of conservation is not possible here, the South African literature on the subject makes the following clear: at stake in colonial contestations over conservation in South Africa were ideas about race, class and property (see Beinart 1989); and scientist ideas that relegated racial difference to the realm of nature underpinned the spatial segregation that culminated in apartheid (Dubow 1995). As I shall argue, nature has also been crucial to the development of gated communities in South Africa, particularly in and around Johannesburg.

Although popular notions of nature may suggest some primordial state prior to human intervention, if something was done by humans long ago, or if it was made by particular kinds of humans (primitive, rural), then it holds a similar status as nature. Furthermore, in so far as popular environmental discourses rely on future generations to justify interventions, nature itself is also a kind of heritage, whose preservation is a birthright rather than an end in itself. 'Heritage has become a construct to conjure with,' write Jean and John Comaroff, especially 'as global markets and mass migration erode the distinctive wealth of nations, forcing them to redefine their sense of patrimony' (2012, 94). Eyal Weizman, describing the architecture of Israeli occupation of Palestine, notes that the Zionist co-optation of subterranean archaeological evidence is a key component of naturalising Israeli claims to land in a broader, vertically integrated architecture of occupation (2007, ch. 1; see also Abu el-Haj 2001). That one's place on the land can be naturalised raises an important point about the politics of nature: as a historically, spatially and situationally variable category, the political work it does relies on a process of naturalisation that transposes features of the material world in between regimes of value delineated by nature. What makes this all the more worthy of consideration is that naturalisation refers to socio-legal processes that adduct foreigners to the body politic, just as easily as it refers to how features of capitalism like the market become taken for granted. 'Naturalisation is integral to the way in which social value is rendered as transcendent truth, just as "denaturing" is key to unmasking the commonsense workings of domination, abstraction, and exploitation' (Comaroff 2017).

Nature, and our place in it, have often been used to legitimate belonging. In the South African context, J.M. Coetzee has noted two sets of representations of the country that have populated landscape art and writing by white South Africans (with, of course, significant exceptions). The first is the pastoral farm, which represented industrious white labour as a way of inscribing the land as the property of whites to the exclusion of blacks. The second is a primordial topography that exists prior to all human toil, a vision 'of South Africa as a vast, empty, silent space, older than man, older than the dinosaurs whose bones lie bedded in its rocks, and destined to be vast, empty, and unchanged long after man has passed from its face' (Coetzee 1988, 7). In relation to the latter representation, what is sought is communing with the land, rather than its domestication, through the crafting of a language that could make the land speak for itself. Coetzee notes that, in the works he studies, nature remains obstinate; when it does come to life, it trembles with vengeance, impossible to control.

Outside literary studies, others have also sought to make sense of the intractability of nature. Nonhumans have a certain 'effectivity' (Bennett 2010); they can intervene in ways that foil or make possible our political projects (Mitchell 2002; Tsing 2014). While I hesitate to grant to nonhumans agency or intention in any strong sense of those terms, their unpredictability provides sites of affective attachment that are well described as anxious because they carry with them the capacity to undermine our best-laid plans. In gated communities, where nature is drawn upon extensively as a way to claim belonging and justify segregation (Ballard and Jones 2011), the nonhuman world is a critical site at which to observe the uneasy affective attachments that characterise the structures of feeling native to gated communities.

Lifestyle estates, many of which are centred around golf courses, equestrian facilities or other leisure amenities, may seem odd places to study the natural world. But they provide ideal crucibles in which to examine how nature, heritage, belonging and capital are currently alloyed in South Africa. If nature is not a category that exists ontologically prior to the human making of it, then it stands to reason that we take it as an emic category rather than looking for significance where we might expect to find it (such as in nature reserves or the 'wilderness'). And if, as already stated, our interest in nature is in large part aesthetic and affective, it matters not so much whether this is 'real nature' (could such a thing exist), but more that gated communities are spaces in which aesthetic and affective sensibilities – and the moral orientations that they engender – are disciplined and made.

In what remains, I outline an argument around nature, naturalisation and belonging. It is based on data collected in an ongoing research project, including interviews with estate managers, developers and residents; ethnographic fieldwork with estate managers; websites, advertising materials and newspaper articles associated with gated communities; magazines and newspapers intended for internal circulation; and an analysis of the magazine *Estate Living*. The last two comprise stories that gated community stakeholders tell themselves about themselves.

LABOUR, ALIENS AND SAVAGES IN THE PRODUCTION OF THE ANODYNE

Although many estates advertise the thrills of various kinds of sporting facilities, they are fundamentally designed to be anodyne, in both senses of the term:

unobtrusive *and* analgesic. Producing what we might call such an *an*aesthetic environment requires an active process of expunging aspects of the world that threaten tranquillity. Anaesthesia in its most literal sense is, after all, as Susan Buck-Morss (1992) reminds us, a way not only to allay the pain of the afflicted, but also to allow physicians to avoid the affective strain of having to countenance that pain. In the South African case, gated communities function as a way for residents to remove themselves from upsetting conditions in the country at large, avoiding emotionally charged interactions with those outside the gates. Sarah described well to me the confronting experiences of inequality that one can avoid behind the walls.[1] A resident of Fourways Gardens, the first gated community in the country, established in 1983 by Anglocorp (an Anglo American Company affiliate), she said to me one afternoon while watching the rain fill the *spruit* (spring, small river) over which the clubhouse restaurant looks:

> Everywhere you turn there's somebody with a hand out … Every time you go to the grocery store, you know, there's beggars on the corner, and every time you reverse out of a parking space there's another hand out. And I think people just get a bit overwhelmed with it all. Like, please can I just go from here to there and go home and not be accosted by somebody for something.

Gated communities permit the making of a life through forgetting those things that might threaten it, a spatial correlate of what Friedrich Nietzsche has argued about history and memory: 'Forgetting is essential to action of any kind, just as not only light but darkness too is essential for the life of everything organic' (1983, 62).

In large part, this is accomplished by homeowners' agreements and enforced by homeowners' associations. These stipulate a set of rules that are more conservative than the laws governing South Africa, and also promise more reliable enforcement. Every resident agrees to abide by these rules when they move in. They govern parking, noise levels, the size and kinds of pets, how fast one can drive. They regulate access so residents don't have to contend with unwanted vehicles, such as passenger taxis or buses, or unsightly people, such as beggars and trash-pickers. In effect, such regulation purifies the aesthetic landscape and assuages guilt.

Gated communities, which are often accompanied by the development of schools and shopping centres nearby, extend these environments beyond themselves. Mithila, a resident of Dainfern Golf Estate, one of Johannesburg's first and best-known estates situated in the Fourways area, bragged to me that she goes for weeks without driving onto William Nicol Drive, a major north–south thoroughfare that provides access to one of the estate's two gates. In order to get to Dainfern, one turns off William Nicol onto Broadacres Drive. Between the turn-off and the Dainfern gates there are other gated communities, shopping centres and a school that has internal gate access to the estate. This particular woman, whose children attended the school, had no need to go all the way to William Nicol: food, entertainment, friends and school were right at her doorstep. Nor, for that matter, did she have to contend with taxi drivers, because the Dainfern Community Association – including most of the estates along Broadacres Drive – paid for security to regulate taxi traffic through the area. Those who do have to leave Broadacres often get in their cars, drive to a shopping centre, house or office park, and only unlock their doors once through another set of gates. They travel from island to island on what might be called an anodyne archipelago.

The maintenance of this atmosphere requires the careful management of multiple phenomena, each with its own ethical valences. I highlight three of them here: labour histories, savages and aliens.

HISTORIES OF LABOUR

Landscape and certain histories of land use are mobilised aesthetically to draw in consumers and to create atmosphere. Several estates, themselves former farms, incorporate old farm structures and equipment – and sometimes even animals – into their landscaping aesthetics, and require that new homes be built in particularly nostalgic styles. Other aspects of historical land use are bulldozed (in the sense of razing) or papered over (in the bureaucratic sense). Dainfern is built on what was the Zevenfontein Farm until the 1980s, when developers began buying and developing the smallholdings north of Johannesburg. Something had to be done with people who lived and worked on the farms, not to mention the generations who may have been buried there. Those who lived on Zevenfontein were forcibly displaced, many eventually taking up residence in Diepsloot, a township created by the ANC government to house the area's growing squatter population, including a proportion of former farm labour. The graves were dealt with in as seemingly careless a manner. According to the funeral services company AVBOB, it was contracted by

Jonnic (then called Johannesburg Consolidated Investment), the developer of Dainfern Golf Estate, to exhume 590 graves. AVBOB's records show that the graves of six white people were moved to individual plots in Midrand Cemetery. The graves of 363 black people were exhumed and dumped into 'waterlogged mass graves' in Mamelodi. The matter of the more than 200 graves not relocated was inherited by the homeowners' association and became the source of considerable confusion and scandal (Mji 2018).[2]

Driving around Dainfern on a golf cart – arguably the most popular form of transport, not only for navigating the golf course but also for getting to school at the adjacent Dainfern College, for visiting other residents or as a pastime – one is hard-pressed to find any trace of the history of the land, let alone the labour and bodies on which it was built. Other gated communities, such as Heritage Hill and Southdowns in Centurion, have maintained farm aesthetics, using some of the original buildings and maintaining old farm equipment as part of the landscaping. All the homes are built in the Old Transvaal style, and some even sport – according to one resident – non-functioning borehole wind pumps and rainwater tanks. Homeowners proudly advertise the fact that structures are built with local rock; it is not just style that creates place, but the material itself. In Southdowns, residents mingle with cattle as approximately a quarter of the land is devoted to grazing for the Irene Dairy Farm. 'A piece of the past has found its way to the future' is emblazoned across the Southdowns website.

Both of these aesthetic sleights of hand – erasing black labourers and reviving a pastoral history made by white labour – are examples of what Williams (1973) called 'a myth functioning as a memory' in his analysis of representations of country life in English literature, in which the country is portrayed – in contrast to the city – as free from conditions of dispossession and exploitative labour. The myths that residents of gated communities fashion for themselves of, as one informant told me, 'what South Africa was like thirty years ago' or, as another told me, 'what it was like to grow up on a farm' are undoubtedly turned to memory.

SAVAGES

The issue of race surfaces in discussions of who is and who isn't a threat to nature and the collective well-being not only of gated community residents but of all life on earth. Black people are figured both as natural threats and as threats to nature. Sara ('Saartje') Baartman's case is emblematic of the dialectical core of comparisons of natives to nature. She was nonhuman in the supernatural sense suggested by her apotheosis as the Hottentot Venus (in many ways analogous to the 'noble savage'), but also in the subhuman sense of a natural object that could be displayed, pricked, prodded and examined. There is a long history of black and brown people being described as closer to or part of nature, as intermediaries between nature and civilisation or, worse, as uncontrollable, savage and unpredictable hordes. Indeed, it was against the savage other of the black native that civilisation was often defined. It is from this unpredictability that *laagers*[3] were meant to protect the Voortrekkers. The presumed wildness of black Africans made *swart gevaar* (black danger) so convincing.

But walls and barricades cannot keep out all conflict, and in June 2011 legislation was passed to establish the Community Schemes Ombud Service (CSOS), a dispute resolution entity mandated to deal with the growing number of community schemes and the conflicts that arise between residents as well as between residents and governing bodies. In August 2018, CSOS released a circular listing a number of rules that it deemed undesirable for sectional title schemes. The circular addressed several situations one might expect – for example, excessive penalties for resident infractions or non-payment of levies and compliance with the National Road Traffic Act. On 8 September, just days before the start of the annual meeting of the Association for Residential Communities (ARC) – a for-profit professional association designed to help with advocacy and management – many of the delegates (primarily estate managers) learned of these rules from an article in the *Sunday Times* entitled 'Ban on Ritual Slaughter in Estates Seen as "Undesirable"'. CSOS was presumably attempting to safeguard the religious expression of the many South Africans for whom slaughter is a fundamental aspect of spiritual and social life, commemorating major life events or periodic festivals.

As we waited for the prize-giving for the golf tournament that marked the start of the ARC conference, I and a handful of estate managers chatted on the veranda of the Serengeti clubhouse over drinks and snacks. When the topic of slaughter came up, Urvashni, the manager of an estate north of Durban, said in an adamant tone, 'We are an eco-friendly estate. We have animals on the property, so slaughter is a no.' I didn't feel comfortable pressing the issue, although, knowing that animals frequently need to be culled on eco-estates, I found her logic puzzling. How did ritual slaughter threaten the other animals on the estate?

In a somewhat analogous scenario, Richard Ballard has explored responses to slaughter in areas of Durban previously reserved for whites (2010). The articles and letters to the editors that he studied draw on explicitly neo-evolutionary ideas in which animal slaughter is evidence of pre-civilised barbarism and primitivism. One of the women quoted mentions the distress that her pets endured as a result of the slaughter, citing their failure to bark as a sign that they, too, determined the slaughter to be barbaric, and were thus capable of making the same moral distinctions as their enraged owner. The nonhuman is brought closer to civilisation through concern for its well-being, and the barbaric black neighbours are distanced from it. Hence, perhaps, Urvashni's assumption that ritual slaughter would be antithetical to the goals of an eco-estate: it may traumatise the other animals.

The relationship between slaughter and race was made clearer in a comment by Lizette, who manages an estate near Vereeniging: 'They want to bring Soweto into the estate. No, I'm sorry.' The tranquillity of the estate might be threatened by the excesses of practices like slaughter, excesses native to black townships. Later in the conference, when a legal expert on community schemes was asked a question about the slaughters, she confirmed that, while it is important to appear otherwise, for at least some homeowners' associations the question of rules is explicitly ethnocultural: 'I've seen one estate that we've got down in KZN [KwaZulu-Natal] that basically says in their rules that "We don't care about religious rights, you can't have fireworks".' This proviso is related to the Diwali celebrations of the province's considerable Indian population. 'The minute you've framed it saying "our conservancy laws supersede any religious rights that you might have", that's gonna be struck down. Frame it a little bit differently.' The tricky part is to create a 'civilised' community ethos that regulates or proscribes forms of offensive ethnocultural expression without seeming overtly racist.

That our conversation occurred around snack plates full of biltong illustrates a point. Industrial meat production, arguably consigning cattle to a fate far worse than ritual slaughter, modulates its violence through spatial displacement and the aesthetic forms of commoditisation that turn animal flesh into supermarket meat. Culling is justified as a conservation effort. But slaughter carries with it all of the township.

ALIENS

John and Jean Comaroff have noted how discourses about nature, and particularly about the indigeneity of flora and fauna, can readily 'jump species' to comment on human distinctions made between native and alien (2012, 91–107). Most of the gated communities I have visited have rules regarding what can and cannot be planted, with an emphasis on indigenous plants in public spaces and private gardens (see also Ballard and Jones 2011). The most prominent exceptions to this are golf courses, which rarely use indigenous grasses. Still, the landscaping along golf courses and throughout golf estates attests to a decidedly African palette of flora, never mind that they stay lush when the rest of the Highveld is dry. The Africanness of the aesthetic is important, using as it does the conservation of indigenous landscape as a branding tool. As a pamphlet for the Hills Game Reserve and Lifestyle Estate states, 'The majority of the estate is dedicated to the game reserve, natural parklands and greenbelts that create an authentic African bushveld experience for the residents and their guests.'

An article in the October 2018 issue of *Estate Living* brings anxieties about 'aliens' into panicked clarity. 'Joburg is being eaten by aliens, and we should be panicking but we're not. At least not yet,' we are told. The article is about the shot hole borer, an invasive beetle of Asian origin that harvests fungus in trees ranging from the non-indigenous (but non-invasive) London planes and oaks to a range of indigenous trees. 'Given that we might lose enormous swathes of our urban and indigenous forests,' the article continues,

> which are some of our most important buffers against climate change and also add enormous value to properties around the country, perhaps now's the time for government, individuals and private enterprises to start finding the funds to resource FABI [the Forestry and Agricultural Biotechnology Institute] to do just that. Which would truly be a good way to panic.

I would not claim that the borer is *not* a threat to biodiversity. Rather, the pitch of the article, and its call to arms, signal a kind of stewardship of the indigenous, which I discuss further in the next section. Here, stewardship of the environment requires the expurgation of the alien. There are echoes of nationalism as well in the collective call to unite against the invader. This is not so much an article as it is an advertorial, paid for by Servest, a contractor that provides landscaping (among other facility management) services. This commercialisation of fighting aliens is at once an acknowledgement that the problem is marketable and thus already widespread, and an acknowledgement that it is currently spreading to the detriment of our natural flora.

OWNERS OF LAND OR STEWARDS OF SOIL?

Finally, I suggest that nature is central to the justification of the continual occupation of land. No longer understood as worthwhile agricultural capital, the landscape is claimed as a natural resource in a nostalgic mode: a source of both biodiversity and the raw materials for a pastoral aesthetic. But more than that, residents cultivate a kind of affective kinship with nature on their estates that signals a change in how they relate to property.

Current autochthonous claims to landownership are made on the basis of past dispossession and the idea that black South Africans are 'of' the land. These came to a head in 2018, when parliament voted to support a resolution promising to expropriate land without compensation, with President Cyril Ramaphosa vowing to change the Constitution to make this power of government more explicit. Although the president has vowed that land expropriation would be done in a way that would neither harm property rights nor discourage foreign investment, the Lockean (1690) justification forwarded by some white South Africans nonetheless seems under threat, especially at a time when many liberal white South Africans repent publicly for the past. Organisations like AfriForum[4] argue that white South Africans obtained much of the land through legal agreements, and have a right to ownership because they rendered that land productive and habitable through technological interventions (see, for example, Kriel 2015). Indeed, Ernst Roets, the deputy CEO of AfriForum, claimed during the land reform parliamentary hearings that in order to dispute the legitimacy of white land claims, one needs to 'surpass the geological and biological fact that it isn't possible to survive on more than 30 percent of South Africa's surface if you do not have the technology to dig a borehole'.[5] In his view, it was only through technology that parts of South Africa were rendered habitable. However, such interventions are no longer tenable as entitlements to ownership, and in gated communities new idioms of landownership are emerging that allay white and elite fears about land and belonging, but are in turn fraught with their own anxieties.

Environmental stewardship obfuscates land-as-capital, in effect reversing the logic of liberalism, which saw proprietary claims made on the basis that soil could be worked into land. Here, land is argued back into soil, whose sanctity and primordial value justify its development and ownership not in the idiom of capital accumulation but in the idiom of stewardship. Gracious property developers of eco-villages will transform property into posterity. Despite continuing to be incredibly lucrative, land in its post-productivist fecundity justifies development with a value higher than that of autochthonous right or liberal property-through-toil. Precisely at a moment when the Anthropocene makes the apocalypse seem imminent and environmentalism urgent, justification of exclusionary urban forms through environmental stewardship can be read as a discursive refashioning of soil that trumps all other claims to land precisely because it is not a claim *to* land, but a claim *on behalf of* the land itself. Moreover, such efforts to delay environmental collapse cut across race and class by including themselves in a global effort to redeem all of humanity, saving it from natural perils by absolving it of the very sins against the environment that brought about such calamity.

The extent to which stewardship as an idiom of property ownership coincides with a new affective relation to the land is made clear not only in marketing materials but also in the internal dialogues that residents have about nature. The website of one eco-village notes that 'residents indulge in nature as their neighbour on a daily basis'. 'Conservation', counter-intuitively, justifies human habitation. Although environmental impact assessments required by municipalities are often grossly misleading, as Manfred Spocter (2015) has shown, the impression of conservation is attractive to both municipalities and potential residents. The magazines that circulate within gated communities similarly focus on nature. Most have sections on the flora and fauna in the estate, and many publish residents' photographs of wildlife. These attest to the affective investment that residents make in the flora and fauna around them.

Fourways Gardens describes itself as 'The Garden of Eden of Estates', presumably because it was the first gated community proclaimed in the country – Eden as primordial utopia – and because of its focus on nature – Eden as paradise. The connection to nature is everywhere apparent. In a commemorative edition of the estate magazine, the nature reserve is described as 'a little bit of untamed paradise right in the middle of the suburbs ... a unique piece of Africa in our midst'. The section on the environment in this magazine includes articles on bats, the eradication of invasive weeds, and the barn owls, spotted eagle owls and blue cranes that have been released on the estate. The article on blue cranes 'lovingly named Jack and Jane' addresses them directly: 'Welcome to your new home, Jack and Jane, we hope you enjoy many happy years in Fourways Gardens Estate and that you will produce many babies for our reserve!'

There is a kind of kinship with nature and plant and animal life that is suggested here, an intimacy that is cultivated through the circulation of these kinds of materials. Nature is a 'neighbour', another member of the community. Part of this sense of kinship is encouraged by direct experience of nature. At Waterfall Estate, for example, 'in keeping with the Estate's emphasis on environmentally-friendly living and awareness, a number of viewing decks have been incorporated into facilities and great care has been taken to ensure that the landscaping on the estate is completely indigenous'. Here natural aesthetics are a form of soulcraft that can transform residents into ideal environmental citizens.

With regard to heritage, traces of human habitation can be a problem for homeowners and investors. Take, for example, the graves in Dainfern, mentioned above. When I brought up the case with a manager of an estate in Midrand, he seemed sceptical: 'What they do is they steal gravestones and put them on the farms so they can say their ancestors are buried there.' Despite this, evidence of early human settlement can actually work in favour of gated communities. The November 2018 issue of *Estate Living* includes a feature article on the Pinnacle Point gated estate in Mossel Bay in the Western Cape. Excavations since the year 2000 have revealed caves occupied by humans between 170 000 and 40 000 years ago. The archaeological sites show evidence of stone tool making, symbolic behaviour and exploitation of marine resources. Acknowledging that heritage can sometimes be a problem for development, the article continues, 'With the increasing emphasis investors and residents of estates place on sustainability and environmental responsibility, these are now considered to be assets that need to be nurtured, both for their intrinsic value and also for their marketing appeal. And heritage resources are just as valuable as natural ones.' In 2012 the caves were declared a provincial heritage site, and there are efforts under way to declare them a UNESCO World Heritage Site, with the estate as a protective buffer. According to its

CEO, 'International buyers are purchasing homes at Pinnacle Point Estate because of the presence of the caves, and our residents and owners take great pride in this priceless resource. It's a huge selling point.' Capital investment is here refashioned as an investment in humanity itself, a humanity that comes prior to histories of racial domination, thus justifying presence and belonging through the stewardship of purportedly non- or pre-racial human heritage.

BETRAYALS

That nature is also a source of anxiety is made clearer by looking not only at how nature is mobilised, but also at how it resists attempts at its own co-opting. One resident told me that she couldn't sleep some nights because the frogs that have returned to Dainfern after being undetectable for many years croak so loudly. They were most likely not giant bullfrogs – Anton Harber (2001) has noted how the giant bullfrog, ubiquitous in much-maligned Diepsloot, is an indicator species that disappears once developers start building the very properties that claim to be natural havens. In another Dainfern case, some pet rabbits that were let loose caused havoc in residents' gardens, and have now multiplied and displaced the native scrub hares. Other residents have complained about the mosquitoes from the Jukskei River and the smell caused by upstream pollution. In a most extreme case, the Mount Edgecombe Country Club Estate in Durban was a few years ago overcome by monkeys who harassed children and dogs and broke into homes to steal food. Oddly enough, the estate's website describes it as a place where 'Buck wander through the Estate, cars drive slowly and carefully, children play and ride bikes, guinea fowl scatter as golfers appear on the horizon, and monkeys watch it all from the trees'. The monkey problem caused a small stir in the local press when residents started to shoot them with pellet guns. *National Geographic* has even made a documentary about the warring troops of monkeys in Mount Edgecombe.

Returning to Fourways Gardens, it is indisputable that nature sits at the heart of its identity. One of the major roads that runs through the estate is named Camdeboo, after the area in the Karoo. Every other road is named after trees, most indigenous to South Africa, and roads are often landscaped with their eponymous trees. Now in its fourth decade, the estate's trees' mature root systems have begun cracking roads, pavements and walls.

Sarah, whose family was one of the first to move into Fourways Gardens, recalled to me the original view from the clubhouse as we walked along its patio.

'You could look out over the lake, you know, and it was all very swish-swish.' Minutes before, driving up to the clubhouse in her car, she had explained to me that the river was dammed to create an open body of water. 'Then erosion happened, and now it's more a wetland than a dam.' The homeowners' association was removing the silt in order to try to restore that initial aesthetic. 'They want to recreate the open water. Because we used to have pontoon races and silly, you know, events. But with all the reeds and things you can't really do that. And all of these people were very upset because when they bought their house it was on an open water and now it's like on the lawn essentially.' Gesturing towards the river and a morass of reeds, she continued, 'And now it's just grass, because the silt has come from upstream and filled it in. And then Fourways Gardens paid for all of this brick stonework et cetera, because things kept getting washed away. And again, they've messed with the river, which they should not have done. 'Cause a river is a living thing. You can't control it.'

In response to 2017 fires in Knysna and George, the editor of one of Dainfern's magazines wrote:

> We need to pause for a moment and send compassionate thoughts out to all those down at the coast who have experienced the devastation of runaway fires that have gutted their homes; those who have lost vehicles as they were blown over and crushed due to the gale force winds; and those who were victim to the destruction caused by the monstrous waves and floods. It's sobering to think that, despite all our concerted efforts to continually raise our standards and strive for improvements, it just takes a few catastrophes and natural disasters to bring the true essence of life back into perspective.

Here, nonhumans assume the potential for unpredictability: 'runaway fires', 'monstrous waves and floods'. The same kind of unpredictability, manifested variously in crime, unreliable state provision of services and other seemingly mysterious phenomena, has driven many residents into gated communities. As several of the examples given above illustrate, the best-laid plans of developers and residents – the trees that they plant, the fauna-hospitable habitats that they create – go awry. There is a latent anxiety about imminent and immanent chaos that persists in secured gated estates, of disorder that is projected onto the entropy and seemingly agentive capacities of nonhumans.

***

There are two points that I have tried to establish during the course of this chapter. Firstly, I have claimed that evolving affective attachments to nature signal political changes in South Africa. Aesthetic manipulations of the environment, including architecture, traffic, and flora and fauna, are exercises in making a world that is liveable, in which heated interactions can be avoided and guilt can be assuaged. But more than that, affective attachments to the natural world and to heritage serve as claims to sovereignty, territory and belonging that are not generally articulated as such by elite South Africans. I have described these affective attachments as anxious because of the possibilities of betrayal and the fundamental intractability of nature with its potential to destroy or betray.

Secondly, and more importantly, I have tried to establish a place for inchoate affects such as anxiety in our analytical crosshairs. In a field marked primarily by analyses of fear, I have argued that other kinds of politics at work are revealed in attempts to read emergent and incomplete affective states. Analyses of fully formed emotions with clearly articulated referents are, I suggest, doomed to excavate ossified political structures. Rather, the evolving political future must be read in the developing affective worlds we create for ourselves. The anxieties that justify spatial segregation and various forms of enclosure, in Johannesburg and around the world, are shifting in response to an acute sense of ecological peril. Our analytical gaze must shift with them.

ACKNOWLEDGEMENTS

I would like to acknowledge the Fulbright-Hays Doctoral Dissertation Research Award, and the Emslie Horniman/Sutasoma Award (Royal Anthropological Institute), for funding this research. In addition, the following grants from Harvard University made this research possible: Frank Knox Memorial Traveling Fellowship; John C. Hansen and Katherine Vogelheim Research and Travel Grant; Center for African Studies Summer Grant; and Graduate Society Summer Predissertation Fellowship. Finally, I would like to thank the Association of Residential Communities for their cooperation in data collection.

NOTES

1   All names of interlocutors are pseudonyms. To the best of my ability, I have chosen pseudonyms that index the ethnic and linguistic backgrounds of the interlocutors.

2   Representatives of the Dainfern Homeowners' Association dispute this account of the graves. They claim that journalist Zanele Mji did not pay satisfactory attention to their responses to her questions, and they resent the portrayal of the estate as an unfeeling bastion of privilege. The homeowners' association was, after all, trying to address demands that should have been made to the developer. In their view, they tried their best to do the right thing.

3   *Laagers* refer to the wagon-forts that the Voortrekkers, Afrikaners who left the Cape Colony to settle elsewhere in South Africa, used for protection.

4   AfriForum is a non-governmental organisation that claims to defend the human rights of South Africa's white minority. They have strongly testified against land expropriation without compensation.

5   See the debate documented at https://www.youtube.com/watch?v=04Ttlo_vrHs (*AfriForum vs EFF [Shivambu] and Others – WATCH IT ALL – Land Debate* n.d.).

REFERENCES

Abu el-Haj, Nadia. 2001. *Facts on the Ground: Archaeological Practice and Territorial Self-Fashioning in Israeli Society*. Chicago: University of Chicago Press.

AfriForum vs EFF (Shivambu) and Others – WATCH IT ALL – Land Debate. n.d. Accessed 15 November 2019. https://www.youtube.com/watch?v=04Ttlo_vrHs.

Ballard, Richard. 2010. "'Slaughter in the Suburbs': Livestock Slaughter and Race in Post-Apartheid Cities." *Ethnic and Racial Studies* 33 (6): 1069–87.

Ballard, Richard, and Gareth A. Jones. 2011. "Natural Neighbors: Indigenous Landscapes and Eco-Estates in Durban, South Africa." *Annals of the Association of American Geographers* 101 (1): 131–48.

Beinart, William. 1989. "Introduction: The Politics of Colonial Conservation." *Journal of Southern African Studies* 15 (2): 143–62.

Bennett, Jane. 2010. *Vibrant Matter: A Political Ecology of Things*. Durham: Duke University Press.

Berlant, Lauren Gail. 2011. *Cruel Optimism*. Durham: Duke University Press.

Breetzke, Gregory D., Karina Landman, and Ellen G. Cohn. 2014. "Is It Safer behind the Gates? Crime and Gated Communities in South Africa." *Journal of Housing and the Built Environment* 29 (1): 123–39.

Buck-Morss, Susan. 1992. "Aesthetics and Anaesthetics: Walter Benjamin's Artwork Essay Reconsidered." *October* 62: 3–41.

Coetzee, J.M. 1988. *White Writing: On the Culture of Letters in South Africa*. New Haven: Yale University Press.

Comaroff, Jean. 2017. "Invasive Aliens: The Late-Modern Politics of Species Being." *Social Research* 84 (1): 29–52.

Comaroff, Jean, and John L. Comaroff. 2012. *Theory from the South: Or, How Euro-America Is Evolving toward Africa*. Boulder: Paradigm Publishers.

Comaroff, Jean, and John L. Comaroff. 2016. *The Truth about Crime: Sovereignty, Knowledge, Social Order*. Chicago: University of Chicago Press.

Dubow, Saul. 1995. *Scientific Racism in Modern South Africa*. Cambridge: Cambridge University Press.

Durington, Matthew. 2009. "Suburban Fear, Media and Gated Communities in Durban, South Africa." *Home Cultures* 6 (1): 71–88.

Harber, Anton. 2011. *Diepsloot*. Johannesburg: Jonathan Ball.

Kriel, Kallie. 2015. "Defending Afrikaners' Land." *News24*, 27 January 2015. http://www.news24.com/Archives/City-Press/Defending-Afrikaners-land-20150429.

Landman, Karina, and Martin Schönteich. 2002. "Urban Fortresses: Gated Communities as a Reaction to Crime." *African Security Review* 11 (4): 71–85.

Locke, John. 1690. "Second Treatise of Government." http://www.earlymoderntexts.com/assets/pdfs/locke1689a.pdf.

Mitchell, Timothy. 2002. *Rules of Experts: Egypt, Techno-Politics, Modernity*. Berkeley: University of California Press.

Mji, Zanele. 2018. "'Those Graves Were Our Title Deeds.'" *AmaBhungane*, 18 April 2018. http://amabhungane.co.za/article/2018-04-18-those-graves-were-our-title-deeds.

Nietzsche, Friedrich Wilhelm. 1983. *Untimely Meditations*. Translated by R.J. Hollingdale. Texts in German Philosophy. Cambridge: Cambridge University Press.

Spocter, Manfred. 2015. "Gating in the Western Cape, South Africa: Post-Apartheid Planning and Environmental Agency." In *Beyond Gated Communities,* edited by Samer Bagaeen and Ola Uduku, 130–53. London: Routledge.

Tsing, Anna Lowenhaupt. 2014. "More-than-Human Sociality: A Call for Critical Description." In *Anthropology and Nature,* edited by Kirsten Hastrup, 27–42. Routledge Studies in Anthropology 14. New York: Routledge.

Weizman, Eyal. 2007. *Hollow Land: Israel's Architecture of Occupation*. London and New York: Verso.

Williams, Raymond. 1973. *The Country and the City*. London: Chatto and Windus.

———. 1976. *Keywords: A Vocabulary of Culture and Society*. New York: Oxford University Press.

———. 1977. *Marxism and Literature*. Marxist Introductions. Oxford: Oxford University Press.

7 THE CHINATOWN BACK ROOM: THE AFTERLIFE OF APARTHEID ARCHITECTURES

MINGWEI HUANG

When I was in Johannesburg conducting fieldwork on Chinese migration in South Africa, I spent my days with Chinese migrant traders at China malls, popular wholesale shopping centres for low-cost Chinese goods, and lived with the 'Chinatown boss', whom I call Mr Zheng, in Cyrildene Chinatown.[1] Among the wave of Chinese migrants who came to South Africa in the early 2000s, Mr Zheng was an early pioneer, arriving in Johannesburg in the late 1990s. Unbeknown to me when I moved in, he was also formerly a mafia boss and South Africa's reigning 'snakehead', a Chinese human smuggler named after the way snakes slither under fences. In his glory years he helped Chinese migrants cross into South Africa through clandestine routes, playing a central part in the making of this migration wave while establishing a fortune and reputation for himself. As new migrants streamed into the fledgling Chinatown, he became Chinatown boss, informally appointed by and among a network of local Chinese businessmen.[2]

How I came to live with Mr Zheng was by happenstance. One of my interlocutors, another respected Chinese businessman and a friend of Mr Zheng's, arranged my accommodation. With a spacious two-storey house, Mr Zheng rented rooms out to Chinese traders and had a vacancy. For one winter I stayed in the upstairs guest room adjacent to Mr Zheng's bedroom. When I returned the following year, I stayed in the only empty room downstairs. That first winter, the Chinatown office was in his house, in a room on the other side of the living room. Through the security bars of the living-room window I could watch real-time surveillance footage from CCTV cameras around Cyrildene displayed on the monitor in the office. This chapter is about Mr Zheng's house, which is both representative of and exceptional to the world of Chinese migrant entrepreneurs, a microcosm of and literally a window into Chinatown. It explores the house, its architecture, spaces and the social interactions between its residents and the people who maintained it. Mr Zheng employed black South African security guards who were stationed outside 24/7, a Malawian gardener, two Zimbabwean nannies to care for his employees' children, and Sarah, a black South African live-in domestic worker who resided in the small detached back room in the house – or the apartheid-era 'maid's room'.

To give some context, South Africa is home to the oldest and largest Chinese diaspora in Africa, a population estimated at around 300 000 in total with roots in the late nineteenth century. 'New' mainland Chinese migrants arriving after 2000 constitute the largest group (Huynh, Park, and Chen 2010, 289–90; Park 2009, 160). Constituting a formation distinct from First Chinatown in the downtown central business district along Commissioner Street, new migrants have clustered in the formerly Jewish and Portuguese suburb of Cyrildene on the city's east side (Accone 2006; Harrison, Moyo, and Yang 2012). The emergence of Cyrildene Chinatown is a post-apartheid phenomenon in two ways: white middle-class flight from Cyrildene coincided with the arrival of Chinese newcomers, and the post-apartheid state pursued economic liberalisation and foreign trade, specifically with the People's Republic of China after diplomatic normalisation in 1998 (Xu 2017). Since 2008, China has become South Africa's largest import and export partner (Alden and Wu 2014, 14). While Cyrildene's petty entrepreneurs are worlds apart from large-scale bilateral dealings, they are nevertheless part of – and the everyday face of – this post-apartheid geopolitical moment.

While the recent migration wave is indeed a post-apartheid phenomenon, the historical and material afterlives of apartheid persist in peculiar ways in the Chinatown maid's room. Julietta Singh (2018) reflects on the fall of Confederate monuments in the American South and the Jim Crow toilet in her basement, writing: 'More than the monuments themselves, it is this toilet that makes history manifest to me, that summons me to remember this particular past, and the ways this past endures now in other social, political, and material forms.' In this vein, I read the post-apartheid present through what Sharad Chari calls 'apartheid remains', 'asking what does not transform' in the transition from apartheid (2013, 134). To do so, as Ann Laura Stoler insists, involves 'tactical methodologies keenly attentive to the occluded, unexpected sites in which earlier imperial formations have left their bold-faced or subtle traces and in which contemporary inequities work their way through them' (2013, 3). The Chinatown back room is one such site of apartheid's remains. In a study of the social and material afterlives of apartheid among Chinese who came after its end, the back room tells a story of continuity and rupture, and the residual and emergent nature of everyday racial regimes.

In Johannesburg, the suburban house has historically been a contact zone between black domestic workers, white men and white madams, and an intense site of racial anxieties about intimacy, domesticity and privacy. As Lindsay Bremner points out, 'The house, as it was under apartheid, is a signifier and an instrument of categorisation and segregation ... it is the site where the most intimate of apartheid's violences – the domestication of the black person – is re-enacted' (2004, 465). In post-apartheid Johannesburg, the house remains the primary site of white middle-class anxieties about race and crime (Bremner 2004). Fear of crime is not only directed towards unknown racial others but fixates on those in close quarters, whether domestic workers, gardeners or workers' partners. The more intimate, in the sense of sustained proximity and deep familiarity, the more anxious. Likewise, in Chinatown, the home is where black bodies, racialised as criminal and in need of domestication, are paradoxically a threat to domestic space and crucial to the reproduction of domestic space through labour, and where particular anxieties about race, crime and intimacies manifest themselves. As Chinese spaces in Africa are hybrid and liminal (Dittgen 2015), I read Mr Zheng's house as a hybrid between South African and Chinese architectural forms and aesthetics. The post-apartheid Chinatown back room is a resolutely material hybrid site where Chinese migrants inherit and refashion apartheid architectures, while it persists in effect as the apartheid era 'maid's room' by shoring up the anxious intimacies of domestic labour.

Initially, I regarded Mr Zheng's house as merely a place to stay, tangential to and even a reprieve from the long hours I put in at the China Mall. Only after moving out did I have the critical distance to make sense of the apartheid architecture of the house, and to see that, all along, the house was a site of inquiry. Accordingly this chapter is not based on data I collected about the house while living there, but draws from an incidental archive: fleeting encounters with residents, squabbles over banalities such as washing machines, and minor events of misplaced keys or power outages that I felt compelled to write about in my notes; photographs of rooms I took to capture a scene; and my memory of inhabiting these spaces. Rather than interviews with residents and employees, my account is based on interactions I witnessed as a participant observer. Such an ephemeral archive and retrospective analysis require some methodological creativity (Muñoz 1996; Manalansan 2014). In lieu of the empirical veracity of blueprints, for instance, I speculate about the peculiarities of corners and gates. I must also clarify that among the estimated 35 000 people (Ho 2013) living in flats and houses in Cyrildene Chinatown, live-in domestic labour is not the norm but the exception. Thus, this is not a systematic study of Chinatown back rooms, or of the relation between South African domestic workers and Chinese employers. And yet this is more than a story about a single room in a unique house. The Chinatown back room is an example of what happens to architectural structures, and the anxieties they were designed to contain, when they are remade by new actors and the uneven transformation of the 'elusive metropolis' (Mbembe and Nuttall 2008).

FORTIFIED CHINATOWN

The transition to democracy has been marked by an increase in crimes such as residential burglaries and car hijackings, and with it the privatisation and regulation of public space, which further exacerbates existing geographies of racial segregation (Murray 2011). Bremner observes, 'It is around the violation of the white body in domestic space that the image of the criminal has been most potently deployed, that an entire security industry has been created and the space of the city has been reconfigured.' With the house as the centre of private life, middle-class residents have adopted a multitude of defensive practices, from 'burglar proofing, burglar alarms, electric fencing, high walls, steel gates, automatic garage doors' to hiring private security to patrol and restrict access to suburbs. The house and the criminal are imagined through the binaries of 'an inside and outside, good and evil, black and white', while the boundary wall has become a 'new portable instrument of control' (Bremner 2010, 464, 170). Preoccupations with crime and security are not unique to South Africa but are pervasive in places of intense socio-economic inequality throughout the global south. As Teresa Caldeira describes in Brazil, a 'fortified enclave' is a socially homogeneous, physically isolated, monitored – through the use of armed guards and security systems – private residential and commercial space for the middle and upper classes. Oriented inward, they are 'physically isolated by walls or empty spaces or other design devices' (1996, 308).

The boundary wall in Johannesburg's Chinatown also needs to be understood in the historical context of walls in Chinese cities. As Duanfang Lu chronicles, from the traditional to late-imperial eras, walls were the main feature of the city. 'City walls' and gates acted as a barrier to foreign invasion and peasant rebellions, while 'inner walls' bounded villages, temples, gardens and houses. Lu emphasises, 'Symbolising authority, order and security, the wall was so central to the Chinese idea of a city that the traditional words for city and wall were identical, the character *cheng* standing for both' (2006, 128). In the socialist urban environment, city walls – seen as a limit to urban development and a mark of 'feudal' tradition – fell, while walls around work units were constructed to optimise production and administration, becoming an architectural norm again (133). In the rapidly developing post-socialist city, the socialist-era unit wall has remained a main feature. Amid widening class inequalities in the post-Mao era, new urban residential and commercial projects are securitised through perimeter walls, controlled gates, security guards, alarms and identification systems (139).

Walking around Derrick Avenue, Cyrildene's main throughway, homes, shops, restaurants and businesses are protected with razor wire, wire netting, spiked palisade fences, bars on windows, and boundary walls. Cars fitted with dark-tinted or bulletproof glass are a common sight. Unlike the nearby affluent suburb of Houghton and its sleek electric fences sitting atop stylised gates and ivy-covered walls, Chinatown's fences and bars are rusty and reinforced with unsightly but cheap razor wire. While Chinatown shares practices of fortification with its suburban counterparts, it does not attempt to reconcile aesthetically the form and function of security technologies. In recent years, two camouflage-clad guards from a private security company, previously Bad Boyz Hillbrow, circle the area in an armoured car 24 hours a day. In the four short blocks of Derrick Avenue, there are two elevated guard chairs, usually unoccupied, and numerous signs for CCTV camera surveillance. A bilingual street sign in all-capital letters warns residents and visitors: 'Caution: China Town Johannesburg Community Committee has already authorised the security company to combat the crime happening in Derrick Ave, including illegally [*sic*] usage of firearms, kidnapping, fighting, stealing and robbery, etc.' Cyrildene incorporates many of the security hallmarks of the most affluent gated suburbs, but differs from them with its shoddy building exteriors, handwritten signs and heaps of garbage. It is, and is not, like other northern suburbs.

As my interlocutors recounted, during Chinatown's early years in the 1990s and early 2000s, Chinese mafia groups ruled the street, demanding protection fees from business owners, kidnapping businessmen and robbing traders. Strong ties between the African National Congress, the Chinese Embassy and Chinese leaders facilitated Chinatown's institutional formalisation. Its day-to-day governance is now carried out through the work of a management committee, community association and the Cyrildene Chinatown Community Police Forum, a collaboration between local Chinese leaders and

Figure 7.1
Razor wire protecting luxury cars and residences. Photograph by the author

Figure 7.2
Boundary walls and razor wire on Chinatown residence. Photograph by the author

Figure 7.3
Bad Boyz makes its mark on Derrick Avenue. Photograph by the author

the South African police (Harrison, Moyo, and Yang 2012). Concurrently with a crackdown on the mafia, private security companies have become the main provider of public security. Until a recent change in leadership, Bad Boyz used to report directly to Mr Zheng, while footage from security cameras went to his office. While Chinatown residents were once fearful of the mafia amid them, the criminal is now solely figured as black Africans working in and passing through Chinatown. In spite of arriving after the end of apartheid, Chinese migrants share with white middle-class South Africans the criminalisation of black bodies while inheriting the suburban built environment of walls and fences.

There is a great resemblance in discourses and practices around crime and security between Chinese migrants and middle-class suburbanites. However, they are not the same. Chinese discourses of crime and security practices emerge from the specific vulnerabilities they experience as traders, and articulate with Chinese racial discourses. A large part of my fieldwork consisted of listening to Chinese migrants talk about crime and public security. Chinese traders and workers are widely known for cash-based wholesaling, are geographically concentrated in Cyrildene and China malls, and are racially hypervisible, a triad that makes them vulnerable to robbery in their shops, at home and on the motorway. Discourses of crime are inextricable from Chinese discourses of blackness. While perpetrators are from all racial backgrounds, including Chinese, criminals are always already figured as black South Africans and African migrants. Chinese migrants often call black Africans, specifically men, *heigui*, a pejorative term meaning 'black devil', to connote criminality.[3] In its usage the term is akin to the racialised masculinist figure of the gangster or criminal, colloquially the *tsotsi*, in South African imaginaries.[4] Fear of crime and anxiety about proximity to black bodies dominate how Chinese migrants conduct everyday life, from how they carry themselves on the street and guard their belongings in public spaces to the driving routes they choose between home and shop – for instance, by taking the roundabout way through Houghton instead of driving through the inner city.

In addition to fearing strangers, Chinese traders are most anxious about those closest to them, a collective paranoia about 'inside jobs'. Although most robberies involve petty stealing, violent inside jobs disproportionately dominate anxieties about crime. At China malls, African employees – undocumented migrants exploited as low-wage labour without legal recourse – are familiar with traders' business practices and daily routines, and are resentful. In some instances, long-term employees, the most knowledgeable and bitter, provided information to criminal syndicates to carry out robberies, resulting in critical and even fatal injuries. Sometimes security guards were involved. The more intimate and long-term the relationship, the more anxious Chinese traders are about the possibility of an inside job. To summarise, racialised anxieties about crime are directed towards racial strangers and those closest to them. Anxieties from the shop spill over to domestic labour at home, an intimate space of interracial encounter on the other side of the wall, fence or gate.

MAIDS AND BOSSES

'Viewed historically,' Charles van Onselen begins his chapter on 'The Witches of Suburbia', 'the South African labour market has always been dominated by three major sectors of employment – mining, agriculture, and domestic service' (1982, 1). *Maids and Madams* (1980), Jacklyn Cock's landmark sociological study of domestic labour during apartheid, documented the ways in which domestic service was a microcosm of racial inequality in South Africa. Cock writes: 'Domestic workers play an important role in the reproduction of labour power, the capacity to work … not only physical maintenance (through the preparing of meals and the laundering of clothes) but also ideological maintenance' (1980, 8). At the time of Cock's study, domestic service was the second-largest source of employment for black women, a predominantly black female institution. Domestic labour continues to be a major part of the post-apartheid labour landscape, and still is the second-largest source of employment for black women (Falkof 2016). Even today, 'Hidden away in the homes and kitchens of suburbia, they are an open secret – such a normalised part of South African life that they are hardly noticed' (Ally 2009, 2).

Since the end of apartheid, domestic labour has been formalised, modernised and professionalised as domestic workers are covered under labour protections – a shift from 'servant', 'maid' and 'houseboy' to domestic worker with nominal rights. However, paid domestic work still retains colonial relations of servitude, depending on the individual employer. Today there is a generational split between older domestic workers who can negotiate live-out and part-time work with their experience, and younger full-time live-in domestic workers who have less experience to leverage (Ally 2009). There has also been a shift from the employment of black South Africans to precarious

African migrants (Kiwanuka, Jinnah, and Hartman-Pickerill 2015). The end of apartheid has also changed the face of employers. While most scholarship on domestic labour in South Africa has dealt with white employers, some has documented the post-apartheid rise of middle-class Muslim coloured employers, previously excluded from participating in white suburban ways of life (Bonnin and Dawood 2013). Amid these changes, Sarah is from an older generation of black South African live-in domestic workers, working not for a white madam but a Chinese boss.

In her fifties, Sarah is from Limpopo and has been a domestic worker for most of her working life. While I lived in the house, she had worked for Mr Zheng for almost fifteen years, nearly the entire time he lived in the Cyrildene house. Sarah is quiet and private. Because she worked in the house while the residents were at the malls, I only interacted with her on the rare days I stayed home. I was aware that she interacted minimally with the Chinese residents, because of language as well as social expectations. At China malls I noticed that Chinese traders, aware of the fraught relations between themselves and their employees, became guarded when I spoke with African workers. Accordingly, Sarah and I made small talk but I never interviewed her, which would have drawn excessive attention to us both and could have compromised her employment and my housing.[5]

Chinese migrants share with white middle-class South Africans anxieties about the interracial intimacies of domestic labour, and accordingly draw boundaries within the household. With black women in the intimate and private spaces of white households, 'few other institutions disrupt and concretise the tensions of racialised intimacy as much as domestic service'. Anxieties about domestic work are profoundly 'anxieties of intimacy' (Ally 2015, 56, 47). Nannies, au pairs and domestic workers work within the intimate spaces of family life; paid to take care of families, they also can develop attachments to them and be treated as fictive kin. This was not the case with Sarah, as paternalistic gestures of inclusion were rare. In the eight months I lived at Mr Zheng's house I only witnessed Sarah's inclusion once, when Mr Zheng invited her to his daughter's twentieth birthday party, a huge banquet that filled an entire restaurant. Most of the time she was an outsider in the house, never interacting with the Chinese residents and only rarely with Mr and Mrs Zheng. Relations were cordial on the surface. Showing respect, she addressed Mr Zheng as 'boss', and Mr and Mrs Zheng politely called her 'Auntie' or by her name. Everyone else referred to her as *heipo* among themselves, a term meaning 'black woman' used to describe African female employees at China malls. As the racialised hierarchies from work carry over to home, Sarah was treated as a racial outsider in an otherwise all-Chinese household. While she kept her family life private, her most immediate social world comprised other domestic workers, nannies, gardeners and security guards nearby.[6]

While domestic work has reproduced suburban life for white middle-class South Africans, among an elite Chinese minority it also makes possible the reproduction of trader households that are transnational and flexibly organised. As the family is integral to transnational capitalist practices across the Chinese diaspora (Ong 1999), Chinese trader families in South Africa integrate home, family and business.[7] Traders assemble immediate and extended family members into a network of businesses and collective living arrangements to pool funds and share the demanding responsibilities of staffing a shop every day. They periodically go to China for weeks or months at a time to import stock and visit family, creating gaps in the maintenance of the home and shop. Other family and shop members fill these gaps, and when this is not possible, traders hire temporary Chinese employees (including myself) to look after the shop. When traders have children, they often raise them until they can send them to live with family in China. As children accompany their parents to the mall, African shop workers and nannies take on the labour of cleaning and child-rearing; in some cases, African domestic workers continue this labour at home, but in most cases, it falls to Chinese women. In the house and shop, the work of caring for children is naturalised as the domain of African and Chinese women.

The organisation and social dynamics of domestic work in Chinatown resemble, but also depart from, traditional black–white contexts in South Africa. In lieu of the nuclear family and the white madam there are the flexible transnational Chinese family and the Chinese boss. Unlike the case of a single-family household, Sarah's labour encompassed Mr Zheng's family and the revolving door of traders at his house who worked full-time at China malls, including his relatives who lived upstairs and ran his businesses, and Mrs Zheng and their elementary school-aged son who lived in China during the school year and returned to Johannesburg every winter. Sarah cleaned the entire house and washed for Mr Zheng and his relatives living upstairs. Monday to Saturday, when the tenants were all at their China malls, she would mop the floors and hand-wash clothes. On Sundays she rested. If the other tenants paid her

R20, she would wash their clothes too. In the late afternoons when the traders returned, she would retreat to her room, performing a vanishing act while traders occupied the clean common areas. The preparation of meals exemplifies how gendered and racialised household labour – Chinese and African, paid and unpaid – was organised around Mr Zheng and his family. The patriarchal head of the family and a Chinatown leader, Mr Zheng was the *laoban* or 'boss' of the house, someone the Chinese residents, and not only Sarah, were required to revere. When Mrs Zheng was home with their son three months of the year, she prepared meals for Mr Zheng and the family members but never did any cleaning or washing. For the other nine months, some of the tenants took on the labour of cooking for him, leaving breakfast covered on the kitchen table before they left for the day. The rest of Mr Zheng's meals came from the Chinatown office and his brother-in-law's household across the street. In white households, the domestic worker typically prepares three meals a day while the kitchen is her domain (Ginsburg 2011). However, preparing food for Mr Zheng was never one of Sarah's tasks, and the kitchen was an exclusively Chinese space.

Just as Chinese traders were concerned with African shop employees stealing from or plotting against them, they were similarly concerned about African domestic workers at home, where cash is kept and where the surveillance of guards and cameras ends. Speculation about the betrayals of security guards who allegedly facilitated home break-ins was common. From a security guard at Sandton City, I heard a rumour about a live-in domestic worker running off with laundry sacks of cash from her Chinese employer in the wealthy suburb of Fourways. At Mr Zheng's house, downstairs tenants, who most likely kept large amounts of cash on site, always locked their doors, but Mr Zheng's relatives upstairs did not. I frequently heard other tenants disparage the security guards as 'black devils', criminalising the men who protected them. During my stay, a Malawian gardener was accused of stealing and was fired. However, I never heard concerns about Sarah. As one resident explained, she knew Mr Zheng 'would kill her' and would never dare to steal. The criminal was figured as masculinist, with more attention paid to security guards and gardeners than domestic workers and nannies. Anxieties about crime were mitigated by locking doors and having faith in the boss to maintain order.

Domestic work in Chinese homes is also governed by meticulous boundary-making practices around hygiene and contagion and the racist belief that black bodies are dirty. There is a long history of colonial discourses on 'black germs' and sanitation in South Africa that has affected domestic labour. Nicky Falkof points out the day-to-day contradictions of domestic work during apartheid: 'Black women were expected to cook a white family's meals but were not considered sufficiently clean to eat off the same plates as them … Black workers could clean a white family's bath and make their beds but the entry of a black body into a family's swimming pool would in many cases have been experienced as a pollutant' (2016, 632). At Mr Zheng's house, there were numerous spatial boundaries and divisions of labour to limit racial mixing. For example, while cooking was never Sarah's responsibility, taking out the kitchen trash and cleaning the kitchen were. While she cleaned common spaces, she never set foot inside individual bedrooms, whether they were locked or not. She washed Mr Zheng's and his family members' clothes by hand, which dried on lines outside, but she never washed underwear, which soaked in bathroom tubs and dried on bedroom balconies. Bedrooms and underwear encompass the body's lower region and are where the public–private line is drawn within the intimate nature of domestic work.[8] The social boundaries of treating Sarah as an outsider and the division of labour between her and Chinese traders were intended to alleviate anxieties around intimacy, and the unsettling reality that Chinese traders depended on African labour for (re)productive, family and household labours.

I now turn to the spatial organisation of Mr Zheng's house, where racial anxieties around domestic labour and crime collide with apartheid architecture.

THE MAIN HOUSE AND BACK ROOM

On the corner of the street away from the bustling activity of Derrick Avenue, Mr Zheng's two-storey white house stands apart from the others. Through the employment of a gardener, the grass and shrubs in the front yard are neatly trimmed, and in the summer roses bloom alongside two concrete swans. Affixed to the fence, with its white bars and deadly sharp tips, are signs for tactical security response and surveillance cameras. On the far corner is a stall with a pitched roof for a security guard. Given Mr Zheng's relationship to Bad Boyz, it is the only guarded private home in Chinatown. In front of the yard, on the street side of the gate, is a series of chairs where security guards and their acquaintances working nearby linger between shifts. While the house is different from others in the area, it is also easily familiar, with laundry hanging from lines off the balcony, and in the driveway and front

Figure 7.4
The house from outside the boundary fence, with chairs for security guards and domestic workers. Photograph by the author, edited to remove house number

yard. Around the back there is a small outbuilding, common in Cyrildene houses, that sits behind the house and does not have the same terracotta roof.

When Mr Zheng bought the house over a decade ago, he renovated it to accommodate the needs of transnational Chinese families, including his own, and to establish the Chinatown office. Upon closer inspection the house, a product of apartheid-era housing stock and Chinese dwelling forms, is riddled with architectural peculiarities. There are two entrances for this house: one for the residents living in the house and another for the former Chinatown office. From the outside it appears to be seamlessly attached to the house, but it is actually fully cordoned off through separate entrances inside and outside. If one looks in from the outside, the changes are difficult to discern, as the new additions inconspicuously blend into the original house structure. The interior, however, leaves clues to where the original architecture ends and the new begins. For instance, when I lived downstairs my window, which shared the same design as others in the house, did not open into the yard but into the living room. The new living room was built around my bedroom, originally a corner of the house. Unlike most Johannesburg living rooms, it has its own entrance, a strong metal door the colour of dark cherry wood, similar to ones for sale at China malls. The spacious room next to the main door has a large window facing the yard; it appears to be the original living room but is now one of three downstairs bedrooms that Mr Zheng rents out.

The house is a hybrid as it has been thoroughly remade to fit the day-to-day mundanities and aesthetics of Chinese domestic life. In front of the main entrance is a staircase with rows of plastic slippers for Chinese residents and visitors. The living room is the face of the house and acknowledges Mr Zheng as the boss. The walls are decorated with rows of plaques commemorating his service as the chairman of Chinese organisations. The centre of the room is a wooden tea table with chipped cups strewn about and an old tin for collecting cigarette ash. In the evenings, traders gather after dinner to watch Chinese television programmes, smoke and drink tea; the next day, Sarah cleans it. In the corner there is a luggage scale, a fixture in many trader abodes. On one side of the living room is the old Chinatown office, and on the other side is Mr Zheng's private office; both are quiet since the establishment of the new Chinatown office across the street. Open to the rest of the house, his home office boasts additional plaques and photographs of him and his family. The large desk is orderly, dustless and unused except for occasional late-night meetings to go over the wholesale business, during which there is the whirring sound of a cash machine. Moving up, halfway up the stairs there is a locked gate. Most likely part of the original house, the gate takes on new meaning by symbolically separating the two hierarchical groups in the house: Mr Zheng and his relatives in the five bedrooms upstairs; and the three bedrooms downstairs and several rooms for rent around the back. The social dynamics of upstairs and downstairs underpin all the informal house rules of who takes priority in using common areas such as the living room and kitchen.

The kitchen is ostensibly the most hybridised and contested space in the entire house. In many suburban South African homes, the kitchen is at the back of the house. This is also the case at Mr Zheng's house, except there are three. The main house kitchen is where everyone, upstairs and downstairs, takes turns eating around the single square table; a stack of plastic stools in the corner makes it easy to accommodate a range of people, from Mr Zheng alone to a hotpot celebration. Fully inside the main house, it is the cleanest of the three kitchens, tiled with white linoleum and fitted with new appliances. Adjacent to the table is a semi-transparent glass brick window and sturdy wooden door that, instead of opening into a backyard, opens into a second, semi-enclosed kitchen outside. With a gas burner holding well-seasoned woks and a corrugated tin roof, the space immediately recalls the format of an open-air kitchen in China; it reminded me of my grand-parents' kitchens I visited as a child. The kitchen was creatively built in the space between the main house and detached outbuildings, and its makeshift design is visible in its idiosyncrasies. It is physically circumscribed by the exterior walls of the main house and outbuilding walls; shelves and counters are resourcefully improvised from used furniture and covered in the same low-cost vinyl sheets that traders wholesale, to hold pots, pans, cleavers and crates of vegetables. Sharply contrasting with the cream and brick walls of the main house and outbuilding is a single wall of blue tiles to catch the grease from the stove. The small sink is connected to an outdoor spigot and is rusting from exposure to the outdoor elements. On the floor, the rubber tiles outside are distinct from the white linoleum tiles in the main house.

Figure 7.5
The outdoor kitchen and outbuilding wall viewed from the main house door. Photograph by the author

Finally, on the other side of the outdoor kitchen is the third kitchen, which is in the outbuilding. Dimly lit with grey ceramic tiles, the small room has an old electric stove and a communal refrigerator of meats and vegetables deemed too pungent to mingle with the contents of the boss's refrigerator. On the shelves are maize, tea, sugar, and a few dishes and pots that belong to Sarah. While Sarah cleans the other two kitchens, this is the only one she is permitted to use. On each side of the kitchen are two back rooms, or 'maid's rooms', that complete the outbuilding. The design of suburban homes and the 'maid's room' were intended to reduce the anxieties of domestic labour. While white family members occupied the living room towards the front of the house, the domestic worker occupied the kitchen and the detached back room, her labouring body out of sight but still easy to monitor (Ginsburg 2011). In Mr Zheng's remodelled home, Sarah lives in one 'maid's room' while a Chinese tenant lives in the other, the least desirable room for rent because of its small and detached location.

Rooms like Sarah's remain an invisible part of present-day Johannesburg. Sarah's room is a standard feature of middle-class suburban homes with origins in the Black Peril panic of the 1910s about 'houseboys' sexually assaulting white women (Van Onselen 1982). In the 1910s, a special committee appointed to investigate African housing in Johannesburg found that most middle-class households provided detached yard rooms and back rooms for African domestic workers. Additionally, back rooms popped up with the demolition of stables and the construction of garages as automobiles gained popularity. In an architectural history of Johannesburg's northern suburbs, Rebecca Ginsburg documents the process: 'Architects included such detached back rooms in new homes, and the white residents of older houses without such quarters converted structures like fowl houses and fodder rooms for African use or constructed purpose-built rooms' (2011, 10).

Later, the back room became part of the architecture of apartheid. The 1950 Group Areas Act assigned racial groups to different urban areas and, in so doing, made it illegal for black workers and white employers to reside under the same roof. Consequently, the back room and its counterpart, the hostel, became indispensable to maintaining a gendered and racialised labour force. As Achille Mbembe explains the existence of the maid's room: 'The role of architecture and planning was to trace partitions within well-defined spaces with clear protective boundaries so as to avoid the disruptive effects – real or potential – of race mixing' (2004, 385–6). Ginsburg details the back room at some length:

> The main house was designed for nuclear family occupation (white residents): a driveway to a garage and a walkway to the front door; the backyard was a cluster of service buildings – toolshed, storage bin, a servant's back room or two, and a toilet and shower stall for African staff. Backrooms varied only slightly in size and plan, generally measuring about eight by ten feet, almost always constructed of brick, with concrete floors and no ceilings. They rarely had electricity. Furnishings consisted usually of the cast-offs of the employer. A twin bed, wardrobe, and a small bench were standard. Not much more could fit inside. There was a single door that locked with a key, usually held by both the worker and her white employers, and, typically, a single, small window. One generally had to walk through the front gate of the property and along the side of the main house to reach the back room. (2000, 87)

At Mr Zheng's house, I caught a few glimpses of the interior of Sarah's room by chance. With a curtain on the window in the door, her room is narrow and dim, lit by only a small window or light bulb, with rust spots on the walls. Inside are a twin bed, a few shelves and a small television, while her clothes hang from a line along the wall. Just outside the outbuilding are a few old chairs, cracking and taped over, where she rests. In most blueprints of suburban houses from the 1960s, the main house sat in the middle of the lot and the garage, shed, work room and back room were behind or adjacent to it (Ginsburg 2011, 11). In the outdoor kitchen area, there is an enclosed bathroom that Sarah and the downstairs Chinese residents share. With a single toilet and shower that drains onto the tile floor, it resembles both a toilet for domestic workers and a bathroom in China. Adjacent to the bathroom is a wide utility sink with a wooden washing board, a fixture of the yard, where Sarah fills up buckets for cleaning and washes clothes.

Interestingly, while apartheid-era suburban homeowners used landscaping to partially block their view of the back room from the main house (Ginsburg 2011, 87), the outdoor kitchen is a liminal space between the main house and the outbuilding, conjoining them through a roof. It is a hybrid space, one that is South African and Chinese in design and aesthetics. Used by all the Chinese residents, upstairs and downstairs, it is the social heart of the house, and also

Figure 7.6
From left to right wall, the back room, toilet and washing sink in the outdoor 'Chinese-style' kitchen. Photograph by the author

a contested space in the different claims that residents and Sarah make of the
house. While the outbuildings and common areas of the house are Sarah's
domain as she labours during the day, when the traders return to cook she
retreats to the hidden back room, maintaining the fiction of racial homogeneity.
Even as the other back room is rented out, hers is indeed the maid's room as it
retains its apartheid-era form and function of managing racial anxieties while
concealing the reliance on African domestic labour in reproducing everyday life.

CONCLUSION

With roots in apartheid architecture, the back room persists as a feature of
suburban homes in post-apartheid South Africa. And yet, as sensibilities
towards domestic labour change and as more workers live out rather than in,
the back room also changes. Back rooms are now rebranded as garden cottages
for white middle-class renters, an attempt to whitewash the lived histories of
racial segregation and exploitation sedimented in them (Falkof 2016). If the

figure of the servant embodies the 'intractable colonial residue of race' (Ally 2015, 57), the back room is the concrete residue embedded in the built environment, apartheid's material remnants. As Mbembe notes, the attempt to limit interracial encounters in the racial city led to 'the emergence of diverse urban worlds within the same territory – strange mappings and blank figures, discontinuous fixtures and flows, and odd juxtapositions that one can still observe in the present-day South African urban landscape' (2004, 386). As is evident in mismatched tiles and windows opening into other rooms, Chinese migrants arriving after the end of apartheid inherit and refashion the back room and all of the 'strange mappings' of the house, while creating peculiarities of their own and reinscribing the racial anxieties the back room was designed to contain. The Chinatown back room, although not common, attests to how deeply racialised structures of everyday life persist even as they are transformed. This is not to make an ahistorical argument, but to recognise the way that racial inequalities and anxieties endure even as racial relations mutate from black and white to black and Chinese, and the role the 'material infrastructure of racism' plays (Chari 2013, 134).

While hybridity is often associated with cosmopolitanism and minor transnationalism, the hybridity of the Chinatown back room is not celebratory. It arises from a confluence of structural factors: the lack of mobility for black South African women and their ongoing employment in domestic work (and, likewise, black South African men in the private security industry), white flight from Cyrildene that made room for Chinese newcomers, the flexible organisation of transnational Chinese trader households, and the form of the single-family suburban home, securitised and designed to accommodate domestic labour. Meanwhile, although traders do not arrive with the same colonial and apartheid ideologies of race, they bring racial ideologies from China to bear on new realities in South Africa and, in turn, produce anxieties around blackness, crime and interracial intimacy that manifest similarly to those of middle-class South Africans across racial backgrounds. In this way, the gate separating upstairs and downstairs and the back room perform similar functions of securitising the home from racial others, as before. While the kitchen is converted into a Chinese format, living rooms are turned into bedrooms, and a Chinatown office is added, the back room intractably remains, a pre-existing infrastructure for racial anxieties old and new.

ACKNOWLEDGEMENTS

Many thanks to Nicky Falkof and Cobus van Staden for their editorial guidance and encouragement, the anonymous reviewer for comments, Eric Worby, and the many people in Johannesburg who let me into their living spaces and lives. This research was made possible with funding from the Wenner-Gren Foundation for Anthropological Research and the University of Minnesota, in addition to support from the Centre for Indian Studies in Africa at the University of the Witwatersrand.

NOTES

1   I conducted 16 months of fieldwork in South Africa between 2013 and 2020, during which I lived at Mr Zheng's house for eight months. All names appearing in this essay are pseudonyms and follow local conventions, including how people are differently addressed by first name or surname. While I have kept the names of public places intact, I have omitted and altered some details in order to protect my informants.

2   Despite the illegality of human smuggling, snakeheads are seen as providing a 'fundamental social good' and become trusted community leaders or 'brotherly' figures. Snakeheads are part of diffuse transnational networks connecting China and Chinatowns around the world, and Chinatown gangs and triads are sometimes involved in the snakehead trade (Keefe 2009, 34, 38). Hence, it is no surprise that Mr Zheng embodied these roles.

3   Blackness in Chinese discourses is negatively associated with the dark, immoral and illegal. Scholars have noted, 'There is no Chinese translation for the highly derogatory English word "nigger". However, "black devil" functions in Chinese in a similar, intensely derogatory way', and is only used to describe men (Pfafman, Carpenter, and Tang 2015, 548).

4   Pertinent to the *tsotsi*, in post-apartheid Johannesburg 'the stranger and the criminal now assume, more than ever, greater prominence in most citizens' imaginations'. Crime is gendered and quotidian: 'The criminal, we could say, moves between the surface and the underneath. Striking at the everyday – the woman leaving her garage, the man asleep in his bed, the young girl on her way to the shop – he navigates the ordinary surfaces of life by attacking from a darker, more underneath place' (Mbembe and Nuttall 2008, 23).

5   Participant observation is both incredibly generative for capturing a social world and ethically complicated. While Mr Zheng, the head of the house, gave me blanket permission to live there and write about him, not all of the residents and employees,

because of their social positions, could provide such consent. What I write about the house and the people living and working there is based on my observations and interactions. In the case of Sarah, I have not only anonymised her but also avoided all reference to her life, focusing solely on her roles in the house.

6   Ginsburg explains, 'Given the workers' social isolation, all interpersonal relationships assumed great value. The conversations they struck up with the next-door worker over the backyard fence, friendships with the part-time gardener, and the collegiality of fellowship with other workers who congregated in neighborhood parks ... helped considerably.' As it went, 'You tell her your address. Just like that. Now she's your friend' (2011, 115).

7   As Aihwa Ong has written about Chinese diasporic subjects under late capitalism, logics and practices of flexibility 'are produced within particular structures of meaning about family, gender, nationality, class mobility, and social power' (1999, 6).

8   Shireen Ally elaborates, 'They work within the emotion-laden intimate spaces of other people's most private lives – they wash underwear, overhear (and sometimes become part of) family arguments, and are often the first ones to discover intimate family secrets' (2009, 13).

REFERENCES

Accone, Darryl. 2006. "'Ghost People': Localising the Chinese Self in an African Context." *Asian Studies Review* 30 (3): 257–72.

Alden, Chris, and Yu-Shan Wu. 2014. "South Africa and China: The Making of a Partnership." South African Institute of International Affairs, Occasional Paper 199.

Ally, Shireen. 2009. *From Servants to Workers: South African Domestic Workers and the Democratic State*. Ithaca, NY: Cornell University Press.

———. 2015. "Domesti-City: Colonial Anxieties and Postcolonial Fantasies in the Figure of the Maid." In *Colonization and Domestic Service: Historical and Contemporary Perspectives*, edited by Victoria K. Haskins and Claire Lowrie, 45–62. New York and London: Routledge.

Bonnin, Debby, and Quraisha Dawood. 2013. "The Domestic Worker's Place in the 'Madam's' Space: The Construction of the Workspace in the Home of Muslim Madams." *South African Review of Sociology* 44 (1): 55–71.

Bremner, Lindsay. 2004. "Bounded Spaces: Demographic Anxieties in Post-Apartheid Johannesburg." *Social Identities* 10 (4): 455–68.

———. 2010. *Writing the City into Being: Essays on Johannesburg, 1998–2008*. Johannesburg: Fourthwall Books.

Caldeira, Teresa. 1996. "Fortified Enclaves: The New Urban Segregation." *Public Culture* 8 (2): 303–28.

Chari, Sharad. 2013. "Detritus in Durban: Polluted Environs and the Biopolitics of Refusal." In *Imperial Debris: On Ruins and Ruination*, edited by Ann Laura Stoler, 131–61. Durham: Duke University Press.

Cock, Jacklyn. 1980. *Maids and Madams: A Study in the Politics of Exploitation.* Johannesburg: Ravan Press.

Dittgen, Romain. 2015. "Of Other Spaces? Hybrid Forms of Chinese Engagement in Sub-Saharan Africa." *Journal of Current Chinese Affairs* 44 (1): 43–73.

Falkof, Nicky. 2016. "Out the Back: Race and Reinvention in Johannesburg's Garden Cottages." *International Journal of Cultural Studies* 19 (6): 627–42.

Ginsburg, Rebecca. 2000. "'Come in the Dark': Domestic Workers and Their Rooms in Apartheid-Era Johannesburg, South Africa." *Perspectives in Vernacular Architecture* 8: 83–100.

———. 2011. *At Home with Apartheid: The Hidden Landscapes of Domestic Service in Johannesburg.* Charlottesville: University of Virginia Press.

Harrison, Phillip, Khangelani Moyo, and Yan Yang. 2012. "Strategy and Tactics: Chinese Immigrants and Diasporic Spaces in Johannesburg, South Africa." *Journal of Southern African Studies* 38 (4): 899–925.

Ho, Ufrieda. 2013. "The Arch Angle of Booming Chinatown." *Mail & Guardian*, 12 July 2013.

Huynh, Tu T., Yoon Jung Park, and Anna Ying Chen. 2010. "Faces of China: New Chinese Migrants in South Africa, 1980s to Present." *African and Asian Studies* 9 (3): 286–306.

Keefe, Patrick. 2009. "Snakeheads and Smuggling: The Dynamics of Illegal Chinese Immigration." *World Policy Journal* 26 (1): 33–44.

Kiwanuka, Monica, Zaheera Jinnah, and Becca Hartman-Pickerill. 2015. "Getting the House in Order: Foreign Migrant Workers in the Domestic Work Sector in South Africa." The Migrating for Work Research Consortium, African Centre for Migration and Society, University of the Witwatersrand.

Lu, Duanfang. 2006. *Remaking Chinese Urban Form: Modernity, Scarcity and Space, 1949–2005.* New York: Routledge.

Manalansan IV, Martin F. 2014. "The 'Stuff' of Archives: Mess, Migration, and Queer Lives." *Radical History Review* 120 (Fall): 94–107.

Mbembe, Achille. 2004. "Aesthetics of Superfluity." *Public Culture* 16 (3): 373–405.

Mbembe, Achille, and Sarah Nuttall. 2008. "Introduction: Afropolis." In *Johannesburg: The Elusive Metropolis*, edited by Sarah Nuttall and Achille Mbembe, 1–33. Durham: Duke University Press.

Muñoz, José Esteban. 1996. "Ephemera as Evidence: Introductory Notes to Queer Acts." *Women & Performance: A Journal of Feminist Theory* 8 (2): 5–16.

Murray, Martin J. 2011. *City of Extremes: The Spatial Politics of Johannesburg*. Durham: Duke University Press.

Ong, Aihwa. 1999. *Flexible Citizenship: The Cultural Logics of Transnationality*. Durham: Duke University Press.

Park, Yoon Jung. 2009. *A Matter of Honour: Being Chinese in South Africa*. New York: Lexington Books.

Pfafman, Tessa M., Christopher J. Carpenter, and Yong Tang. 2015. "The Politics of Racism: Constructions of African Immigrants in China on ChinaSMACK." *Communication, Culture & Critique* 8 (4): 540–56.

Singh, Julietta. 2018. "Monumental Extinctions." *Social Text Online*, 7 June 2018. https://socialtextjournal.org/periscope_article/monumental-extinctions.

Stoler, Ann Laura. 2013. "Introduction. 'The Rot Remains': From Ruins to Ruination." In *Imperial Debris: On Ruins and Ruination*, edited by Ann Laura Stoler, 1–35. Durham: Duke University Press.

Van Onselen, Charles. 1982. "The Witches of Suburbia: Domestic Service on the Witwatersrand, 1890–1914." In *Studies in the Social and Economic History of the Witwatersrand, 1886–1914*, vol. 2: *New Nineveh*, 1–73. London: Longman.

Xu, Liang Xu. 2017. "Cyrildene Chinatown, Suburban Settlement, and Ethnic Economy in Post-Apartheid Johannesburg." In *China and Africa: A New Paradigm of Global Business*, edited by Young-Chan Kim, 81–104. London: Palgrave Macmillan.

8 SHIFTING TOPOGRAPHIES OF THE ANXIOUS CITY

ANTONIA STEYN

Hillbrow is a residential inner-city neighbourhood to the north of the downtown business district, on the historical border between city and suburbs. In the 1970s it was a playground for chic white urbanites. By the 1980s it had gained a reputation as a hotbed of vice: a 'grey area', where the Immorality Act banning interracial sex was no longer enforced, and a site of homosexual and other 'deviant' sociality. By the 1990s it housed expanding communities of migrants from elsewhere in South Africa and the continent. In the twenty-first century Hillbrow is vibrant and cosmopolitan but also overpopulated, poorly serviced and dangerous. Home to people from all over Africa, it is, ironically, considered a no-go zone by many locals.

Hillbrow is the locale of two of Johannesburg's most memorable buildings, immortalised in artistic and tourist visual discourse as part of the city's famous skyline. The so-called Hillbrow Tower, on the corner of Goldreich and Banket streets, was built in 1968–71. At a height of 269 m, it is the highest structure in Johannesburg and the tallest tower in Africa. Originally designed for telecommunications and named in honour of apartheid prime minister JG Strijdom, it once housed a revolving restaurant and observation deck. These attractions have been closed to the public since 1981, although the City of Johannesburg has repeatedly discussed plans to renovate and reopen them. Ponte City on Joe

Slovo Drive, 173 m and 55 floors high and crowned by a distinctive red band advertising the mobile phone company Vodacom, was built in 1975 as luxury accommodation for the wealthy. It was the first cylindrical skyscraper and is the tallest residential building in Africa. When white and middle-class residents began abandoning the inner city for the malls and gated communities of the northern suburbs, Ponte deteriorated into a site of almost legendary crime and violence. At its worst, in the early 2000s, one entire floor was used as a pimp-controlled brothel and the building's central well piled up with uncollected rubbish to about three floors high. Local legend insists that more than one dead body was left to rot here. In recent years, Ponte has been 'cleaned up' by new owners, and now features extremely stringent security and entry conditions.

In their peaks and their troughs, their reputations for crime, glamour and decay, their Anglo-modernist aspirations and late-apartheid disintegrations, Ponte and the Hillbrow Tower can function as metonyms of the city overall. Alongside this, their physical and geographical aspects suggest some of the uncertainties of living in the anxious city. Both buildings are visible from high points around Johannesburg. However, depending on where one is located, their relation to each other and to the ground below can look radically different to the viewer. Sometimes one is strikingly taller than the other, sometimes they appear to be the same height. Sometimes they are nestling neighbours, sometimes they are separated by urban skyscapes. From the rooftops of Rosebank, the Hillbrow Tower soars miles above Ponte; from the streets of Ellis Park, Ponte looms menacingly over a small and distant Hillbrow Tower; from Kensington, they seem clustered together and about the same height. It is as if the ground on which they stand is in motion and unreliable.

What may this topographical insecurity mean for imaginings of Johannesburg, for those who live in the area, those who are afraid of the area and those who view the towers as nothing more than distant shapes on the skyline? For a city that is always already unstable – subject to violence, migration, development and the geological weaknesses caused by over a century of intense mining – these shifting monuments to its many incarnations can only further suggest the unreliability of the anxious city.

Words by Nicky Falkof, based on an idea by Joe Walsh. All photographs taken on Saturday, 15 June 2019, with a Nikon D850. With thanks to Shireen Ally and Eric Worby, Petra Ross and Niren Tolsi, Ruth Sacks, Hotel Oribi and the Troyeville Hotel.

Figure 8.1
Bertrams Rd, Troyeville

Figure 8.2
Niobe St, Kensington

Figure 8.3
Miller St, Ellis Park

Figure 8.4
Westminster Mansions, Highlands Rd, Yeoville

Figure 8.5
Hotel Oribi, Commissioner St, Jeppestown

Figure 8.6
Rosebank Mall, Baker St, Rosebank

Figure 8.7
Melville Koppies, Kloof Rd, Melville

Figure 8.8
Majestic Towers, Clarendon Place, Parktown

9 PHOTOGRAPHY AND RELIGION IN ANXIOUS JOBURG

JOEL CABRITA AND SABELO MLANGENI

his chapter is an edited rendition of a series of conversations between Joel Cabrita and Sabelo Mlangeni that took place on the phone, in person and over e-mail, in Johannesburg, Mbabane and New York, between June 2017 and July 2018. Cabrita's recent work has focused on the history of Zionism in southern Africa – one of the largest African Christian movements in the region with an estimated 15 million adherents – and Mlangeni has a longstanding interest in photographing Zionist communities. Their collaboration has taken the form of two exhibitions of Mlangeni's photographs of Zionist Christians, at the Museum of Archaeology and Anthropology in Cambridge, England, in 2017 and at Wits Art Museum (WAM) in Johannesburg in 2018. The theme of 'anxiety' – defined here as a state of being existentially and materially unsettled or 'out of place', also akin to a state of liminality – has pervaded many of their conversations surrounding religion and photography in contemporary Johannesburg.

JOEL CABRITA: Sabelo, much of your photography has focused on two areas: Driefontein in Mpumalanga, the small village you're originally from, and Johannesburg, the city you moved to in 2001, to pursue studying and work. With regard to Driefontein and surrounding small towns, I'm thinking of series like your *Country Girls* and your recent body of work on Zionist

Christianity, *Umlindelo wamaKholwa*. Series like *Invisible Women* and *Big City* were shot in Johannesburg, while *Umlindelo wamaKholwa* has images taken in both Driefontein and Johannesburg. I'm struck by how your continual oscillation between Driefontein and your life in the city seems to be a productive creative force for you. You never quite belong in either place, but rather than creating anxiety in any stereotypical sense, this feeling of perpetual displacement is a generative and positive dynamic for you and for your work. And I think the title of this volume – *Anxious Joburg* – captures something of those liminal complexities: of both belonging and not belonging to a city like Joburg, an experience that surely you share with very many of the city's inhabitants, both historically and in the present day. So, let's first focus on that somewhat unsettled state of existing between two places and two homes. Leaving aside your experiences in Joburg for a moment, can you tell me about growing up in Driefontein?

SABELO MLANGENI: Yes, I grew up in Driefontein, a village in eastern Mpumalanga. I was estranged from my parents and raised by my aunt from the Msibi family. In fact, for many years of my childhood, I thought that my aunt was my mother. This was only something I realised wasn't the case in later life.

Figure 9.1
'Lungile Mndebele', Sabelo Mlangeni, 2016

JOEL: So your childhood home was itself never really a secure place for you, and what we're here calling 'anxiety' seems to pervade even that early experience. I'm also struck by the contrast between your unsettled relationship with your own biological family and how your photography has become the medium for you to explore a sense of the Zionist church as a new family and a kind of new home. Of course, this experience has powerful historical precedents in a country like South Africa, where for many people – displaced by the massive social changes of the twentieth century including urbanisation and labour migration centred in the city of Johannesburg and its many industries – increasingly found new solidarities in the city via the church, whether that was a Zionist church or any other denomination.[1] That sense of the church as a new family emerges very powerfully in your work. For example, many of the photographs in your recent *Umlindelo wamaKholwa* series evoke your intimate relationships and close ties with your fellow believers in the Zionist church, both in Driefontein and in Johannesburg. How did you come to be involved in the Zionist church?

SABELO: My home church in Driefontein is the Christian New Stone Apostolic Church.[2] My first encounter with them was when I was 17 years old. I remember the moment very well: it was during a church night vigil, or *umlindelo*. I was born into a Christian family – my family in Driefontein went to the Swazi Zion church – but at this time I was in a very disconnected state with the church. But at that night vigil I especially remember the singing. I was sitting outside the tent at the fire, but when the choir started to sing, I ran in immediately. I left the fire [outside] to listen to them. It was another experience. The singing was beyond … I can't explain how the singing was. But the strong bond I formed with the church created problems with my family at home. Joining another church outside of the one my family went to was a challenge at home.

JOEL: Given that you titled your series on Zionist Christians *Umlindelo wamaKholwa*, or the Night Vigil of the Believers, clearly the night vigil, or *umlindelo*, is something that is important to you and central to Zionist identity.

SABELO: Yes, there are different ways of viewing night vigils in the Zionist community, the act of waiting. I think we could even relate it to what we've been discussing about anxiety and unsettlement. In the moment of waiting nothing is exactly clear, and so we find ourselves between things, between the old and the new, between the night and the dawn. There are those night vigils where people are celebrating something. Or when someone has lost a family member, and then the whole church comes for a night vigil. Also, you have *umlindelo*, a night vigil where it's just *siguqho* [praying and dancing in a circle], people are using *umoya* [the Holy Spirit] and they are prophesying throughout the night. So there are these different levels of *umlindelo*. I am especially interested in the Zion church as a community, where people gather like spiritual sisters and brothers. And *umlindelo* is very central to the creation of this; it's a time when a community is created by the experience of waiting together.

JOEL: This notion of 'waiting' – the time of between, or a liminal space – is central to your identity as a Zionist. But it also strikes me that 'waiting' is integral to your craft as a photographer. I know that the physical process of developing film is very important to you, and that you value the materiality of it. And 'waiting' for the image to emerge is part of this. Thinking more explicitly about photography, by the time you were a teenager you were fully immersing yourself into the new family of the church. How did photography fit into all of this?

SABELO: The time that I started attending church was the same time when I started working with local photographer Mrs C.S. Mavuso. She was an important figure in the Driefontein community who was a teacher and also had a photographic studio. She photographed all elements of the community, including Zionist baptisms, marriages and funerals. I began assisting C.S. in the studio, first delivering photographs to her clients, but soon starting to assist her in making photographs.

JOEL: So from an early age photography for you was about working from a position of belonging to the community of Driefontein, but also to the churches themselves. You were photographing people that in some sense you were intimately tied to; these were your own communities. But as we've already been discussing, belonging is never entirely straightforward. For me, this complex shifting between proximity and distance is encapsulated by this wonderful photograph of you taken in 2009 in Driefontein. In it, you're standing at the back of a group of Zion church youth after a Good Friday service. What's especially interesting to me is that this photograph of you was actually taken by one of the church members with your own camera. I read that image as underscoring your conflicted sense of belonging, your continual movement back and forth between observer and participant: between observing the community with your camera, on the one hand, and being part of the community, on the other, and even having the camera turned on you. Maybe we could even see this image as a commentary on the anxiety of both belonging and not belonging to a church.

SABELO: Photography and a strong – even if complicated – sense of belonging to a community have always been intertwined for me. Moving to Johannesburg gave that a whole new dimension. It was in 2001, around May, when I moved to Johannesburg from Driefontein. It was my first time in the city. I was 21. I arrived in Noord Street at the taxi rank and had to go to the house of my father who jointly owned a few bottlestores and taverns in

Figure 9.2
'Sabelo Mlangeni at the Good Friday church service', Bong'musa Dube, 1999. Courtesy of Sabelo Mlangeni

Fordsburg as well as in Booysens. No one came to pick me up and I got a bit lost. I wasn't scared but I was quite excited. The city was totally different to Driefontein, everything was different, all the buildings. I felt so disorientated.

JOEL: Your journey from Driefontein to Johannesburg echoes a historical connection between these two places in the history of Zionism in South Africa, something that I've explored extensively in my own research [Cabrita 2014, 2018]. I describe how Zionist missionaries from the United States arrived in Johannesburg in 1904, and the area around Driefontein was one of the first areas outside of Johannesburg where they concentrated their energies. So the two areas of growth for Zionism in South Africa were originally Driefontein and Johannesburg. The site of the first independent black-led breakaway Zion church was in Driefontein, led by Daniel Nkonyane around the 1920s. And it was due to Johannesburg and its growth throughout the twentieth century as a mining hub that Zionism spread across the region via migrant labour routes.[3] I find it fascinating that your own personal journey back and forth between your two homes – Driefontein and Johannesburg – exactly mirrors the geographical dynamic through which Zionism first took root in South Africa.

SABELO: Yes, we can look at the history of Zionism in a double way: my own personal history between Driefontein and Johannesburg, and also the bigger history of the church between these two places. And, of course, both are marked by an unsettled state. One of the things we've discussed at some length in our conversations is that there have always been differences between Zionists in Johannesburg and our church members in the rural areas. We'll return to that later on in this particular conversation.

JOEL: For the moment, then, returning to your personal trajectory between Driefontein and Johannesburg, why had you come to the city?

SABELO: This was after my matric and I knew I wanted to study. In fact, because of my experience with C.S., photography was one of the things I thought about studying. But at my school in Driefontein, when we received career guidance from our teachers, studying photography was not one of the things they had information on. And I knew I didn't have the finances to do a course like journalism where we would also have learned about photography. So in my first few months in Johannesburg I was walking about on foot looking for a job and I just happened to pass the Market Photo Workshop. This is when it was one room in Newtown, really like a workshop, right opposite the Market Theatre in the passageway. When I walked in there, they told me they offered classes for beginners, and there was this great excitement for me in finding out I could study photography. It was around R300 to register, and my friends from Driefontein helped me raise enough. I thought I already knew how to make photographs from my time with C.S., but I was surprised to be introduced to totally different ways of making photographs, and also to go deep into learning about the equipment. During my time at Market Photo Workshop it was about going out, making a photograph, coming back and talking about it. It was very practical. Alongside the history of photography we learned in the classroom, photography was something I also learned outside the classroom, in the community I was taking the photographs in.

JOEL: It sounds like your apprenticeship as a photographer was also an apprenticeship in the city itself – newly arrived from Driefontein, moving around the city and learning more about its multiple communities (and, as a side observation, still supported and buoyed up by your friends in Driefontein, who generously helped you with your new life in Johannesburg).

SABELO: Yes, and after living with my father in Fordsburg for a time, I moved into my own place in Hillbrow, an open space I shared with my friends. Hillbrow was this place where people who were new to the city, people who were immigrants, first thing they arrived, it was straight to Hillbrow. Nigerians were there, Ghanaians, people from the upper part of Africa; later the Zimbabweans came.[4] My friends and I were all paying rent for this flat, and we divided it with curtains. I met these friends in clubs and bars in Hillbrow. But we all went to church together (at that time I was attending the Johannesburg branch in Germiston of my Driefontein church, New Stone Christian Church). We would drink together on Saturday night and on Sunday we'd go to church in the morning, and then afterwards someone would cook dinner or lunch; you go to church and come back to someone's house and they braai. It was just a fantastic community we had in Hillbrow. And Friday and Saturday evenings we'd have people coming to stay from all over, Daveyton, coming in to party from different parts of the city and they didn't have a place to stay, so our house would become a place where you wake up in the morning on Sunday and there were an extra ten people in the house. Everyone is here and you don't know what is what. You don't have control of things. Anyone can just go to the fridge. It was that kind of environment.

JOEL: I notice these were friends you also went to church with, and, to me, it sounds like a riff on the biblical idea of church: a communitarian space where no one has private property and everything is equally owned and shared. Did you feel that when you moved to the city, you discovered a whole new network of relationships – a new 'family', perhaps – wider than your Zion church from home in Driefontein?

SABELO: Yes, definitely, I remember that I explored a lot of different Zion churches in the city when I first arrived. Sometimes, I'd just be walking in the city and hear something from a building, and go up the stairs. Many of these churches meet in schools in the city centre, that are several-storey buildings. There was one that I went into one Sunday coming from my own church, on the corner of President and End Street. You're in a Zion uniform, they're in a Zion uniform that's completely different to yours. So there's this kind of barrier. Also, there was a language barrier. This was a church that was almost entirely Zimbabwean, so I couldn't really understand the things they were talking about. But then there was this moment of *siguqho*, where they all were singing and they started using *umoya*. That's when I had the feeling that we were all united in speaking to a higher power somewhere.

JOEL: The other thing that strikes me from what you've said here and about your church in Hillbrow is that the boundaries of what is a 'church' in the city become quite fluid, perhaps more so than when you were in Driefontein. Meeting in a school, rather than in a dedicated church building; partying together Saturday night, attending a service Sunday morning; eating and relaxing together Sunday afternoon: everything becomes an aspect of what it means to be in communion with your church.

SABELO: One thing I've always noticed with churches in the city is that they are somehow quite open spaces, and that the divide between what is church and what is not church becomes very blurred. Perhaps this also links to this theme of liminality that we've been raising throughout. Where does the line between belonging and not belonging to a church get drawn when the boundaries of the church are themselves so open and unclear? For example, there are many churches that meet in spaces that weren't designed for worship, like churches gathering in the basements of parking buildings downtown. There are also those open spaces like Melville Koppies, or a space that is now gone in Yeoville, right up there on the hill. These spaces are open for people just to walk in and be part of the worship. There's also that big church between Claim Street and Wolmarans, or maybe it's Smit. They meet in an old Jewish synagogue, and many people go there with water to get healing there, they use a lot of *umoya*. If you go there on a Sunday, you'll find it's so popular that people are even standing outside. One story is that traffic officers try and remove people waiting on the street and on the pavements because the church inside is so full. But you also find the other extreme: Zionists worshipping in small private houses. When I was living in Hillbrow there was a small Zion church that had services in someone's flat. That was very new to me coming from Driefontein, to have church in such a small space, and in such a personal intimate space.

JOEL: I think of the difficulties that churches like the Zionists and other independent churches have historically faced in gaining access to sites to worship in Johannesburg. The paradox was that the city became many people's new home (including finding new religious networks there), but at the same time the government was determined to restrict permanent African urbanisation. So this gives us yet another perspective on the anxiety of not belonging in a city like Johannesburg. Legislation affecting so-called native churches was passed in the 1920s that was explicitly designed to halt the spread of independent churches by denying them the right to erect dedicated church buildings. And then there was the legislation of the 1960s that mandated the removal of churches that weren't 'recognised' by the government from urban spaces.[5] So what you describe as this 'make-do' character of Zionist churches, using whatever space is available and to hand to worship in (even old synagogues), seems to me a product of the historical and political pressures on Zionist communities in cities like Johannesburg.

SABELO: And you know, even in a dense, built-up city like Johannesburg, the use of open landscapes, open spaces and nature for worship is very, very important. I've mentioned Melville Koppies and that hill in Yeoville. You can also think about Wemmer Pan. So, the relation between nature and spirituality is important with the Zion church. And this question of the land also links to the idea of waiting – *ukulinda* – that we've already discussed. I think of waiting in a very open-ended way. How do I relate waiting to a South African landscape?

JOEL: A lot of your work in the *Umlindelo wamaKholwa* series features borders and boundaries of some description: walls, bushes, fences, or bushes that make a fence, gates. Is that part of what you're saying about land? Are your depictions of borders speaking to the current anxieties surrounding how access to the land is still so unequal in present-day South Africa, and the way in which many ordinary people are still struggling to stake their claim to territorial belonging?

SABELO: Yes, I'd say so. That's also why in this work I was experimenting with including borders [around the images] that are both open and closed. They do have a meaning in this work. What does it mean to have these open or closed borders around the images?

JOEL: It brings to mind the 1913 Land Act, when borders were drawn to determine European and African ownership of the land, and these historical borders still influence South Africa today. I don't know if that's too much of a stretch, or if that's where you could go with that.

SABELO: I think that's how far I was going when I created those borders around the images. There was a moment when I thought to myself, should I close them? Should I have images that are fully closed with borders? But I felt like closing them wouldn't speak to the past, a time when Africans did have access to the land, when borders weren't closed yet and things were more hopeful.

Figure 9.3
'KwaMtsali, Bhekumthetho, Nongoma', Sabelo Mlangeni, 2016

JOEL: And, of course, alongside the Zionist communities we've been discussing, the city has so many other types of communities who struggle to gain a foothold or are in some sense marginal, who feel shut off from full inclusion, who don't belong or have a highly unsettled and anxious existence there. I'm thinking here of your first body of work, *Invisible Women* [2006], that focused on the female street cleaners who remove rubbish from the inner city at night. I recall you told me that you encountered this community on foot, at the time when you were regularly walking home from the Market Photo Workshop at night and coming across a group of women cleaning in the inner city.

SABELO: Yes, seeing these women as I walked around the city at night was my starting point. And while at first I followed many different women around, by the end I was following a single group who were cleaning between Kerk Street and Eloff Street. It's a very dense part of the city with a lot of street vendors. It was a group of about five women, and they'd start cleaning around seven or eight and knock off at midnight. They all lived in different parts of the city, one lived in Soweto, another in Orange Farm, another in Alexandra.

It took about three months for them to accept me. I was constantly show-ing up and hanging around, and at first they thought I was coming from a newspaper and were a bit suspicious of me. But eventually I had a bond with them, and some days I would leave my camera at home just to spend time with them and help them to clean sometimes. Sometimes they would even have a broom ready for me …

JOEL: In other words, you somehow became a part of their community, albeit in a limited and transitory way. And there is something highly liminal about this community. As the title of your work suggests, they are 'invisible', they are active at night while others sleep, and their labour is almost always unacknowledged and hence undervalued by the residents of the inner city.

SABELO: Exactly. As with everyone else who lived there, my experience was of waking up in a clean city every morning. And we would never ask ourselves, 'Who are these people? Who are these ghosts, who come when we are asleep and clean for us?' Because if you go to Johannesburg in the after-noon it is always messy, but you come back in the morning and everything is clean. It reminded me of growing up in Driefontein where we'd all see the role of our mothers: you'd play soccer in the yard, and leave things out like that, and she'd come in the morning and clean and move things around, and then we'd come back. I felt like they were our mothers, our mothers in Johannesburg, cleaning for us overnight. I also felt that there was something important about their work in the present-day city contrasted against the historical reality of Johannesburg when women weren't encouraged to be in the city.[6]

JOEL: We're back at the topic of family once again, and we're discussing your own memories and perceptions of the physical labour that contem-porary mothers undertake or are expected to undertake. This is especially interesting to me given your own experience of your mother was so fraught. It also intrigues me that you're describing these city women in terms of family relationships back home in Driefontein, comparing them to your mothers there. I imagine that surely these urban street cleaners would also have had strong ties to rural areas outside of Joburg. What were their stories?

Figure 9.4
'Low prices daily', Sabelo Mlangeni, 2006

SABELO: Well, in fact, they were all mothers, one was even pregnant during the time I spent with them. And yes, their children were outside of the city, in their home areas. It was difficult for them. I remember one of the women telling me a story of her daughter at home in Pongola failing at school and she felt her mother's absence as the reason why she did not get good results. Because her mother was away here in Johannesburg cleaning streets, and maybe the daughter was looking after the other kids. There are just kids at home, and their mother is in the city, working.

JOEL: So this community of women were liminal or anxious in a further sense: they were not only an uneasy part of the urban landscape, largely invisible as 'ghosts' who appeared and disappeared during the night, but they were also themselves conflicted about working in the city away from their families at home. Building on that idea, I'm curious to know how you negotiated the experience of being in the city and of geographical distance from your family and your church 'family'.

SABELO: Well, at the time I was taking photographs for the *Invisible Women* series I had already stopped attending my Zion church in the city. For some years, I stayed at home without attending any church. I was thinking about many things at the time. Partly it was linked to questions of sexuality. But it was also about my relationship as Sabelo with religion.

JOEL: You mean you had doubts about your faith? That strikes me as really suggestive and important given what we've been discussing about the importance of the church as a new home for you. In other words, doubts (another form of anxiety, I would say) continually shadow security, even within the new setting of the church.

SABELO: I still have doubts. I didn't go to church for some time, even after I rediscovered my faith in around 2008. After then I started attending church again, not my old Zion church from Driefontein, but a different Zion church, Twelve Apostolic Church of Southern Africa Ekuthuleni. And now I participate in church, but I don't participate in such a way that I want to preach or talk. Before I had no problem to stand up and talk about the Bible and find different ways of explaining it. But this time it's not something I want to do. I think about Christianity and the disruption of African spirituality. All those pictures that we grew up seeing of Jesus as a white man. Why should the Jesus that I worship look different from me? Another thing that bothers me is the position of women in our churches. I've been to so many different Zion churches in Johannesburg, and in all of them, all the prophets, they are mainly focused on the problems that women have, as if it's only the women who have problems. I find it a little bit disturbing. And in our Zion churches we find more women, yet men still keep the important positions. I notice that when we have a prayer and the men stand up, the women still have to kneel. And I think, why are we still doing these kinds of things?

JOEL: Thinking about how you're describing your doubts, and your own uneasy sense of belonging to the church, I see a tension in many of your photographs about your two churches linked to your two homes, New Stone in Driefontein and Twelve Apostles in Joburg.[7] Many of your images offer the viewer very direct and intimate access to the faces of the people you're photographing, emphasising your close ties with your subjects and your privileged access to the community as a Zionist yourself. But I also notice that there are many photographs that hide rather than reveal people's faces. There are many images with obscured faces, turned backs, indistinguishable silhouettes. Of course, the most striking example of this is 'In time, a morning after Umlindelo', where the heads of your three subjects seem to have been cropped off. We can see their bodies up to their shoulders, but not their faces. It's a very powerful image.

SABELO: Actually, Jo, it's one of those images where I intended to have a full frame. So I overlooked it for some time.

JOEL: Then this wasn't deliberate, that the heads were cut off?

SABELO: No, no, it wasn't deliberate. It's the end of the film; there are things that are happening when I'm processing in the darkroom and waiting for the results. I've always been very committed to the material process and the

Figure 9.5
'In time, a morning after Umlindelo', Sabelo Mlangeni, 2016

slow pace of older, more traditional ways of developing images. Maybe for me it's like the waiting of the *umlindelo* we were discussing earlier on. Sometimes at the end you have that kind of an image where you weren't expecting the outcome. But it suddenly opens up or stretches the work in ways you couldn't have seen before. With an image like this one, you can think of lost identity, because suddenly you have the bodies, but you don't have the faces, so you can't identify who these people are. And how does this photograph fit into this whole set of questions that I have about religion? What does it mean? There's the idea of loss. A loss of identity perhaps. You know, when we think of this whole idea of *umlindelo*, or *ukulinda*, this waiting, and how in this process a community is formed, so the church is a community, yes, of course. And to some point you can even think of it as a family. But you also have to think of it as not really a family. So it's having this family, having this community, but not really. It's your family, but not your family.

JOEL: It sounds like you're talking about the limits of relationships. And that even the church isn't all that you hope it to be. Speaking about alienation, what about the act of taking photographs? Did you ever find that taking photographs contributed to your sense of distance from the church and from church members?

SABELO: Well, the kind of photography I'm doing is not the kind of photography where I photograph you today, and then tomorrow I bring back the photographs and you pay me R10 for them. People see you time after time making photographs, and they don't get to see them. The questions start: 'What are you doing with our photographs?' They know what kind of work I'm doing, but there's always that question. 'You keep on taking them, and we don't see the end results of what you do.' And when people see a camera, they have the feeling that their problems are solved, or that you're coming to change their lives in a way that whatever issues or problems they have are suddenly going to be out in the world. So you have that kind of responsibility too, while at the same time that isn't the direction of the photographs that you're making.

JOEL: I interpret what you're saying in terms of not being aligned in any straightforward way with the people you're photographing. Rather than using your camera to 'represent' communities, or to use your photography to proclaim your membership of the Zionist community, you're in a much more complex conversation with what they might mean and represent in your own imagination. It seems to me that your identity as a photographer makes your belonging to your own Zionist church much more anxious than it might otherwise be.

SABELO: In a way it's even bigger than that. It's also this sense of not being at home or settled anywhere, not in the church, not in the city, not even at home in Driefontein. The idea of displacement has become very, very rich for me. I've recently been working on a series about South African soldiers who were involved in the First World War, and died overseas. Their bodies are still there, in France, rather than at home in South Africa. In Johannesburg, I often think about how for many people it's a hard thing to think of the city as a home. It's just a place where we come to work, and we have a home somewhere else. For example, where I live right now on Joubert Street, I've been there since 2014. All the people that I've met in that space have come and gone, arriving and leaving. Living in a city like I'm doing doesn't give you a sense of home. In a city we're continually moving. Maybe we've even moving around within the same city. But the fact is we're not keeping one structure as home.

JOEL: But there are some people who've lived in Johannesburg for many, many generations. There are people for whom Johannesburg is home.

SABELO: Yes, yes, of course. But as much as Johannesburg is home, it's not home like my home in Driefontein was a home that was formed by my grandfathers. Even for people who've been in Johannesburg for a very long time. We have people who've been in the city, living in one house, for generations, maybe in places like Soweto. But right in the inner city where people are living in small apartments, they're always moving around.

JOEL: So when people pass away in the city, where are they buried?

SABELO: They go home. People don't get buried in Johannesburg. Of course, I wouldn't say that completely. Some people do. But most people go to their villages, where they come from, other towns and even in other countries. There's one Zion church that meets in a big building near me on Lilian Ngoyi Street; I think during the week the building is used as a crèche for children. These members are South Africans, of course, but their homes and families are in Zimbabwe. When they come out of church, they stand around outside on the street. I've been photographing them through my apartment window. I'm thinking about using these images to create a contact sheet. This is when you photograph with film, and then you process it, and there's a page where you have all the images, but as small thumbnails. So I'd blow up this contact sheet until it was very large, and then I'd do an intervention. I'd cut out some of the images from the contact sheet and leave those open spaces there. And then I'll present those images that I've moved out – maybe next to the contact sheet; maybe somewhere else. And I'd leave these holes right there. Perhaps it's a way for me to talk about displacement and about the anxiety of a place like Johannesburg.

JOEL: I'm interested to hear more about what that displacement, or double belonging – at home both in Johannesburg and somewhere else, whether within or even outside of South Africa – might mean for churches that are based in the city. It must mean that Zion churches in Johannesburg are always travelling outside of the city on Saturday nights for night vigils for funerals and other occasions?

SABELO: Yes, of course. Take the example of the event at Wits Art Museum on the Saturday in July where four Zion choirs came to sing.[8] Two of the choirs were from my Joburg church (Twelve Apostles) and from my Driefontein church (New Stone). That evening, the Twelve Apostles choir went to Ermelo for a night vigil. Babe Msibi, the pastor of Twelve Apostles, is from Ermelo. He has a house in Rosettenville, where he lives with his wife. But his family lives past Ermelo in a very small place whose name I can't remember. And, in fact, the evening before they came to sing at Wits Art Museum, they had come from Newcastle, where they had another night vigil for a funeral. And New Stone had a funeral for a church member's brother, so they all travelled back from Joburg for the night vigil in Driefontein. If I think back to the time when I was living in Driefontein, of course we always had trips to Joburg for church occasions. But, really, it was the church members in Joburg who were making a lot of trips to us in Driefontein as well as in other rural places. In the city, as much as you're part of a church in the city, you are coming from somewhere. So if something happens at your home, you go home.

JOEL: If members of Zion churches in Johannesburg are always going away for weekends and funerals and significant events, they must spend a lot of time travelling with church members. That must be a significant part of Zion identity. And you know, a lot of the times when we speak on the phone, you're always about to go somewhere with the church, or have just come back from somewhere. The time travelling with the church seems like one of the significant parts of being a Zionist, that you're travelling together and that you're on the road a lot. And in fact, many of your photographs are about travelling and this experience of being on the road with your spiritual brothers and sisters … it sounds like another variation on the liminal space of the *umlindelo*, the night vigil, the time of waiting, or of being in between two states.

Figure 9.6
'USipho Mathunjwa noScara',
Sabelo Mlangeni, 2015

SABELO: Ja, because when we look at other Christian churches like the Born Agains and the Charismatics,[9] they're different to Zionists in that they don't have all these services and ceremonies like *imilindelo*. One thing about the Zion church is that we support each other through the vigils when someone passes away. Almost the whole year round, the church's calendar is full with things that are happening. It involves a lot of money, and this is something that people sometimes get frustrated about. It's so much money that is used in our church specifically for travelling. And of course, when we get to the place, you also have to buy presents for the person, and in most cases the person with the job is expected to give more money.

JOEL: So what would a present look like?

SABELO: For example, this time for the pastor's wife, for the ceremony of her coming out of mourning, they bought a very expensive couch. Or it could be a fridge and cupboards. Maybe all the members contribute R20. But those who are working are expected to give more. You have agreements between yourselves. If anything happens to my parents, to my brothers, to my sisters and they pass away, each church member will contribute R20 as a support.

JOEL: Do you find that you struggle with mixed allegiances in being torn between your belonging to two different churches, one in Johannesburg and one in Driefontein? Does this cause any kind of tension or conflict between you and your two churches? Is there a sense of competition or rivalry between the two of them, both fighting for your loyalty and your support?

SABELO: Well, that can sometimes be the case. But when both choirs from both my churches [Driefontein and Johannesburg] were in Johannesburg for the concert at the Wits Art Museum exhibition, something amazing happened. When New Stone from Driefontein saw the beautiful cloth sewn by Londiwe from Twelve in Johannesburg, they called me saying they wanted Londiwe to make them new uniforms [for church] because she sews so wonderfully.[10] This is so beautiful. This is something I really want to see. And maybe they'll even meet up outside of Johannesburg. Twelve even has a branch in Piet Retief, which is very close to Driefontein and to where New Stone meets.

JOEL: Sabelo, this seems like a lovely and hopeful way to end our conversation. Much of what we've been talking about relates to things that could be construed negatively: anxiety, displacement, dislocation, liminality, not belonging. Our discussion has especially focused around the fraught complexities surrounding home and belonging, whether to a city like Johannesburg, a biological family in Driefontein, or to a Zion church that is continually moving between sites. But what you've just said about your two churches coming together through this event at Wits Art Museum in Joburg is a reminder that occasional moments of togetherness, peace and belonging do emerge from the midst of all these displacements that so characterise a place like Johannesburg. I suppose the point is that the movement between belonging and not belonging (or between anxiety and peace) is such a productive one. The two states are inseparable; perhaps they actually constitute each other in some mysterious way. Thank you so much for the privilege of having these rich conversations with you over the last months.

NOTES

1   Belinda Bozzoli's *Town and Countryside in the Transvaal* (1983) is a classic treatment of the wide-scale migration of Africans to work in the new mining metropolis of Johannesburg. See also Charles van Onselen's *New Babylon, New Nineveh* (2001). For a treatment of new religious affiliations in the city, see Deborah Gaitskell (1983). Wilhelm-Solomon et al. (2016) offer a contemporary perspective on the intersections between migration and religion in the city.

2   This organisation loosely identifies itself with the Zionist Christian tradition. Rather than being a single church, the Zionist movement in southern Africa is a decentralised federation of thousands of different churches, many of which practise some form of healing prayer. The single largest Zionist organisation in southern Africa is the Zion Christian Church (ZCC) with approximately six million members.

3   Usually thought of as a religious movement entirely local to southern Africa, in fact the Zionist church had its roots in a late-nineteenth-century Protestant faith-healing movement centred in the small industrial hub of Zion City, located on the banks of Lake Michigan just north of Chicago. Under the leadership of the charismatic preacher and healer John Alexander Dowie, Zion's faith-healing teachings circulated the world, largely thanks to the dissemination of the movement's popular periodical *Leaves of Healing*, as well as through the work of missionaries from Zion City. Although

Zionism took root in other areas of sub-Saharan Africa (most notably in the Gold Coast), it was within the post-South African War Transvaal that Zionist faith healing most spectacularly flourished among Africans and – for a limited phase only – white Afrikaners and Britons (Cabrita 2018).

4   For a historical perspective on Hillbrow's changing demographic composition from the 1970s onwards, see Alan Morris (1999), or see AbdouMaliq Simone (2004) for a more recent treatment of Hillbrow as a hub for local and international migrants.

5   The Native Churches Commission passed its recommendations regarding independent black-led churches in 1926, including outlining the almost always insurmountable criteria churches had to fulfil in order to access the right to construct a dedicated church building (Cabrita 2014).

6   Throughout the twentieth century, white urban administrators allied with conservative African patriarchs to keep African women domiciled at home in the rural areas across southern Africa, thereby hoping both to discourage permanent African settlement in cities such as Johannesburg and to avoid the perceived undesirable consequences of a female urban population emancipated from the supervisory control of fathers and husbands at home (Simelane 2004; Bonner 1990).

7   This and all future references to 'Twelve' or 'Twelve Apostles' denote the Twelve Apostolic Church of Southern Africa Ekuthuleni.

8   Mlangeni's *Umlindelo wamaKholwa* was exhibited at Wits Art Museum from 26 June to 28 October 2018. On 28 July, four choirs from four different Zion churches based in Johannesburg and Driefontein performed a concert in the WAM café in response to the photographic exhibition.

9   'Born Again' and 'Charismatic' refer to a variant of Protestant Christianity loosely identified with Pentecostal theology and characterised by an emphasis on speaking in tongues, faith healing and the so-called prosperity gospel.

10 Londiwe Xaba, a member of Twelve Apostolic Church of Southern Africa Ekuthuleni in Johannesburg, designed and made two Zionist altar cloths (*iladi*) as part of an installation for the exhibition of *Umlindelo wamaKholwa* at Wits Art Museum.

REFERENCES

Bonner, Philip. 1990. "Desirable or Undesirable Basotho Women? Liquor, Prostitution and the Migration of Basotho Women to the Rand, 1920–1945." In *Women and Gender in Southern Africa to 1945*, edited by Cherryl Walker, 221–50. Cape Town: David Philip.

Bozzoli, Belinda, ed. 1983. *Town and Countryside in the Transvaal: Capitalist Penetration and Popular Response.* Johannesburg: Ravan Press.

Cabrita, Joel. 2014. *Text and Authority in the South African Nazaretha Church.* Cambridge, England: Cambridge University Press.

———. 2018. *The People's Zion: Southern Africa, the United States and a Transatlantic Faith-Healing Movement.* Cambridge, MA: Harvard University Press.

Gaitskell, Deborah. 1983. "Housewives, Maids or Mothers: Some Contradictions of Domesticity for Christian Women in Johannesburg, 1903–1939." *Journal of African History* 24 (2): 241–56.

Morris, Alan. 1999. *Bleakness and Light: Inner-City Transition in Hillbrow, Johannesburg.* Johannesburg: Wits University Press.

Simelane, H.S. 2004. "The State, Chiefs and the Control of Female Migration in Colonial Swaziland, c.1930s–1950s." *Journal of African History* 45: 103–24.

Simone, AbdouMaliq. 2004. "People as Infrastructure: Intersecting Fragments in Johannesburg." *Public Culture* 16 (3): 407–29.

Van Onselen, Charles. 2001. *New Babylon, New Nineveh: Everyday Life on the Witwatersrand, 1886–1914.* Johannesburg: Jonathan Ball Publishers.

Wilhelm-Solomon, Matthew, Lorena Lunez, Peter Kankonde Bukasa, and Bettina Malcomess, eds. 2016. *Routes and Rites to the City: Mobility, Diversity and Religious Space in Johannesburg.* London: Palgrave Macmillan.

10 MAROONED: SEEKING ASYLUM AS A TRANSGENDER PERSON IN JOHANNESBURG

B CAMMINGA

When I come here for me, my perspective about South Africa is that it is a gay-friendly country … when I … get in the plane I was crying because I felt relieved. I say, 'Oh my God!' and I cried. There was a … woman on the plane who said, 'Why are you crying?' I know why I am crying. I know because I was feeling, when we land to Johannesburg I will say, 'Thank you, God, now I am safe!' (Alex, 10 August 2012).[1]

South Africa is the only country on the African continent that recognises sexual orientation and gender – including gender identity and expression – as human rights, enshrined within the country's Constitution (1996).[2] Although other countries across the continent have increasingly begun to decriminalise homosexuality, most recently Angola and Botswana, South Africa is the only country that offers particular rights and protections to transgender people, including access to affirming health care. In recent years, in part owing to these far-reaching constitutional protections, the country has seen the emergence of a relatively new class of refugee – those who identify as transgender or 'gender refugees'.[3] In essence, these are people who *can* make claims to refugee status, fleeing their countries of origin based on the persecution of their gender identity.

As the opening comment from the East African refugee Alex suggests, for transgender people who journey to the country from other parts of the continent, South Africa is synonymous with safety, possibility and protection. Indeed, so wide is this reputation for constitutional protection that some gender refugees have even been told by assailants in countries of origin, 'We will kill you … go to South Africa.' Two primary cities or sites structure this notion of safety: Cape Town and Johannesburg. The former has a prominent place within the global queer imaginary as the African continent's not uncontroversial 'gay capital', while the latter maintains an identity as a 'world-class African city' and economic hub (Narsee 2013). As a country of asylum, South Africa does not practise encampment but rather a system of local integration, meaning that asylum seekers experience freedom of movement. It is perhaps unsurprising that the majority of those entering the country who identify as transgender, like Alex, have in the past chosen not to remain in Johannesburg. Rather they have chosen to journey to the place 'for visitors who are out and proud, and looking for a city that embraces this freedom' – Cape Town (Cape Town Tourism 2018).

In recent years, owing to changes in asylum policy in South Africa, moving to Cape Town has become difficult if not impossible for transgender asylum seekers. These policy shifts have left many with little option but to remain in Johannesburg. Drawing on my ongoing research work begun in 2012 with gender refugees living in South Africa, this chapter forms a companion piece to a chapter published in *Beyond the Mountain: Queer Life in 'Africa's Gay Capital'* (Camminga and Matebeni 2019).[4] In 'Being and Longing in Cape Town' I focused on Cape Town and the dire impact of the closure of the city's Refugee Reception Office (RRO). The current chapter situates itself in Johannesburg. In it I unpack what it may mean for transgender people, who can no longer move directly to Cape Town owing to the RRO closure, to have to stay in Johannesburg. This is a city which, given the density of migrants from all over the continent and beyond, the lack of trans-specific support structures and high rates of criminality, is often punitively experienced by those considered socio-economically weak or less able to defend themselves. Being 'marooned' in Johannesburg can leave gender refugees deeply fearful, anxious and apprehensive.

Work in the area of emotional geography has highlighted how emotions are not 'entirely interiorised mental states' (Held 2015, 34) but are also the outcome of socio-spatial relations between people and environments. Alongside this, more recent work in transgender studies has shown that geographies can and do have a critical impact on how transgender people are able to actualise themselves and how they experience or can express their gender (Shakhsari 2014; Aizura 2018). In this chapter, I consider the socio-spatial relations that affect migrants in Johannesburg, in particular the impact of the generalised anxiety over economic migrants and what this has meant for transgender people who seek asylum in South Africa. I argue that the system of asylum, as it is currently managed in South Africa, induces particular kinds of anxiety for transgender asylum seekers directly linked to their status as both transgender people *and* migrants marooned in a city that is profoundly unwelcoming and unable to support them.

SEEKING ASYLUM IN JOZI

In Pretoria, Joburg's neighbouring city, at the corner of Es'kia Mphahlele and Johannes Ramokhoase streets, lies the Desmond Tutu Refugee Reception Centre. Formerly Marabastad, the Centre was relaunched in 2017 by President Jacob Zuma with updated software, a digitised ticketed queuing system and a refurbished interior. It was renamed 'Desmond Tutu' with a picture of the archbishop erected over its entrance to invoke, according to Zuma, the spirit of someone 'who fought tirelessly for justice, equality, human rights and freedom' and to inspire those within to provide exemplary service (Rushin 2017).

Isobel, a trans woman from East Africa, fled her country of origin after a near-fatal attack and arrived in Johannesburg in 2018. The Desmond Tutu Refugee Reception Centre has a website indicating which nationals may be seen on which days: Monday–Tuesday: 'SADC, North Africa and Asians [*sic*]'; Wednesday: 'Ethiopia, Burundi, Rwanda, Uganda, Eritrea and Ghana'; Thursday: 'Somalia, Cameron [*sic*], Senegal, Eritrea and Ethiopia'; and Friday: 'English only' (DHA 2019). The country that Isobel comes from is not on the list. The first time she went to the Centre, she was told that she had arrived on the wrong day and that she would need to return on a Tuesday with 'other North Africans'. This is not her region, let alone her country of origin. Since her arrival, she has returned to the Centre on several occasions to begin the process of gaining access to an asylum-seeker permit. Each time, after a day of queuing with other migrants, many of them hostile, she has not made it through the doors to even begin the process of applying for asylum (Camminga 2018).

As with many asylum seekers who have had to return to the Centre on several occasions because they could not make it through the front doors, Isobel's visa, allowing her to be legally present in South Africa, is about to expire. She is being supported by a transgender organisation that has stepped in to assist her but does not usually do refugee work. Refugee organisations, who are already working under challenging conditions in South Africa, struggle to assist transgender people seeking asylum because of the dual precarity they face. For transgender people there is a general lack of support in the city. While Cape Town has the Pride Shelter, Johannesburg does not have any dedicated LGBTQI equivalent. The lack of general transgender support in the city means that transgender people are vulnerable to becoming homeless. Most shelters in the city are either single-sex or run by organisations that are religious and therefore not inclusive. According to Joshua Sehoole from Iranti, a Johannesburg-based media organisation that works with and champions the rights of lesbian, transgender (including gender-nonconforming) and intersex persons in Africa:

> There is also a lack of understanding, support and information, which affects the lesbian, gay, bisexual, transgender and intersex community in general, but particularly transgender people. I can't say I know of any shelters that are inclusive in terms of policy or their practice. In our experience, trans people are only granted access when they can hide their gender identity. (Collison 2018)

Without shelter or community support, transgender asylum seekers are forced to stay with country-of-origin communities. Individual prejudices held by these communities are often not altered by progressive legislation and protections. A comparative analysis of the experiences of LGBTQI refugees made by the Organization for Refuge, Asylum and Migration (ORAM 2013) notes that though South Africa has some of the most progressive legislation in the world addressing the rights of LGBTQI people, there continues to be 'a stark disparity between official legal rights and their practical enjoyment'.

Shelter is not the only service that transgender asylum seekers require. Unlike other asylum seekers and migrants, or even other LGBTQI people, transgender people have specific health-care needs. In Cape Town, in part because of the presence of the Transgender Clinic at Groote Schuur Hospital, transgender constituents and organisations, there is some focus, however insufficient, on transgender-related health care and access. Nadzeya Husakouskaya's

(2015) study of transgender South Africans who had migrated to the city from elsewhere in the country notes that the focus on trans-related health care is less salient in Johannesburg. Health concerns of LGBTQI organisations more generally have tended to focus on HIV/AIDS and gender-based violence, with less attention given to other health concerns including trans-related health care and mental health. Public hospitals in Gauteng which offer trans-related services include Steve Biko Academic Hospital in Pretoria, the Chris Hani Baragwanath Hospital and Charlotte Maxeke Johannesburg. Of these three, only Steve Biko offers comprehensive care while the other two offer some services but not others (Husakouskaya 2016, 93, 98). Alongside these three hospitals there continues to be only one official non-governmental transgender organisation, Transgender and Intersex Africa (TIA). Based in Shoshanguve, Pretoria, TIA is predominantly focused on the needs of black transgender and intersex people in townships and rural areas (Anon n.d.). They certainly have assisted and supported transgender asylum seekers, and continue to do so, but asylum is not a focal point of their advocacy or work.

Husakouskaya (2016, 102) highlights that the lack of access to health care and community support coupled with the perceived high cost of living and unemployment makes life in Johannesburg especially difficult for transgender South Africans who migrate to the city. Along with this, given widespread discrimination experienced on public transport, in medical settings, with local communities and in the job market, many consider returning home. Home here means other areas of South Africa. For transgender asylum seekers like Isobel, returning home is simply not an option. The question becomes: why, as a transgender asylum seeker, is Isobel applying in Johannesburg at all?

ASYLUM IN SOUTH AFRICA

After crossing the border into South Africa an asylum seeker has fourteen days within which to get to a Refugee Reception Centre (RRC) or Refugee Reception Office (RRO) and apply for asylum. This entire process is overseen by the Department of Home Affairs (DHA). By law, a decision should be made within 18 months of application. At this point, the applicant is either awarded or denied refugee status and can challenge the latter decision. If they have no intention of doing so, they are required to leave the country.

During the time of application and awaiting a decision, asylum seekers have freedom of movement within the country and are allowed to look for employment. The only requirement during the 18-month adjudication period is that they return to an RRO or RRC every three to six months to renew their papers. In the past asylum seekers did not have to return to the RRO/RRC at which they had first applied, as long as their file had been transferred to a new centre or office. RROs function as the critical entry point to the South African system of asylum. To further facilitate this freedom of movement, the South African Refugees Act of 2000 makes 'provision for the establishment of as many RROs across the country as is deemed necessary by the Director-General' (Khan and Lee 2018, 1208). After the Act came into force, RROs were established in Cape Town, Pretoria, Durban, Port Elizabeth and Johannesburg. During that time South Africa became one of the top ten refugee-receiving countries in the global south, with applicants predominantly coming from elsewhere on the African continent (ANA 2018). To increase access and implementation, additional offices were opened in Musina and Tshwane.

The growth in applicants has over time placed an incredible strain on the asylum system. It has also fostered accusations that those applying are not actual asylum seekers but rather economic migrants using the system as a means to remain in South Africa. Several studies indicate that the DHA believes that the system is being abused or used in bad faith by economic migrants (Amit 2012; Crush and Williams 2001; Amit and Kriger 2014). Since 2010, there have been notable shifts in the DHA's approach to asylum seekers in South Africa – a turnaround from the previous implementation and access model – including scaling back on the number of RROs. The first RROs to be closed were the Tshwane and Johannesburg offices. After this, both Cape Town and Port Elizabeth were earmarked for closure as 'wind-down' facilities. As I show further on, the impact of these decisions on transgender refugees has been brutal.

The closures also coincided with a change in policy, which thereafter required asylum seekers to complete their applications at the RRO at which they first applied. This means that applicants need to remain in the vicinity. In addition to restricting freedom of movement, this practice also places an 'enormous financial, economic and social burden on refugees and asylum seekers who [are] … now expected to travel for thousands of kilometres to continue to access their asylum application, including renewing their permits' (Khan and Lee 2018, 1214).

The closing of offices has left only three fully functioning RROs open to first-time applicants. These three remaining facilities have also been expected to deal with the shortfall from the closures and their own renewal load. For the singular office servicing the Johannesburg and Pretoria area – now the Desmond Tutu Refugee Reception Centre – this is a workload far beyond its capacity. Fatima Khan and Megan Lee note that, given the way in which this new strategy in the management of asylum in South Africa has unfolded, it appears as though the DHA is deliberately trying to ensure 'that all migrants, including refugees and asylum seekers, remain undocumented in an attempt to facilitate their classification as illegal immigrants and subsequent removal from South Africa' (2018, 1205). This not only acts as a deterrent to potential migrants and asylum seekers but has coincided with an increase in deportations (Hiropoulos 2017). This shift and arguable hostility towards migrants more broadly can be traced back to a series of ANC proposals which emerged in 2012, suggesting the relocation of all RROs to the borders (Khan and Lee 2018, 1208). In essence, this would force applicants to remain in areas close to the border with little access to opportunities or support, thereby creating a system of encampment by default.

CLOSURES

Initially all RROs across South Africa were open to new or first-time applicants. Given its location as the first major city close to the country's borders, Johannesburg has, for many transgender-identified asylum seekers, often been a site of application, but not a place in which they had planned on remaining. Many, if not the majority, hoped to move to Cape Town. There are several reasons for this; critically, unlike Johannesburg, Cape Town is perceived to offer safety, community, support structures, access to affirming health care and fewer asylum seekers, refugees or migrants from transgender people's country-of-origin communities. As Sasha, a trans woman from East Africa, explains:

> We reached South Africa, Johannesburg … It was night … I did not have nowhere to go and I call one of my friends, I have his number, he stays in Johannesburg in a place called Ellis Park … I stayed there for one night and I just buy a tickets from Johannesburg to Cape Town because even my friend … told me I must go to Cape Town because Cape Town is more freedom than other areas in South Africa. (Sasha, archive interview, 2008)

Cape Town's reputation as the 'pink capital' is largely a tourism sales pitch but not entirely, for the city also hosts the most significant number of support structures for transgender people, including migrants and asylum seekers (Rink 2013). Gender DynamiX, the oldest transgender organisation on the continent, has its offices in the Cape Town suburb of Observatory. Transgender asylum seekers, once recognised as such, have access to all the same rights as South Africans, barring the right to vote. This means they are also able to access affirming health care at the Transgender Clinic. The support group which works as the feeder scheme for the Transgender Clinic is run with the assistance of an LGBTQI health organisation, the Triangle Project. The country's only LGBTQI refugee advocacy and support group – PASSOP (People Against Suffering, Oppression and Poverty) – is also based in Cape Town.

Sasha arrived in South Africa in 2006 and applied for asylum in Cape Town. In July 2012 the Cape Town RRO closed its doors to newcomers. Criticised for undermining 'the entire refugee framework' (Sonke Gender Justice 2018), the closure was particularly harmful to lesbian, gay, bisexual and transgender asylum seekers who sought to live in Africa's 'gay capital'. The DHA has been taken to court several times regarding the closure and was eventually ordered to reopen the RRO by March 2012. The Supreme Court of Appeal found that the DHA's closure of the office was 'substantively irrational and unlawful' (Sonke Gender Justice 2018). As of 2019, almost seven years after the initial closure, the RRO still remains closed to first-time applicants.

RROs are the crucial access point to South Africa's asylum system. As Khan and Lee note, 'restriction of access to the RROs ultimately leads to a restriction of access to the entire asylum process' (2018, 1210). The Cape Town RRO's ongoing closure has meant that many of those who would wish to reside in Cape Town can no longer do so legally. In essence, should LGBTQI asylum seekers choose to live in Cape Town there is a high possibility that, though ostensibly legally present in the country, they might end up becoming 'illegal'. To choose to reside in Cape Town would mean having to commute to the closest RRO every three to six months for the renewal of papers. This is affordable for only a small minority of individuals. As trans woman Stella, also from East Africa, explains:

> I have a problem … My folder is in Pretoria. He [the DHA official] doesn't want to see me here in Cape Town … I can't go there because my situation.

I don't have the money, transport, and I am not working. I don't know how am I going to travel and where am I going to stay? Maybe it takes time when I go there. Maybe the same day I am going I am not going to get in so that time where am I going to stay? I don't have money, I don't have budget to stay in the hotel. (Stella, 15 August 2012)

When asked why she left Johannesburg, Stella explains:

It was … homophobia. I was staying in Kensington and the house I rent, the room was very expensive and also taxi was very hard to me. If the homophobia come to stay in the house, how am I going to pay rent? How am I going to eat? I am going to die here. I say let me solve my life I go to Cape Town. I hear Cape Town is better than Joburg.

Stella is clear that she does not want to move to or return to Johannesburg. In Cape Town she has support as a transgender sex worker, as a transgender woman, and as someone requiring access to affirming health care. It is also a space that she believes is less dangerous to her and less homophobic. She believes that if she had stayed in Johannesburg, she would ultimately have died. However, Stella cannot afford to travel to Johannesburg regularly to renew her documents. She has by extension allowed her asylum papers to lapse and now remains in Cape Town illegally. Such is her anxiety about leaving her support base and the type of life Joburg presents, even for a brief stay, that she would 'choose' to become illegal rather than relocate. What is it about Johannesburg that elicits such fear that a transgender asylum seeker would choose illegality, with the possibility of exposure to arrest and the concomitant danger of navigating prisons, police and possible deportation, over relocation to Johannesburg?

WHAT IS JOHANNESBURG?

What is and is not Johannesburg for the people who come to inhabit it is not easy to define. Much of what would be officially marked on a map as 'not Johannesburg' in fact forms part of its imagined limits for those who have to traverse the city. A place like Tshwane (or Pretoria), in its administrative capacity and its facilitatory bureaucratic role, is as much part of Johannesburg as Sandton is. Zethu Matebeni, in her 2011 work "Exploring Black Lesbian Sexualities and Identities in Johannesburg", noted a similar tension in the definition of the city limits for her participants, as she explains: 'delineating spaces and areas seems easy in geographical terms, but this proves physically impossible at times in the local imaginary ... It is difficult to tell the meaning and demarcation of Johannesburg when one talks about Johannesburg ... Johannesburg as a location ... an imagination' (2011a, 109).

The map of Johannesburg, much like the city's residents, is ever moving. Its clear limits are indiscernible except by those making the definitions – and the same can be said for the definition of who does and does not belong. Johannesburg is home to an

> enormous variety of peoples and social groups, often competing for the same space by virtue of the dense spatial juxtaposition that constitutes city life. Such social diversity in close proximity, with all its cultural variety and cultural strains, has the potential of producing new identities and meanings forged out of mixture. (Amin 2003, 240–1)

Such mixing also has the potential to re-inculcate particular identities and meanings for particular cultural groups as a means to create common bonds in a foreign place. Since the discovery of gold in the Witwatersrand, Johannesburg has long been home, sanctuary and site of employment for migrants from all over the continent. From 1913 to the 1980s Johannesburg provided temporary or permanent resident permits to white foreigners only (Peberdy, Crush, and Msibi 2004, 11). This did not mean that black migrants did not enter the country and make their way to the city but rather that their movements were mostly unregulated. Racial restrictions on movement were finally lifted in 1986, but those granted legal status to reside in the city continued to be mostly white. As Sally Peberdy (2009) notes, black people from southern Africa have always entered South Africa without documents and migrant labour, documented and undocumented, has always formed part of the city's infrastructure.

It is difficult to know the exact numbers of migrants, both in terms of those who are in the country legally and those who are here in a way in which the South African state might deem 'illegal'. This is in part due to historical patterns of irregular migration, a lack of available data, and the fact that 'both governments and non-governmental organisations have a vested interest in exaggerating immigrant numbers, either to justify stricter immigration controls or secure increased donor funding' (Meny-Gibert and Chiumia 2016). It is notable that the data do suggest that the population of cross-border migrants in Gauteng is higher than the population of cross-border migrants '*in all other provinces combined*', with the highest concentration in Johannesburg and surrounding municipalities (Meny-Gibert and Chiumia 2016; emphasis in original). Furthermore, it is estimated that 47.5 per cent of all international migrants coming to South Africa settle in Johannesburg (Statistics SA 2018).

The areas in Joburg known as Little Mogadishu, Little Addis and Little Lagos are all markers of a city that indicate the density and visibility of its migrant population. It is clear that the imagination of Johannesburg is also mapped by the multiple bodies not born within its physical or imagined limits. Alex illustrates this when they talk about their first day in Johannesburg: 'When I came to South Africa and we landed in Joburg the place where I was staying … it was like "Am I in [the capital city of my country of origin] or what?" There were many [country-of-origin community members]' (19 August 2012).

The city's relationship with migrants, be they refugees, asylum seekers, 'illegal' labourers or legal labourers, has always been fraught with tension. During apartheid, this was often due to race. In post-apartheid South Africa, this has often been due to issues regarding resources.

Loren Landau (2018) notes that, much as during apartheid, in post-apartheid South Africa the state has played a keen role in naturalising what can be understood as pervasive anti-foreigner sentiment. News images of inner-city buildings being raided by the 'Red Ants' (a private security company relied on by the city to remove people considered 'illegal' invaders from city properties) are only one example of what successive mayors and civil servants of the city have referred to as 'crime prevention measures' (Khumalo 2017). In a recent raid on inner-city buildings, mayor of Johannesburg Herman Mashaba took part in the sweep, 'asking people to show their IDs in a neighbourhood known for African immigrants' (Chutel 2017). This followed on the heels of former Johannesburg mayor Parks Tau's 'Operation Clean Sweep', which some detractors referred to as a 'purge of the poor' from the inner city (Nicolson and Lekgowa 2013). These kinds of operations have led to increased tension between South African citizens and migrants – who are almost always perceived as foreign and not white.

This kind of rhetoric on the part of the city mayors has elided migrants more broadly with poverty, criminality and the deterioration of the city. Raids inevitably cause insecurity for both South Africans and migrants who live in the city. The direct link made between raids and migrants, as shown by the mayor asking for IDs, naturalises the resentment South Africans feel towards migrants as the perceived cause of their physical insecurity (eNCA 2018). Moreover, as Landau (2018) explains, the link to criminality has also 'naturalised anti-outsider' or xenophobic violence, 'the natural resentment poor South Africans feel towards those they perceive as "stealing" opportunities from them'. The xenophobic attacks that swept the country in 2008 (though they found their initial concentration in Alexandra, a township in Johannesburg) are but one outcome of this.[5] Online xenophobic violence-monitoring platform Xenowatch recorded '529 xenophobic violence incidents that resulted in 309 deaths; 901 physical assaults, 2,193 shops looted and over 100,000 people displaced' between 1994 and 2018. More than 40 per cent of this has taken place in the Gauteng area (Mlilo and Misago 2019, 3).

MAPPING LGBTQI JOBURG

Surprisingly, perhaps, given the community focus on Cape Town, Johannesburg has a long history of gay and lesbian activism, so much so that at one point the City of Johannesburg's official website publicised a Queer Johannesburg Tour:

> The tour takes in all of gay Johannesburg's famous landmarks: Harrison Reef Hotel in Hillbrow, the oldest gay bar and home to the first gay and lesbian church for blacks; Forest Town, where a gay party was raided by police in 1966, leading to the implementation of harsh measures aimed at stamping out homosexuality; Simon Nkoli Corner, on the corner of Twist and Pretorius streets in Hillbrow, dedicated to the memory of the gay anti-apartheid crusader, who was tried for treason; and the Soweto homes of gay and lesbian activists. (Brand South Africa 2003)

The city also continues to host the Gay and Lesbian Memory in Action Archives (GALA), the custodian of South African (and in some sense sub-Saharan African) LGBTQI history. Matebeni (2011b, 53) suggests that given the 'numerous historic queer spaces' in the city it might seem, at first glance, that Joburg is a space of ease for people of varying sexual and gender identities. She stresses that in reality this is not the case, and that navigating Johannesburg for LGBTQI people is bound up with risk, complexity and contradiction.

If anything, Johannesburg offers a clear indication that LGBTQI history does not an LGBTQI community make. For those with financial constraints, navigating Johannesburg is often tempered by a series of circumscribed decisions 'based on emotional, financial, and physical accessibility' (Canham 2017, 102). Hugo Canham, in his essay 'Mapping the Black Queer Geography of Johannesburg's Lesbian Women through Narrative', notes that class and race are particular variables affecting movement, access and emotional response to the Johannesburg city space. Canham concludes his study by arguing that in Johannesburg there has been a 'classed commercialisation of queer identities', and those who find themselves black, queer, working class or poor struggle to survive 'annihilation in a patriarchal anti-poor and anti-black heteronormative society' (2017, 103).

In Matebeni's work mapping the city, she follows the movement and experiences of South African transgender model Vanya through the streets of the city. Matebeni explains: 'Vanya felt both the pleasure and the danger of being consumed in the streets and shopping malls of the city … she walks and occupies the streets as an exoticised and desired figure.' Matebeni points out that this ability to occupy the city securely is challenged when men find out that Vanya is transgender. The outcome of this has not been pleasant, leaving Vanya with 'physical and emotional scars, as a survivor of rape and hate crimes' (2011b, 55).

Looking at the experiences of transgender and intersex internal migrants living in Johannesburg, a study by Husakouskaya noted that though LGBTQI groups and individuals in Johannesburg had made substantial contributions to policy dialogues, community building and support in South Africa, the majority of these interventions 'barely included' transgender individuals. Moreover, at the time these groups and individuals had not considered issues of internal migration, let alone cross-border migration, as a relevant policy and community issue. As a result, Johannesburg's transgender internal migrants were less integrated 'into local "queer" community and social networks' than their LGB counterparts. In part owing to this, they experience a severe lack of support, emotional distress and social isolation (Husakouskaya 2015, 20, 21).

Many of the participants in Husakouskaya's study shied away from even identifying as migrants, associating the term with a 'lack of freedom (to choose whether and/or where to move) and lack of support/family structures … Additionally, language barrier and cultural shock have been attributed to "a migrant experience"' (2015, 113). The study suggests that even internal migrants are unwilling to adopt the term 'migrant' due to the stigma it carries in the city. The issues experienced by transgender people like Vanya are only compounded when one is an asylum seeker like Isobel.

Akraam, a trans woman from the Horn of Africa, fled her country of origin when her father wanted to arrange her marriage to her female cousin. She could not tell him she was trans for fear that he might kill her. In explaining her experiences of coming to Johannesburg Akraam, much like Alex, high-lighted the high concentration of people from her country of origin: '[There are] lots … [they are] conservative, they even got a huge mosque' (Akraam, 13 January 2013). One of the critical anxieties for transgender asylum seekers in Johannesburg is the predominance of migrants, especially those from their country of origin. Owing to the lack of shelter and support networks, Akraam did eventually end up staying with her 'conservative' in-country community in Johannesburg. Rumours about her being in South Africa because she was 'gay' soon began to spread. Following a particularly horrific incident in Johannesburg in which she was beaten up by her community and left for dead, she was resettled in Canada. Her explanation of the reasons why her resettlement was accepted, an almost unheard-of occurrence given that South Africa is considered a 'safe country', highlights why Johannesburg can be an anxious space for transgender asylum seekers:

> In Johannesburg I was beaten up, I was stabbed and a friend took me to the hospital. So I had to report to UNHCR [United Nations High Commissioner for Refugees] … This Canadian lady [the UNHCR official] … ooh I love her so much. The interpreter, my interpreter, that was working for the organisa-tion said 'he is gay, he is evil and he is in our community' and she told him 'hello, you are working here as interpreter, you are not here to tell me that he is evil, that he is gay' … So she put me on an emergency case at the UNHCR. (Akraam, 13 January 2013)

Akraam's experience makes clear that other migrants' ability to deny the humanity of transgender refugees is so deeply ingrained that even a person employed by an organisation involved in the protection of people like her might be so brazen as to call her 'evil' while simultaneously acknowledging that she is part of his community. This was a veiled threat powerful enough to ensure Akraam's resettlement. For transgender asylum seekers, experiences like Vanya's and Akraam's are part of their knowledge of Johannesburg – it is a space associated with other migrants, with homophobia and transphobia. Kelly, a trans person from East Africa who lives in Cape Town, goes so far as to suggest that in South Africa Johannesburg is the place where homophobes *should* live. After an incident with other foreigners in Cape Town, Kelly explains that she confronted them: 'I told them … Cape Town is a town for gay people and you should know that … If you don't want gay people, you go to another city … go to Joburg' (15 November 2012).

ETERNALLY OUTSIDE

Shifts in policy have made it difficult for asylum seekers more generally to access the South African asylum system. Within the global asylum regime, it is widely acknowledged that some groups are more vulnerable than others. In South Africa, as this chapter has illustrated, this is true of transgender asylum seekers, in that they are both transgender *and* migrants, sitting at the interstices of a deeply anxious and precarious space. Research shows that the vast majority of LGBTQI asylum seekers in South Africa are undocumented. Only 4 per cent have officially been awarded refugee status. Of those who have not, 48 per cent are living in South Africa in ways in which the state would deem illegal. As Khan and Lee note:

> By restricting access to the asylum process and placing undue obstacles before individuals wishing to apply for asylum, or even regularise their existing permits, the Department [of Home Affairs] is attempting to deter applicants from the asylum system and often leaves them with no choice but to 'go underground' and remain in South Africa undocumented and hidden from authorities. (2018, 1218)

Isobel is not unique in her difficulties with regard to access and legality. As Daniel, a transgender asylum seeker from East Africa, explains, trying to access asylum in South Africa is a repetitive process marked by 'you go, you come back, you go, and you come back' (22 August 2012). The consequence of this is that many are vulnerable to arrest and exploitation. If something should happen to them, it is highly unlikely that they would report it to the police (Chikalogwe 2018). As a participant in a recent exposé by Carl Collison, entitled 'Africans Say SA's Queer "Haven" Is Hell', told about her engagement with the police:

> Even the police sometimes calling us names like moffie.[6] I'm not a moffie, I'm a human being. I didn't wake up one morning and say I want to be like this. No … And some people don't understand trans women … For me, sometimes I feel I want to kill myself. But sometimes I think why must I kill myself for these people? I say, that's me; I can't kill myself. I'm tired. I don't know where I can go … I don't have peace here in South Africa … I'm not safe. (Collison 2019)

As Matebeni notes, transgender people experience space and place in particular ways and will often move 'from one place to another … looking for safer and more conducive areas, zones or landscapes' (2011b, 50). The current siting and concerns of the RRO, which is meant to service Johannesburg and its connected areas, coupled with the continued closure of the Cape Town RRO, have effectively blocked this possibility for LGBTQI asylum seekers. For people like Isobel, being in Johannesburg is not a choice: it is in some sense to be stuck, marooned. This visibility, lack of community support, and isolation leave transgender asylum seekers in a particularly anxious and vulnerable position. As Alex explains:

> I was thinking there is no hope anymore. I was thinking that this is another country, a free country and everything will be better for me but there was no support group, the LGBTI community they are not supportive for people who have come from other African country. They see us as foreigner. We face xenophobia. We face homophobia. We face all kind of problem. (12 February 2013)

Johannesburg is currently not a city, zone or landscape safely available to transgender asylum seekers. Though this is the case for many migrants, as evidenced by the city's history of xenophobia and overall social exclusion, there is something particular about the precarity and inescapability that transgender people, who come to South Africa seeking refuge, experience in Joburg. The city continues to treat migrants as a broadly unwanted category of persons within its boundaries, but those with particular kinds of vulnerabilities arguably experience this most acutely. The most Isobel has seen of the possibility of security, safety and protection for transgender people in South Africa is the shining promise of Desmond Tutu's face hanging over the entrance to the RRO. She has not been able to tell anyone inside her story. She has not even seen the inside of the building.

NOTES

1 Pseudonyms, along with regional instead of national origins, have been used to protect the identities of the participants who took part in this project.

2 Section 9(3) of the Bill of Rights in the South African Constitution, referred to as the 'Equality Clause'. The clause affirms the rights to non-discrimination and equality on the basis of sexual orientation and gender respectively, among other grounds.

3 The 1951 UN Convention relating to the Status of Refugees defines a refugee as 'any person who is outside their country of origin and unable or unwilling to return there or to avail themselves of its protection, on account of a well-founded fear of persecution for reasons of race, religion, nationality, membership of a particular group, or political opinion'. Prior to 1990, claims to refugee status based on sexual or gender-based persecution were not recognised within the Convention. International LGBTQ organisations promoted notions of sexual orientation and gender identity as human rights, building an increasingly influential lobby (Kollman and Waites 2009).

4 This chapter forms part of a wider project, started in 2012, on transgender refugees living in South Africa, some of which has now been published in a monograph titled *Transgender Refugees and the Imagined South Africa: Bodies over Borders and Borders over Bodies* (2019). Interviews were conducted in English with 14 transgender-identified asylum seekers and would-be asylum seekers living in South Africa, originally from other African countries. There were six other participants whom I did not interview directly, for reasons including their death or a concern for their mental health and well-being. In these cases, I was able to access archival interviews.

5 In May 2008 xenophobic violence erupted in Alexandra township in Johannesburg where the businesses of foreign nationals were attacked. Violence soon spread across Johannesburg leaving 62 people dead. The violence soon spread to other parts of the country.

6 A South African slur denoting an effeminate man or male-bodied person.

REFERENCES

Aizura, Aren Z. 2018. *Mobile Subjects: Transnational Imaginaries of Gender Reassignment.* Durham: Duke University Press.

Amin, Ash. 2003. "Street Life." In *City A–Z*, edited by Steve Pile and Nigel Thrift, 240–1. New York: Routledge.

Amit, Roni. 2012. "All Roads Lead to Rejection: Persistent Bias and Incapacity in South African Refugee Status Determination." ACMS Research Report. Johannesburg: African Centre for Migration and Society.

Amit, Roni, and Norma Kriger. 2014. "Making Migrants 'Il-Legible': The Policies and Practices of Documentation in Post-Apartheid South Africa." *Kronos* 40 (1): 269–90.

ANA (African News Agency). 2018. "UJ Holds Summit to Find Out If Refugees Are Welcome in South Africa." *The Citizen* (blog). 20 February 2018. https://citizen.co.za/news/south-africa/politics/2087440/uj-holds-summit-to-find-out-if-refugees-are-welcome- in-south-africa/.

Anon. n.d. "Transgender Intersex Africa." Devex. Accessed 26 June 2020. https://www.devex.com/organizations/transgender-intersex-africa-111278.

Brand South Africa. 2003. "The Queer Johannesburg Tour." 2003. Brand South Africa (blog). 2 December 2003. https://www.brandsouthafrica.com/tourism-south-africa/travel/cities/queerjoburgtour.

Camminga, B 2018. "'Gender Refugees' in South Africa: The 'Common Sense' Paradox." *Africa Spectrum* 53 (1): 89–112.

——— 2019. *Transgender Refugees and the Imagined South Africa: Bodies over Borders and Borders over Bodies.* New York: Palgrave Macmillan.

Camminga, B, and Zethu Matebeni, eds. 2019. *Beyond the Mountain: Queer Life in 'Africa's Gay Capital'.* Pretoria: Unisa Press.

Canham, Hugo. 2017. "Mapping the Black Queer Geography of Johannesburg's Lesbian Women through Narrative." *Psychology in Society* 55: 84–107.

Cape Town Tourism. 2018. "Pink Capital Cape Town Says Hello Weekend." *Capetown*. Accessed 1 April 2018. http://www.capetown.travel/members/member-news/members-blog/pink-capital-cape-town-says-hello-weekend.

Chikalogwe, Victor Mdluli. 2018. "Forward." In *My Home, My Body and My Dreams: Reflections by African LGBTQI Refugees in South Africa*, edited by People Against Suffering, Oppression and Poverty (PASSOP), 1–2. Cape Town: Friedrich Naumann Stiftung. https://drive.google.com/file/d/1d_QAZb-Sp3tn9A-RQj97H3iQTh4mTyfR/view.

Chutel, Lynsey. 2017. "Johannesburg Wants to Be a 'World Class African City' – Just Not for African Foreigners." *Quartz Africa*, 28 July 2017. https://qz.com/africa/1039889/johannesburg-wants-to-be-a-world-class-african-city-just-not-for-african-foreigners/.

Collison, Carl. 2018. "Homeless Trans Folk Out in the Cold." *M&G Online*, 20 April 2018. https://mg.co.za/article/2018-04-20-00-homeless-trans-folk-out-in-the-cold/.

———. 2019. "Africans Say SA's Queer 'Haven' Is Hell." *M&G Online*, 15 February 2019. https://mg.co.za/article/2019-02-15-00-africans-say-sas-queer-haven-is-hell/.

Crush, Jonathan, and Vincent Williams, eds. 2001. "Making Up the Numbers: Measuring 'Illegal Immigration' to South Africa." Southern African Migration Project, Migration Policy Brief no. 3 (January).

DHA (Department of Home Affairs). 2019. "Department of Home Affairs, Pretoria: Desmond Tutu Refugee Reception Centre." Pretoria: DHA. http://www.dha.gov.za/index.php/contact-us/24-refugee-centres/29-pretoria.

eNCA. 2018. "Red Ants Evict People in Randburg Flatlands." eNCA, 17 April 2018. https://www.enca.com/south-africa/watch-red-ants-evict-occupants-in-windsor-east.

Held, Nina. 2015. "Comfortable and Safe Spaces? Gender, Sexuality and 'Race' in Night-Time Leisure Spaces." *Emotion, Space and Society* 14: 33–42.

Hiropoulos, Alexandra. 2017. "Migration and Detention in South Africa: A Review of the Applicability and Impact of the Legislative Framework on Foreign Nationals." Policy Brief 18. Johannesburg: African Centre for Migration and Society.

Husakouskaya, Nadzeya. 2015. "Becoming a Transgender/Intersex Internal Migrant in Urban Gauteng: Challenges and Experiences of Transition while Seeking Access to Medical Service." Master's dissertation, Erasmus Mundus.

———. 2016. "Queering Mobility in Urban Gauteng: Transgender Internal Migrants and Their Experiences of 'Transition' in Johannesburg and Pretoria." *Urban Forum* 28 (1): 91–110.

Khan, Fatima, and Megan Lee. 2018. "Policy Shifts in the Asylum Process in South Africa Resulting in Hidden Refugees and Asylum Seekers." *African Human Mobility Review* 4 (2): 1205–25.

Khumalo, Siphumelele. 2017. "Red Ants Terror." *IOL News*, 9 October 2017. https://www.iol.co.za/the-star/red-ants-terror-11524006.

Kollman, Kelly, and Matthew Waites. 2009. "The Global Politics of Lesbian, Gay, Bisexual and Transgender Human Rights: An Introduction." *Contemporary Politics* 15 (1): 1–17.

Landau, Lauren. 2018. "Xenophobia in South Africa: Why It's Time to Unsettle Narratives about Migrants." University of the Witwatersrand (website), 7 September 2018. https://www.wits.ac.za/news/latest-news/in-their-own-words/2018/2018-09/xenophobia-in-south-africa-why-its-time-to-unsettle-narratives-about-migrants.html.

Matebeni, Zethu. 2011a. "Exploring Black Lesbian Sexualities and Identities in Johannesburg." PhD thesis, University of the Witwatersrand.

———. 2011b. "TRACKS: Researching Sexualities Walking about the City of Johannesburg."
In *African Sexualities: A Reader*, edited by Sylvia Tamale, 50–7.
Cape Town: Pambazuka Press.

Meny-Gibert, Sarah, and Sintha Chiumia. 2016. "Factsheet: Where Do South Africa's
International Migrants Come From?" Africa Check, 16 August 2016. https://africacheck.
org/factsheets/geography-migration/.

Mlilo, Silindile, and Jean Pierre Misago. 2019. "Xenophobic Violence in South Africa:
1994–2018 – An Overview." African Centre for Migration and Society, March 2019. http://
www.xenowatch.ac.za/special-report-march-2019/.

Narsee, Aarti J. 2013. "World-Class African City? You're Kidding." *TimesLive*, 10 July 2013.
https://www.timeslive.co.za/news/south-africa/2013-07-10-world-class-african-city-
youre-kidding/.

Nicolson, Greg, and Thapelo Lekgowa. 2013. "Operation Clean Sweep: Not Just a Clean-Up
but a Purge of the Poor." *Daily Maverick*, 15 November 2013. https://www.dailymaverick.
co.za/article/2013-11-15-operation-clean-sweep-not-just-a-clean-up-but-a-purge-
of-the-poor/.

ORAM (Organization for Refuge, Asylum and Migration). 2013. "Blind Alleys Part III: A
Tri-Country Comparative Analysis: Mexico, South Africa, and Uganda."
Minneapolis: ORAM.

Peberdy, Sally. 2009. *Selecting Immigrants: Nationalism and National Identity in South
Africa's Immigration Policies, 1910–1998*. Johannesburg: Wits University Press.

Peberdy, Sally, Jonathan Crush, and Ntombikayise Msibi. 2004. "Migrants in the City of
Johannesburg: A Report for the City of Johannesburg." Johannesburg: South African
Migration Project.

Rink, Bradley M. 2013. "Qu(e)erying Cape Town: Touring Africa's 'Gay Capital' with the Pink
Map." In *Tourism in the Global South: Heritage, Identities and Development*, edited by
João Sarmento and Eduardo Brito-Henriques, 66–90. University of Lisbon: Centro de
Estudos Geográficos.

Rushin, Daniel. 2017. "Zuma Launches Desmond Tutu Refugee Centre." *News24*, 17 February
2017. https://www.news24.com/SouthAfrica/News/zuma-launches-desmond-tutu-
refugee-centre-20170217.

Sasha. 2008. "Interview with 'Sasha'." Gender DynamiX Collection (GAL108), Gay
and Lesbian Memory in Action Archive, William Cullen Library, University of the
Witwatersrand.

Shakhsari, Sima. 2014. "The Queer Time of Death: Temporality, Geopolitics, and Refugee
Rights." *Sexualities* 17 (8): 998–1015.

Sonke Gender Justice. 2018. "Why Is the Cape Town RRO Being Re-Opened in 2018?"
    Sonke Gender Justice (blog). Accessed 1 April 2018. https://genderjustice.org.za/card/
    the-cape-town-refugee-reception-office-and-south-africas-asylum-policy/why-is-
    the-cape-town-rro-being-re-opened-in-2018/.

Statistics SA. 2018. "Statistical Release: Mid-Year Population Estimates." Pretoria: Statistics
    South Africa.

11 EVERYDAY URBANISMS OF FEAR IN JOHANNESBURG'S PERIPHERY: THE CASE OF SOL PLAATJE SETTLEMENT

KHANGELANI MOYO

One night in 2017 I visited relatives in Bramfischerville, on the western edge of Sol Plaatje, an economically depressed quasi-formal settlement located between Roodepoort and Soweto on the outskirts of Johannesburg. I stayed until late at night and, on leaving, my cousin's instructions were as follows:

> Here in Bramfischerville phase two, we do not have criminals anymore, it is safe, you can walk at night without any problems. The criminals that were troubling us were necklaced by the residents last year and since then we do not have issues of crime, the criminals are afraid. However, on your way, avoid Durban Deep [Sol Plaatje], it is not safe, that is where all the criminals are. They will hijack and rob you or, even worse, they may kill you. Rather, go through Bramfischerville phase one and drive straight to Main Reef Road and you'll be on your way to Johannesburg.[1]

The instruction from my cousin is still vivid in my mind as I remember his demeanour and the concern in his eyes. It is a fear that the residents of Sol Plaatje live with. While my cousin and I live outside the area and can take steps to avoid passing through Sol Plaatje at night, those who live in the settlement do not have an alternative: this space is home to them and their children.

There have been numerous studies conducted in Sol Plaatje since its inception in the late 1990s. These have focused on a range of issues, including HIV prevalence, how people living with HIV cope with their everyday realities, and the treatment regimens that they adopt (see, for example, Decoteau 2008; Carrasco, Vearey, and Drimie 2011). Others have focused on the interlinked livelihood systems of internal migrants from rural parts of South Africa and how they remain connected with their areas of origin while setting roots in the urban environment (see, for instance, Carrasco, Vearey, and Drimie 2011; Vearey et al. 2010). In their work on urban health in Johannesburg, Joanna Vearey et al. (2010) use the example of Sol Plaatje to argue that place (physical location) is central to understanding intra-urban inequalities in the context of migration and HIV. They compare the living conditions of Sol Plaatje, which they describe as peripheral, and those of the inner city of Johannesburg, which they describe as centrally located in relation to service provision. They argue: 'Migrants residing on the periphery of the city are found to experience challenges in accessing water, sanitation, electricity and refuse collection. Those residing in the central city, however, are significantly more likely to be able to access basic services' (Vearey et al. 2010, 699). The point made here is that, by virtue of being informal and located in a peripheral space, far from the core areas of economic activity, people in Sol Plaatje are likely to suffer limitations in accessing the city and the social services guaranteed by the South African Constitution.

In addition to academic writers who have looked at poor service provision and the burden of HIV in the settlement, authors have discussed the informal gold-mining activities of the zamazamas in the area, particularly the associated danger and criminality (see, for example, Nhlengetwa and Hein 2015; Jinnah 2016).[2] The area is attractive to zamazamas owing to a long history of mining dating back to the discovery of gold in Johannesburg in 1886. Informal mining activities have intensified since the cessation of formal mining in the late 1990s. According to Kgothatso Nhlengetwa and Kim Hein, informal miners in the area of the defunct Durban Deep gold mine 'gain access to the abandoned underground mine via old access portals and ventilation shafts, reprocess the surface slime dams, waste dumps or tailings, or pan for gold in small polluted streams that emanate from these' (2015, 3).

Studies of Sol Plaatje have also cast a spotlight on the plight of the urban poor and created nodes on which to build or further deepen an understanding of the lives of people on the margins of large urban regions such as Gauteng, the densely urbanised province in which Johannesburg can be found. In this work I use data from conversations with residents of Sol Plaatje, field observations, semi-structured interviews and focus group discussions to engage with the anxieties of people in the settlement and to interrogate their lived realities. After discussing the context, development and history of Sol Plaatje since its inception, I identify key characteristics of this urban peripheral settlement that produce social vulnerabilities and related anxieties for poor urban migrants, both internal and cross-border. This discussion is informed by issues shared by the residents, which include fear of crime related to the activities of artisanal zamazama miners and anxieties about health concerns related to the mining in the area. Lastly, I connect the anxieties and fears experienced by residents of Sol Plaatje to the general context of Johannesburg and argue that their fears and incidences of ill health are linked to the affective, physical, economic and socio-cultural conditions of the settlement.

SOL PLAATJE IN CONTEXT

Sol Plaatje has gone through numerous transitions. Originally built as part of the vibrant Durban Roodepoort Deep mining precinct, which started operations in the late 1880s following the discovery of gold in Johannesburg, the settlement became a disused and derelict wasteland when mining operations ceased in the 1990s. More recently it has become a built-up Reconstruction and Development Programme (RDP) settlement teetering between formality and informality.[3] Established in 1999 in its current form, Sol Plaatje is located south of Roodeport on former mining land. According to the 2011 census figures, the population stands at 9141 residents consisting of three groups evicted from different informal settlements in Johannesburg.[4] The first contingent came from Maraisburg and settled in 1999, while the second were from Wilgespruit in Honeydew (Corruption Watch 2012). The third and largest group of approximately 1500 families settled in 2002 after they were evicted by court order from Mandelaville informal settlement in Diepkloof, Soweto, at the instigation of the City of Johannesburg (Wilson 2005). Media reports at the time noted that the city sought an eviction order to pave the way for a multi-million rand business development and the court ordered the city to find alternative accommodation for the evictees (see, for example, Ndaba 2002a, 2002b).

Present-day Sol Plaatje is a growing low-cost housing settlement, with renovated mine hostels and RDP housing units replacing the original shacks, though part of the informal settlement still exists in the vicinity and is home to many people without access to RDP housing. They include foreign migrants as well as internal migrants who arrived after the completion of the process of vetting and allocating existing RDP units. The people of Sol Plaatje are ethnically diverse and, according to their own understanding, all the major South African ethnic groups are represented, even though there is a larger contingent of Xhosa-language speakers.[5]

A NOTE ON METHODS

In engaging the different aspects of residents' lives in Sol Plaatje, I draw from observations and historical memory. I have been part of research studies in Sol Plaatje intermittently since 2008 (Vearey et al. 2011; Vearey, Nunez, and Palmary 2009). For the purposes of this work, I held key informant interviews with the clinic manager, the former sister in charge of the clinic and the local NGO representatives, and conducted two focus group discussions with the residents of the settlement. The idea behind the interviews with the clinic manager emanated from an interest in the health and well-being of residents of Sol Plaatje and a desire to understand the main health concerns within the settlement – for example, the most common ailments that people seek treatment for. The local NGO, Mandelaville Crisis Centre (MCC), has been working in Sol Plaatje since 2002 and provides HIV/AIDS counselling and testing services, home-based care for HIV-positive community members, and a range of other skills development training services in the area.[6] They have rich knowledge of the Sol Plaatje community and provided valuable information pertaining to the development of the settlement as well as the key issues that the community grapples with. The NGO also assisted with the recruitment of community members for the two focus group discussions. In addition, I held informal conversations with local residents on each of my field visits to the settlement, extending over 12 months between 2017 and 2018. These conversations were unstructured and included ad hoc encounters with residents on the streets in which they talked about their lives in Sol Plaatje and how the settlement has changed over time as well as the problems that people face in their everyday lives. The individual interviews and informal conversations were held in English and isiZulu while the focus group discussions allowed the participants to speak in isiZulu, English, isiXhosa and Sesotho, which are the main languages spoken in Sol Plaatje. All the recorded interviews were transcribed into English.

PROXIMITY TO ARTISANAL MINING AREAS AND FEAR OF CRIME

There is a sizeable corpus of literature that discusses the effects of natural resources on the economic performance of certain countries as well as the corruption and conflicts associated with their exploitation (see, for instance, Van der Ploeg 2011; Kronenberg 2004; Haber and Menaldo 2011). This literature often focuses on country-level examples and discusses what is commonly referred to as the 'natural resource curse' where the presence of natural resources yields negative outcomes for the economies of the countries where they are found (Auty 1993).

While Sol Plaatje is not a country-level example, the natural resource curse does apply here and involves the informal gold-mining activities of the zamazamas, who often come from outside the community. Thus, the location of Sol Plaatje in the vicinity of the former Durban Roodepoort Deep gold mine creates problems in at least two ways. One is the issue of artisanal mining and the other is the health implications for the population because of dust storms and hazardous waste.

As for the zamazamas, it is important to note that I am discussing them in the context of the experiences of the Sol Plaatje residents and how they are seen to have an effect on community well-being and levels of crime in the area. While they form an important part of society in Sol Plaatje, the intricacies of their activities have been better dealt with and documented in the literature that focuses on artisanal mining, especially in the Durban Deep area (see, for example, Jinnah 2016; Thornton 2014; Nhlengetwa and Hein 2015). Researchers have noted that many of the artisanal miners are irregular migrants from neighbouring countries like Zimbabwe, Mozambique and Lesotho (Thornton 2014; Nhlengetwa and Hein 2015). While academic and media accounts of artisanal mining in the area often associate it with criminality, as Zaheera Jinnah (2016) and Nhlengetwa and Hein (2015) observe, Robert Thornton cautions against what he calls the 'misrepresentation by the

South African press and government'. Thornton's argument is that there is more to this practice than alleged criminality and that the zamazamas 'are better described as "artisanal" miners and entrepreneurs who create significant numbers of jobs and economic value for many local communities' (Thornton 2014, 127). There is no disputing the economic value created by artisanal mining in terms of jobs and adding money to local economies, yet Nhlengetwa and Hein sound a cautionary note, arguing, 'From our study of Zama-Zama activities in the footprint of the Durban Deep mine, it is clear that mining forms an invasive livelihood rather than an alternative livelihood' (2015, 3). This is important in the context of Sol Plaatje owing to its proximity to the zamazama mining activities. Nonetheless, this form of mining is not accessible to everyone in the community and is often the preserve of defined groups of foreign nationals and South Africans from outside the area. None of the interviewees in my research mentioned the participation of South Africans from Sol Plaatje in artisanal mining. These activities are observed from a distance by the community and are seen as a source of fear and crime within the area.

Residents speak of a feared group of artisanal miners known as the BaSotho from Lesotho who control one of the shafts in the settlement. One male participant in a focus group discussion had the following to say:

> Another thing, crimes are different. So if you speak of those BaSothos guarding
> the shaft, some of those things may not affect the community directly … Many
> people might see it that way, including those shaft guards, so if you take action
> to report them they may see it as a threat to their 'peaceful livelihood means',
> so it's those people who in meetings go behind the community to tip off those
> mine shaft operators on who is pushing for their removal, which places com-
> munity members at risk. So the shaft case needs real men not cowards.[7]

The fear of the BaSotho miners who guard the illegal mine shaft was palpable among focus group participants, and the subject was discussed in hushed tones out of concern that some of the participants might pass on information to them. It is important to highlight that, due to its location on former gold-mining land, Sol Plaatje is a proverbial mecca for artisanal gold miners, who live in the informal settlement adjacent to the RDP houses. The settlement lies within the geographical boundaries of Sol Plaatje, yet the informal gold miners are not integrated in the community and do not participate in meetings and other community-building activities. In other words, as Phefumula Nyoni (2017) noted, they form their own networks of solidarity and social support along ethnic and friendship ties in the areas where they operate. The informal mining landscape is riddled with contestations over the control of mining rights to specific shafts, and networks of solidarity ensure the protection of each member's rights and safety against rival groups and criminals who prey on the zamazamas (Nyoni 2017; Munakamwe 2017).

According to the residents, there are occasional visits or raids by the police and there is widespread suspicion that when such visits happen, it is because someone has made a report. That is why the focus group participants and the general public are afraid of being fingered as informants. The preceding quotation from the focus group emphasises that various crimes are seen differently. Informal gold mining is for some residents a crime that does not have a direct consequence for the community, apart from creating secluded spaces where residents are not permitted to intrude. For instance, informal miners are not mentioned as suspects in robberies and petty crimes that directly affect the Sol Plaatje community. The sense is that if people can avoid the informal mining areas and not involve the police, there will not be problems between residents and informal miners. In other words, the zamazamas go about their business without bothering the community unless they are provoked or the police are called out to deal with them. Some residents, however, see this as a limitation on their freedom of movement. For example, one female community member expressed her displeasure in the following terms: 'These people have installed their shack by the mine shaft which they are guarding with arms and we can no longer pass through the place as it is now dangerous. The Sothos who are always guarding their shaft make it very unsafe for us and our children; it will help to close down these illegal mines.'[8]

Considering the sentiments of community members, there is a growing disagreement about how to 'deal with' the informal miners. There is a sense that they are dangerous and should be removed from the community, yet there is also a fear of retaliation by the miners if the police were to be called. For instance, one focus group respondent said:

> It happens, mainly because you are protecting your life, we are talking of crime involving hard-core criminals who are armed. For instance there are Sothos across by the edge of our community who own a shaft and gunfire is heard from

that place. As I passed by, they called me and one of them said that there is some-body who called the police to come after them and the police burnt down their tent with all their belongings. So, he said to me, I suspect that woman who stays there [pointing at the place] and if I discover that it is her, I will deal with her.[9]

The anxiety generated by the presence of the zamazamas in Sol Plaatje is, I would argue, of a particular nature and deserves to be analysed in different terms from the more general emotion that is encapsulated by the fear of crime (FOC) thesis. This concept has been discussed in various forms for decades, with some authors arguing that it 'pertains to a perception about the relative sense of safety against a possible crime' (Piscitelli and Perrella 2017, 180). Rachael Collins argues that 'fear of crime (FOC) is a complex construct that is used to describe a range of both psychological and social reactions to per-ceived threats of crime and/or victimisation' (2016, 21).

Academic researchers have noted that fear of crime is often unrelated to the actual experience of being a victim of crime, and is largely driven by perception (see, for instance, Mistry 2006; Collins 2016; Piscitelli and Perrella 2017; Allen 2002). As Duxita Mistry (2006) remarks, the 2003 South African victims of crime survey noted that levels of crime had declined between 1998 and 2003, yet the fear of crime seemed to have risen. Within the South African context, the effects of crime and the fear generated by criminal activities are disproportionately distributed across society, and the manner in which people react differs in accordance with their socio-economic positions. For example, Danielle Allen argues, 'Fear of crime in Johannesburg has resulted in higher walls, increased security, and fenced-off neighbour-hoods which is reinforcing the compartmentalised nature of the geography of a post-apartheid city' (2002, 55). Charlotte Lemanski supports this proposi-tion and argues that the fear of crime in South Africa creates 'architectures of fear' in which 'individuals assess risk and modify behaviour and urban form to eliminate fear and minimise crime' (2004, 101). These discussions of fear in the urban environment speak to a spatialised notion of city-making in response to crime. Within the Sol Plaatje context, there are two sources of crime-related fear and anxiety: one is the general crime level, which is demon-strable in all of Johannesburg, and the other is generated by the activities of the zamazamas, and is particular to Sol Plaatje and possibly other areas where informal mining activities take place.

THE FEAR OF CRIME IN SOL PLAATJE

The opinions of the residents are split when it comes to crime and safety. There are some who believe that criminals are external to the settlement while others are of the view that criminals are locals and they belong right in the heart of Sol Plaatje: they live with members of the community, walk with them, drink with them and rob them during the night. Thandeka, a middle-aged female resident, expressed a more imaginative explanation of the places where criminals come from when she said, 'I think criminals are just roaming freely. I feel that whenever I read in newspapers of criminals having escaped from law enforcement, they come to hide in this place. We are not safe here.'[10] Thandeka's conviction that criminals hide in Sol Plaatje stems from the community's experiences with law enforcement agents, who do not respond timeously when criminal activity is reported. Her concerns are confirmed by Isaac, an elderly male focus group participant, who pointed in the direction of the informal settlement when talking about the places where criminals come from and bemoaned the lack of police action in dealing with criminality. He stated:

> We must not play hide-and-seek on this matter. These criminals come from here [pointing in the direction of the informal settlement], they are there and we know them here but it is very hard to identify them, and when we call the police we are told there are only two vehicles that are based in Mathole [a neighbouring suburb]; they can't attend to us. For example, last week we caught a criminal jumping over a neighbour's yard at around midnight, and when we phoned the police to attend to us they informed us that we need to see what to do about the person as there was no police van that was going to come to Sol Plaatje. We realised that if we killed this person we would be in trouble, so we had to release him, so there was no police response to this case.[11]

Whether the threats are perceived or real, Sol Plaatje is a space where people are uncertain, afraid, but not sure of what exactly, just a general anxiety that pervades the air as you drive or walk through the area. The afternoons are said to be safe; but at night the criminals come out and they prey on anyone who is on the street.

SPATIAL BREEDING OF ANXIETY IN SOL PLAATJE

There is also concern about the location of the settlement on former mining land, leading to anxieties regarding the health of the population. As I concluded the focus group discussion with residents, an elderly woman walked over to me and said, 'Wherever you go, please, as researchers, do some research and test the suitability of this land for human habitation. This place has minerals and is contaminated.' The request took me by surprise, but having been to the settlement intermittently in the last ten years, I understood the apprehension written in her eyes. The evidence of gold mining is easy to see as the mine dumps rise prominently in the background. The concern raised about contamination of the land is important in the light of reports that some of the mine dumps in Johannesburg contain very high levels of radioactive waste and are a health hazard for nearby communities (Balch 2015; Stassen 2015; Bench Marks Foundation 2017a). The connection between informal artisanal mining activities and the contamination of the land makes for a disturbing possibility since the zamazamas do not only work underground but also mine the uranium-rich abandoned tailings on the surface. Reports have noted that the gold-bearing reefs in Johannesburg also yielded large quantities of uranium and these were disposed of in the mine dumps together with other non-utilised material. Uranium breaks down into radon gas, which is a carcinogen responsible for causing lung cancer (Bench Marks Foundation 2017b; Stassen 2015).

Apart from the health risks posed by the mine dumps, there is also the danger of mercury (Hg) emissions into the environment, since it is the main chemical used by artisanal miners in gold processing (see, for instance, Telmer and Veiga 2009; Drace et al. 2012). Globally, artisanal miners are the largest source of mercury pollution, and according to Wells Utembe et al. (2015), South Africa has one of the highest rates of mercury emission into the environment.[12] 'Inhalation, ingestion, or dermal absorption of Hg can result in neurological and behavioural disorders, tremors, insomnia, hallucinations, memory loss, neuromuscular effects, headaches and cognitive and motor dysfunction' (Utembe et al. 2015, 1214). Consequently, the unregulated disposal of mercury may have catastrophic consequences for communities like Sol Plaatje that are located close to areas with active zamazama mining activities.

During the latter part of the winter season, residents of Sol Plaatje spray water in their yards to mitigate the effects of dust storms. They complain that the air quality is bad and causes respiratory complications. The clinic manager confirmed residents' concerns, highlighting the main diseases that people seek help for: 'Mostly it's coughing, tuberculosis and skin problems. But in terms of coughing, it is mostly caused by the dust in the area, hence many patients coming in for that.'[13] The prevalence of respiratory ailments in areas with mine dumps was also highlighted in a three-year study of four Soweto townships by the Bench Marks Foundation (2017a) in which over 56 per cent of the surveyed population reported suffering from respiratory diseases. In 1998 a newspaper reported the dust problems caused by the mine dumps in the Meadowlands area of Soweto, which is 6 km from Sol Plaatje. The report noted: 'Motorists driving through the sprawling Black township of Soweto at times have to switch on their car lights during the day to drive through the thick dust of pollution descending on the settlement' (see Mutume 1998).

CONCLUSION

The residents of Sol Plaatje are anxious about their future in the urban environment and exasperated by the promise of freedom, which for some is yet to materialise as employment opportunities and decent accommodation. Numerous academic accounts have highlighted as concerns both the unemployment levels and the location of the settlement far from economic activity. While Sol Plaatje is a magnet for informal artisanal miners who profit from mining the gold tailings, it does not provide similar benefits and hope for local residents. Instead it is a space that breeds fear owing to criminality and the perception that law enforcement is absent or, at worst, that the government has forgotten about the community. The area also breeds anxiety because of its location on former mining land, which has resulted in problems such as dust storms and respiratory infections, especially during the winter months. For many of the residents the future is bleak and uncertain, yet they have to continue living with the realities of Sol Plaatje, an environment that breeds both fear and ill health.

NOTES

1   Necklacing refers to a form of mob justice which was commonly used in South Africa during the struggle against apartheid, where a car tyre is forced over the victim's shoulders, mimicking the act of wearing a necklace (see, for example, Fihlani 2011).

The tyre is doused with petrol and set alight. During the apartheid struggle necklacing was used against those seen as informers of the regime. In the present day it is commonly used in townships to fight alleged crime.

2 Zamazamas are informal artisanal miners and the name literally means 'to try'. Their mining activities are largely considered illegal in terms of state law, and 'for the most part, Zama-Zama miners are disconnected from the community' (Nhlengetwa and Hein 2015, 2).

3 RDP refers to the Reconstruction and Development Programme initiated by the first democratic government of South Africa in 1994. The houses are 'developed by government and allocated to beneficiaries with a household income of less than R3500. Beneficiaries of this subsidy receive a once-off grant for land, basic services (water and sanitation) and the house (top structure)' (Landman and Napier 2010, 302).

4 https://census2011.adrianfrith.com/place/798026001.

5 South Africa has nine major African ethnic groups, namely, Zulu, Xhosa, Venda, Tsonga, Tswana, Sotho, Pedi, Ndebele and Swati.

6 http://mandelaville.org.za/home.html.

7 Focus group held with residents of Sol Plaatje, Johannesburg, 13 June 2018.

8 Focus group held with residents of Sol Plaatje, Johannesburg, 13 June 2018.

9 Male focus group respondent, Sol Plaatje, Johannesburg, 14 June 2018.

10 Focus group respondent, Sol Plaatje, Johannesburg, 13 June 2018.

11 Focus group discussion held in Sol Plaatje, Johannesburg, 13 June 2018.

12 https://www.epa.gov/international-cooperation/reducing-mercury-pollution-artisanal-and-small-scale-gold-mining.

13 Interview with the Sol Plaatje clinic manager.

REFERENCES

Allen, Danielle Burger. 2002. "Race, Crime and Social Exclusion: A Qualitative Study of White Women's Fear of Crime in Johannesburg." *Urban Forum* 13 (3): 53–79.

Auty, Richard. 1993. *Sustaining Development in Mineral Economies: The Resource Curse Thesis.* London: Routledge.

Balch, Oliver. 2015. "Radioactive City: How Johannesburg's Townships Are Paying for Its Mining Past." *The Guardian*, 6 July 2015. http://www.theguardian.com/cities/2015/jul/06/radioactive-city-how-johannesburgs-townships-are-paying-for-its-mining-past.

Bench Marks Foundation. 2017a. "Respiratory Ailments Associated with Living Close to Mine Dumps." Bench Marks Foundation, 29 August 2017. https://www.bench-marks.org.za.

Bench Marks Foundation. 2017b. "Soweto Report: 'Waiting to Inhale': A Survey of
    Household Health in Four Mine-Affected Communities." *Policy Gap* 12. Johannesburg:
    Bench Marks Foundation.

Carrasco, Lorena Nunez, Jo Vearey, and Scott Drimie. 2011. "Who Cares? HIV-Related
    Sickness, Urban–Rural Linkages, and the Gendered Role of Care in Return Migration in
    South Africa." *Gender and Development* 19 (1): 105–14.

Collins, Rachael E. 2016. "Addressing the Inconsistencies in Fear of Crime Research:
    A Meta-Analytic Review." *Journal of Criminal Justice* 47: 21–31.

Corruption Watch. 2012. "Informal Settlers Homeless as Housing Dept Stalls." *Corruption
    Watch*, 9 May 2012. https://www.corruptionwatch.org.za.

Decoteau, Claire Laurier. 2008. "The Bio-Politics of HIV/AIDS in Post-Apartheid South
    Africa." PhD thesis, University of Michigan.

Drace, Kevin, Adam M. Kiefer, Marcello M. Veiga, Matt K. Williams, Benjamin Ascari, Kassandra
    A. Knapper, Kaitlyn M. Logan, Vanessa M. Breslin, Ashley Skidmore, and Daniel Bolt
    et al. 2012. "Mercury-Free, Small-Scale Artisanal Gold Mining in Mozambique: Utilization
    of Magnets to Isolate Gold at Clean Tech Mine." *Journal of Cleaner Production* 32: 88–95.

Fihlani, Pumza. 2011. "Is Necklacing Returning to South Africa?" *BBC News*. Accessed
    30 January 2019. https://www.bbc.com/news/world-africa-14914526.

Haber, Stephen, and Victor Menaldo. 2011. "Do Natural Resources Fuel Authoritarianism?
    A Reappraisal of the Resource Curse." *American Political Science Review* 105 (1): 1–26.

Jinnah, Zaheera. 2016. "Between a Rock and a Hard Place: Informal Artisanal Gold Mining in
    Johannesburg." *Africa at LSE: African Perspectives on Migration*. http://blogs.lse.ac.uk/
    africaatlse/2016/01/26/between-a-rock-and-a-hard-place-informal-artisanal-gold-
    mining-in-johannesburg/.

Kronenberg, Tobias. 2004. "The Curse of Natural Resources in the Transition Economies."
    Economics of Transition 12 (3): 399–426.

Landman, Karina, and Mark Napier. 2010. "Waiting for a House or Building Your Own?
    Reconsidering State Provision, Aided and Unaided Self-Help in South Africa." *Habitat
    International* 34: 299–305.

Lemanski, Charlotte. 2004. "A New Apartheid? The Spatial Implications of Fear of Crime in
    Cape Town, South Africa." *Environment and Urbanization* 16 (2): 101–12.

Mistry, Duxita. 2006. "Falling Crime, Rising Fear: 2003 National Victims of Crime Survey."
    South African Crime Quarterly 8: 17–24.

Munakamwe, Janet. 2017. "Zamazama: Livelihood Strategies, Mobilisation and Resistance
    in Johannesburg, South Africa." In *Mining Africa: Law, Environment, Society and Politics*

in Historical Multidisciplinary Perspectives, edited by Artwell Nhemachena and Tapiwa Warikandwa, 155–86. Bamenda, Cameroon: Langaa Research and Publishing CIG.

Mutume, Gumisai. 1998. "Environment-South Africa: Pollution Descends on Soweto." *Inter-Press Service*. Accessed 25 January 2019. http://www.ipsnews.net/.

Ndaba, Baldwin. 2002a. "Mandelaville Squatters Begin Forced Move." *IOL News*. Accessed 25 January 2019. https://www.iol.co.za/news/south-africa/mandelaville-squatters-begin-forced-move-80269.

———. 2002b. "Residents Cheer Squatters' Eviction." *IOL News*. Accessed 25 January 2019. https://www.iol.co.za/news/south-africa/residents-cheer-squatters-eviction-80357.

Nhlengetwa, Kgothatso, and Kim A.A. Hein. 2015. "Zama-Zama Mining in the Durban Deep/Roodepoort Area of Johannesburg, South Africa: An Invasive or Alternative Livelihood?" *Extractive Industries and Society* 2 (1): 1–3.

Nyoni, Phefumula. 2017. "Unsung Heroes? An Anthropological Approach into the Experiences of 'Zamazamas' in Johannesburg, South Africa." In *Mining Africa: Law, Environment, Society and Politics in Historical Multidisciplinary Perspectives*, edited by Artwell Nhemachena and Tapiwa Warikandwa, 133–54. Bamenda, Cameroon: Langaa Research and Publishing CIG.

Piscitelli, Anthony, and Andrea M.L. Perrella. 2017. "Fear of Crime and Participation in Associational Life." *Social Science Journal* 54 (2): 179–90.

Stassen, Wilma. 2015. "Gauteng's Mine Dumps Brimming with Radioactive Uranium." *Health-e News*, 15 October 2015. https://www.health-e.org.za/2015/10/15/gautengs-mine-dumps-brimming-with-radioactive-uranium/.

Telmer, Kevin H., and Marcello M. Veiga. 2009. "World Emissions of Mercury from Artisanal and Small Scale Gold Mining." In *Mercury Fate and Transport in the Global Atmosphere*, edited by Robert Mason and Nicola Pirrone, 131–72. Boston: Springer.

Thornton, Robert. 2014. "Zamazama, 'Illegal' Artisanal Miners, Misrepresented by the South African Press and Government." *Extractive Industries and Society* 1 (2): 127–9.

Utembe, W., Elaine M. Faustman, Puleng Matatiele, and Mary Gulumian. 2015. "Hazards Identified and the Need for Health Risk Assessment in the South African Mining Industry." *Human and Experimental Toxicology* 34 (12): 1212–21.

Van der Ploeg, Frederick. 2011. "Natural Resources: Curse or Blessing?" *Journal of Economic Literature* 49 (2): 366–420.

Vearey, Joanna, Lorena Nunez, and Ingrid Palmary. 2009. *HIV, Migration and Urban Food Security: Exploring the Linkages*. Johannesburg: Regional Network on AIDS, Livelihoods and Food Security (RENEWAL).

Vearey, Joanna, Ingrid Palmary, Liz Thomas, Lorena Nunez, and Scott Drimie. 2010. "Urban Health in Johannesburg: The Importance of Place in Understanding Intra-Urban Inequalities in a Context of Migration and HIV." *Health and Place* 16 (4): 694–702.

Vearey, Joanna, Marlise Richter, Lorena Nunez, and Khangelani Moyo. 2011. "South African HIV/AIDS Programming Overlooks Migration, Urban Livelihoods, and Informal Workplaces." *African Journal of AIDS Research* 10 (sup1): 381–91.

Wilson, Stuart. 2005. *Relocation and Access to Schools in Sol Plaatje*. Johannesburg: Centre for Applied Legal Studies, University of the Witwatersrand.

12 INNER-CITY ANXIETIES: FEAR OF CRIME, GETTING BY AND DISCONNECTED URBAN LIVES

AIDAN MOSSELSON

Fear of crime, real and imagined, is a defining feature of contemporary life in Johannesburg. In the inner city, where crime remains prevalent, fear plays a decisive role in shaping residents' experiences of the area, the ways they move through it, engage with public spaces and with each other. These fears contribute to shaping and restricting their urban subjectivities and ways of living the city. At the same time, broader structural issues are obscured or masked by 'talk of crime' (Caldeira 2000). The ways in which residents articulate fears and concerns about crime also express their positionings within the inner city's social order. In many cases, residents fixate on issues of crime in the absence of long-term attachments to the area or channels for expressing collective identities and aspirations. Intense regulation inside residential buildings shuts down potential avenues for engagement and limits residents' sense of agency. Furthermore, precarious and stressful living conditions and the pressures of everyday life propel residents to disengage and eschew forms of identification, both with each other and with the spaces in which they live. In place of attachments to the area and their neighbours, residents fall back on discourses about crime and longings for physical security when articulating their aspirations. It therefore becomes apparent that crime limits or restricts people's experiences of contemporary Johannesburg in very real ways, but that anxieties about crime are also symptomatic of broader societal inequalities and forms of stratification, and obscure more troubling issues around belonging and ownership of urban space.

This chapter draws on in-depth, semi-structured interviews with 57 residents living in social or affordable housing developments in inner-city Johannesburg. The interviews were conducted by the author between 2012 and 2013 and formed part of a larger study of the urban regeneration process in the area. Interviews were also conducted with government officials, neighbourhood organisers, housing providers, private security personnel and employees of agencies providing finance for housing development in the inner city. Social housing is rental housing which is partially state-subsidised and provided by non-profit social housing institutions (SHIs); households earning between R3500 and R7000 per month qualify for access. Government subsidises social housing primarily through two grant schemes – the Capital Restructuring Grant and Institutional Subsidy. These cover the initial costs of developing social housing, including purchasing land or buildings and carrying out construction or renovation. They are designed to cover only a portion of the start-up costs, and are intended to act as levers so that SHIs can access private sector finance to complete their projects and cover ongoing operations. Once construction is completed, SHIs are required to finance their operations through effective business strategies and cost-recovery measures. As a result, although they cater to people in lower-income brackets, they run on similar lines to private rental housing companies, and conditions and management practices inside social housing developments are the same as those inside private residential buildings in the inner city.

The private rental market in the inner city is dominated by companies which brand themselves as 'affordable'. They generally cater to households earning between R7000 and R14 000 per month. These households are known as the 'gap market': they earn too much to qualify for state-subsidised social housing but still cannot afford to purchase their own homes through the commercial mortgage market. It is estimated that approximately 30 per cent of South African workers fall within the 'gap market', including teachers, nurses, police officers and government officials, as well as those employed in the mining and manufacturing industries (CAHF 2015). In my study, as Table 12.1 indicates, 27 interviews were conducted with residents living in social housing developments and 30 with residents in affordable housing.

Interviewees were chosen from a random sample of residents who were at home during hours in which I was given access to buildings.[1] All interviewees spoke English, were black African and were predominantly South African, but people hailing from Zimbabwe, Nigeria and the Democratic Republic of Congo were also included. Social and affordable housing developments require residents to have stable, regular forms of income. Therefore, although large proportions of the inner-city population are unemployed or earn their living through informal means, my sample consisted of people involved in a range of formal occupations, including domestic workers, nurses, personal assistants, bank tellers, factory workers, entrepreneurs and small business owners, as well as several stay-at-home parents.

During interviews, residents were asked a range of questions which could shed light on their experiences living in the inner city. They were asked how long they had lived in the area; where they were living previously; why they decided to move to the inner city; what their concerns about the inner city were; what, if anything, they enjoyed about their building and neighbourhood; whether they had perceived any changes in their neighbourhood; how they felt about and interacted with their neighbours; and whether they intended to stay in the inner city over the long term. Because the interviews were open-ended, different lines of discussion could be followed as and when they became necessary.

NAVIGATING THE ANXIOUS CITY

Fear of crime is treated as a bourgeois concern in the majority of urban studies and planning scholarship. This body of work discusses how upper-class fears

Table 12.1: Inner-city buildings in which interviews were conducted

Building name	Type	Number of interviews	Location
Cavendish	Affordable	5	CBD
Constantine	Affordable	4	Hillbrow
Gaelic Mansions	Social	18	Hillbrow
Greatermans	Affordable	6	CBD
Lake Success	Social	9	Hillbrow
Ridge Plaza	Affordable	6	Berea
Rochester	Affordable	9	Jeppe

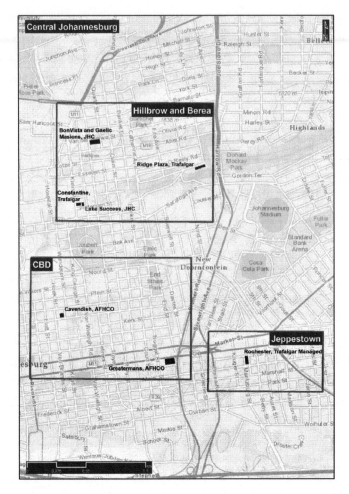

Figure 12.1
Map of the inner city, indicating the locations of buildings in which interviews were conducted

and discourses about crime are usually placeholders for other forms of prejudice and discomfort caused by proximity to 'others' (for example, see Caldeira 2000; Flusty 2002; Lemanski 2006; Sandercock 2005). In Johannesburg's inner city, the majority of the population can be considered as poor or low-to-moderate income earners. According to the 2011 census data, 17 per cent of inner-city households earn between R6366 and R12 816 per month; 21 per cent earn R3500 to R7000 per month; and 49 per cent earn less than R3500 (SERI 2013). These residents fall within a category whose experiences and perceptions about crime have not been extensively researched. Furthermore, while the academic literature pointed to above has generally focused on fear of crime as an expression of white people's racist suspicions and hostilities towards black people (and downplayed the experiences of crime to which people are subject), in the inner city the majority of the population is black.

Despite their general silence in the prevailing literature, poor black people are actually more likely to fall victim to crime and violence, and frequently articulate acute fears and anxieties about this vulnerability. For example, a survey of over 30 000 residents conducted in the greater Gauteng City-Region (GCR) in 2014/15 shows that while concerns about crime are pervasive, with 37 per cent of respondents noting that crime is the biggest problem facing their community and 42 per cent saying that the crime situation in South Africa has deteriorated in recent years, people living in informal settlements reported feeling far more vulnerable to crime than people living in gated communities, formal houses or townhouses (Siteleki, Ballard, and Mosselson 2017). Although these figures do not indicate respondents' race, the continuing apartheid spatial form, in which poverty, physical location and race all overlap, makes it possible to extrapolate racial identities. While it is certainly not the case that all black people in South Africa are poor, it is a fact that the majority of poor people and people living in informal settlements are black (Everatt 2014). Furthermore, residents in poor peripheral parts of the GCR described crime as the biggest challenge confronting their communities with much more regularity than people living in wealthier suburban regions (Siteleki, Ballard, and Mosselson 2017). These figures clearly indicate that crime is a very real concern for poorer (black) communities.

Like informal settlements and former townships, central Johannesburg is home to a majority black, lower-income population, where fear of crime is pervasive. My interviews revealed widespread concerns about safety, and described a social setting that can be characterised by a sense of 'endangerment'. Austin Zeiderman (2016) uses this term to describe how particular urban areas come to be defined by collective atmospheres of fear and risk. The following accounts demonstrate how people come to map spaces of the inner city according to experiences, temporalities and geographies of endangerment.

When comparing the inner city to Soweto, where he is originally from, one resident explains, 'It's very, *very* different 'cause there I know even if I'm in the street at eight o'clock at night, I don't have a problem. But here by six o'clock, seven o'clock, I have to be in the house because it's not safe out there' (Tenant Three, Greatermans). Another tenant living in the central business district (CBD) cautions that 'in town, it's dangerous if you walk at night and all that, but during the day it's safe, you just have to look after yourself … Just to be careful, you mustn't walk outside after eight' (Tenant Four, Greatermans). Living in the inner city, then, necessitates adapting one's routines and movements to prevailing fears and insecurities. Another resident demonstrates this starkly when she explains: 'I saw a person being shot back there at Tudhope Street [one of the main streets in Berea] … It's difficult but you have to learn to deal with it and take care of yourself, you need to put yourself in order; certain time, such things they make you stay in the house' (Tenant Three, Ridge Plaza).

It thus becomes clear that for many people, life in the inner city is lived in relation to feelings of endangerment and anxiety, and their spatial experiences and abilities to use the area and the amenities it offers are circumscribed by these fears. As one Hillbrow resident, who participates in the local Community Policing Forum, explains, 'If you are safe, you feel at home. But the minute if you're not safe you cannot feel at home, you say "no, in this place anything can happen".'[2] Women experience heightened concerns and threats as, even during the day, they are frequently subjected to intrusive and unwelcome comments, touching and harassment on the streets. There has been an improvement in policing in Hillbrow and the CBD, as private security personnel have been deployed and CCTV cameras have been installed to monitor public spaces (see Mosselson 2018). However, the personnel surveilling the streets focus on property-based crimes and elements that detract from the aesthetic quality of the environment, and therefore these pernicious acts go unchecked. This clearly signals how policing efforts in the area concentrate on protecting private property and enhancing the quality (and thus commercial viability) of the environment, while disregarding other pressing social needs and forms of vulnerability. Similarly, residents hailing from other African countries are exposed to South Africa's intense levels of anti-migrant hostility. The volatile situation means that they are in constant states of endangerment; as one resident, originally from Zimbabwe, states, 'You never feel safe in South Africa' (Tenant Eighteen, Gaelic Mansions).

This prevailing sense of endangerment has real consequences for people's experiences of the inner city and the ways in which they engage in public life and relate to others. During the late 1980s and 1990s the area underwent drastic capital flight, demographic change and decline (for various explanations of this process, see Crankshaw and White 1995; Goga 2003; Morris 1999a). What was once zoned exclusively for white people quickly became a predominantly black residential area. This change is significant in terms of South Africa's segregated social geographies, in which apartheid residential patterns largely remain intact, with the majority of black people continuing to live on the margins of large cities, whether in informal settlements, the former townships and newly built RDP communities, or commercial developments (Butcher 2016; Gotz, Wray, and Mubiwa 2014).[3] People generally come to the inner city in search of social mobility, as the area provides better access to economic opportunities, social amenities, transportation networks and public services than former township areas. The changes that have occurred in the inner city therefore stand as one of the few instances of substantive urban transformation and represent the emergence of what Achille Mbembe and Sarah Nuttall (2008) term an 'Afropolis', an urban space which, while built on the remnants of the apartheid past, is home to a 'largely black, highly tensile, intra-African multiculture' (Nuttall 2004, 744). However, the prevalent sense of endangerment in the inner city means that residents are frequently disconnected from the spaces in which they live and, as the quotes above illustrate, drastically limit their movements through the area, particularly avoiding being outside at night. This means that their opportunities to experience urban citizenship in the post-apartheid era – to make something of the city, to stage public forms of social life, or simply to occupy and take space – are circumscribed. The intra-African multiculture is, in fact, shot through with fear, mistrust and social distance which drastically limit the prospects and opportunities for a collective sense of associational life. The situation is exacerbated as endangerment leads residents to be suspicious of one another and to avoid chance encounters with others (Landau and Freemantle 2010; Simone 2008a). A neighbourhood organiser, employed by the Ekhaya Residential City Improvement District, captures this sense of estrangement and relates how it makes organising residents and communal events difficult. She recalls: 'Everyone was minding his or her own business. No one wanted to know what's someone's business. Hence that anonymosity [sic] was what was promoting crime and everything.'

Fear of crime, then, has had significant negative effects on the forms of urban citizenship and experiences that have arisen in the inner city. While substantial changes have occurred and new social relations, identities and ways of inhabiting the area have come into being (Le Roux 2014; Matsipa

2017), opportunities for new urban subjectivities and types of identification have also been constrained. The inner city consequently stands today as a symbol of South Africa's changing social landscape and a setting in which new African forms of urbanity are being realised, as well as a site of fear, anxiety and tense, suspicious social interactions.

GETTING BY IN THE INNER CITY

Constrained social interactions and limited engagement with the inner city are not only the results of crime and endangerment. They also arise out of the forms of resignation and indifference which can be considered emblematic of inner-city residents' habitus. Habitus refers to the set of socially and culturally inculcated values, dispositions, tastes and preferences (Bourdieu 2005, 1984; Crossley 2013; Reay 2015). Importantly, habitus is not only an expression of the effects of social structures and influences, but a framework for acting and expressing one's social position and identity. I have shown elsewhere how habitus is made in space, as people absorb the different dynamics and realities of physical spaces into their ways of being in and relating to the world, as well as their conceptions of self and others (Mosselson 2019). The ways in which people take and make space, or are restricted from doing so, are reflections of their habitus and under-standing of their position in the social hierarchy. Thus, inner-city residents, who are in the area temporarily, lack avenues for collective engagement, orient their lives elsewhere, have learnt not to expect much from the post-apartheid city, are generally in positions of limited power and influence, and act accordingly.

The inner city has long served as a landing area for migrants from other African countries as well as other regions in South Africa. It is a place people settle as they attempt to gain footholds in the urban economy, usually with the hope of moving on once they have achieved some financial success and stability. Various studies emphasise inner-city residents' transience and imper-manence, and highlight how people living in the area constantly harbour plans and ambitions to move (Kihato 2013; Landau 2009, 2006). Caroline Kihato (2013) describes this situation as living 'in between' – being rooted or trapped in one place, but aspiring to live elsewhere. The residents who par-ticipated in my study share this predicament, with few articulating long-term ambitions to remain in the area.

Inner-city residents' in-between situations mean that they are often discon-nected from the spaces in which they live, and orient their social lives elsewhere.

During interviews, several residents referred to other places in South Africa as 'home' and described how they spend the bulk of their free time outside the inner city. They also orient their future plans elsewhere and have not put down roots in the area. As one tenant longingly states, 'The only thing I think about is going home' (Tenant Six, Rochester), while another, when asked if she plans to stay in the area for the long term, declares decisively, 'I'm going anytime!' (Tenant Two, Lake Success). These desires to be elsewhere mean that residents seldom engage in collective life in the inner city. There are few public spaces or recreation facilities which support socialisation. While religious institutions abound and provide important forms of identification and social, spiritual and material sustenance, they generally do not engage in 'secular' forms of public life and have not served as platforms for collective mobilisations around wider issues, such as evictions, housing shortages and poor living conditions (Malcomess and Wilhelm-Solomon 2016).

Reflecting on the lack of social interaction and interest in political engagement, a local councillor points out:

> Here in inner city it's not easy of that [*sic*] [to form community and get people politically involved], because most of the people that are staying in the inner city are from different provinces, they only influx here for a better living, that's the only thing they are here for. They are not interested in anything so if they can get a job and work, after that, by the end of the month they just go home.

Residents are therefore largely disconnected from one another and concentrate on getting by in trying financial situations. While anonymity, detachment and opportunities for financial advancement are important features of urban life and allow many people to free themselves from burdensome attachments, kinship networks and obligations (Landau 2018; Thrift 2005), the prevailing situation in the inner city means that there are few platforms for expressing collective urban citizenship. Civil society has largely not responded to the spate of evictions which have taken place as buildings have been purchased and renovated (COHRE 2005; Wilhelm-Solomon 2016), and the forms of resistance and protest seen in other urban areas in South Africa, particularly the former townships, have not been replicated in the inner city.[4]

Rather, residents continue to occupy in-between geographies and concentrate on maintaining their footholds in the area. Although the rents in formal inner-city buildings are kept within social and affordable rates, and social housing in particular is cheaper as it is subsidised by the state, they remain hard to afford. Consequently, most tenants expend their energy working and finding ways to alleviate economic anxieties. As one resident bitterly complains, 'It's like you are working only for paying the rent. What next about life? [*sic*] Nothing you can do' (Tenant Three, Ridge Plaza). This anxiety limits the energy and time they have to spend on other aspects of life, and can overwhelm them. As one tenant declares, 'The main problem that we are having is the rent issue, it's affecting us big time; it's putting a strain on our lives!' (Tenant One, Ridge Plaza).

However, despite their dissatisfaction and desire to live elsewhere, residents are generally resigned to staying in the inner city. Johannesburg's landscape is still vastly divided and unequal. Living conditions in the former townships are still generally poor, with inadequate housing, infrastructure and services. They are also far from most health-care and education facilities, and employment opportunities are concentrated in the northern parts of the city-region, where housing is expensive and generally beyond the reach of most lower-income households (Gotz and Todes 2014; SERI 2016).

Inner-city residents are caught in a situation of living in an undesirable area, aspiring to be elsewhere, but unable to find somewhere that is better and still affordable. These divisions become absorbed into their dispositions and experiences of the city, and come to define their expressions of urban citizenship. As one resident prosaically reflects, 'For now I'm stuck here, but I don't have a problem' (Tenant Seven, Lake Success). Residents therefore resign themselves to remaining in the inner city, and their experience is characterised by detachment, endurance and acceptance, rather than active assertion of their claims to belong in and reshape urban space. A tenant explains, 'It's just that you have to accept the condition, the way of living where you are. You have to accept' (Tenant Two, Ridge Plaza), while another sums up the way many relate to the inner city by stating pragmatically, 'It's not a place I like, but I can live with it' (Tenant Six, Rochester).

REGULATION AND RESTRICTION

Habitus refers not only to a conception of self and an understanding of one's place in society, but also 'a sense of the place of others' (Bourdieu 1990, 131). The 'others' who occupy the top of the inner-city hierarchy and are most influential in making space in the area are property companies and developers (see Mosselson 2019; Wilhelm-Solomon 2016). There is a robust, very competitive property and housing industry in the inner city. As the urban regeneration process has taken hold, buildings and entire city blocks have been renovated and remade. The changes haven't always been drastic, and the area is still beset with maintenance and infrastructure shortcomings, but they have brought significant improvements to the built environment and social landscape. Property developers and housing companies thus have substantial powers to take and make place.

Housing companies are even more influential inside residential buildings. In these, strict regimes of control and regulation are put in place. The main purposes are to ensure that buildings run effectively, rent is collected seamlessly, and tenant populations are orderly and well behaved. The entrances to redeveloped inner-city residential buildings are fortified with metal turnstiles and electronic access-control systems. Security guards are stationed at the entrances 24 hours a day, and access cannot be gained without residents' and guards' permission. Interior communal spaces are monitored by CCTV cameras. Although they are draconian, residents generally appreciate these security features, which give them a welcome sense of safety and respite from the endangerment and anxieties that characterise their experiences of public spaces in the area. Many of the residents interviewed enthused about the security arrangements and the ways in which they create a sense of order and regulation, in contrast to seemingly chaotic and unruly spaces outside. Improvements made to renovated residential buildings also offer people opportunities to experience comfort and safety, which are lacking in derelict inner-city buildings or urban areas yet to undergo regeneration. For example, one tenant who lives in a social housing building in Hillbrow explains: 'It's very safe; the security access system, the lifts work, it's all fine. It's very clean. Where I was living before was not good, people got killed, mugged' (Tenant Seven, Lake Success). Tenants thus enjoy living in controlled environments and gain assurance from the familiarity of security guards stationed in their buildings.

As people do not feel comfortable or safe moving around the inner city, it still feels like a foreign, unpredictable terrain. The sheer number of people living in the area, combined with the even greater numbers that commute through it, makes it feel unpredictable and threatening. Residents find comfort in the presence of security guards and arrangements in their buildings, as these provide predictability and a sense of routine. As one tenant in a for-profit building in the CBD points out, 'I feel safe, nothing can happen. The security guards are nice people, they don't allow anyone in' (Tenant Two, Cavendish Court). Another tenant living in social housing illustrates the peace of mind tenants gain from security guards being present: 'The security is downstairs, we can sleep with the door open' (Tenant Fourteen, Gaelic Mansions).

The seemingly hostile environment of the inner city also nurtures anxieties about moral failings and deviance. The area has long been notorious for its prolific drug and sex trades, and has a reputation for being lawless and anomic. The strict rules governing behaviour inside residential buildings serve as an antidote to this anxiety, and allow for the formation of a type of moral order or community. Constant surveillance and prohibitions on parties and consuming alcohol enforce codes of behaviour and help people trust their neighbours. As one tenant happily points out, 'Most of us spend the whole day at work and I know nobody is going to touch my daughter while I am away. The security is tops!' (Tenant Eleven, Gaelic Mansions).

However, security measures are also used to discipline tenants and ensure that housing companies' authority goes unchallenged. All buildings have long lists of rules governing residents' behaviour. Loud noise, consuming alcohol in public spaces, and holding gatherings inside apartments are not permitted. The use of rules is not out of the ordinary; collective housing systems, from gated communities to informal occupations and squats, almost always enforce rules that prohibit some activities.[5] In the inner city, house rules help establish cohesion in residential buildings and prevent conflict between residents. However, they also create disciplinary spaces where behaviour is closely regulated and tenants are monitored constantly. Housing companies also keep close watch on the numbers of visitors residents receive and do not permit guests to stay overnight without prearranged approval. This means that residents are not able to make decisions about whom they share their living spaces with and are often unable to assist friends and family members when they are in difficulty. Their agency is therefore constrained, and they are made aware that they are living in a space they do not own or control.

Housing companies capitalise on the endangerment which characterises residents' experiences of the inner city, and implement security mechanisms which, while making people safer, also directly enhance their authority and dominance over space. The security systems inside buildings are used to ensure that rent is collected. When residents fall behind on their rent, their access is deactivated and they are forced to go to company headquarters and begin making arrangements to pay the outstanding amounts. One housing developer clearly explains how access control and security systems are disciplinary mechanisms which have enabled companies to monitor individual residents and establish an order in which commercial arrangements are unquestioned. As he points out, 'There's a culture in the inner city that you pay your rent ... You pay your rent, or you go somewhere else.' He elaborates that this culture has been created by security mechanisms: 'The culture [of paying rent] developed partly because high-rise buildings are still a lot easier to control than spread-out housing estates or suburbs ... We've got biometric systems, security guards sitting downstairs, and the ability to deal with individual tenants is that much easier.'

Dealing with tenants individually is also easier since housing companies refuse to recognise tenant committees. While residents are welcome to make complaints to building managers and at company headquarters, and some housing companies even place suggestion boxes in the foyers of residential buildings, all the companies with which I conducted research were adamant that they do not permit residents to form committees and they will not negotiate with them collectively. These strategies are responses to experiences from the mid-1990s, in which inner-city residents organised to withhold rent and challenge landlords. In part, these actions were continuations of the anti-apartheid movement's boycott campaigns in the townships (Morris 1999b). They were also responses to malicious landlords who exploited their tenants, charging high rents and refusing to invest any money in building maintenance. These forms of collective mobilisation were often effective ways of confronting slumlords and helped assert black communities' new political identity and right to belong in the inner city. At the same time, many boycott campaigns paved the way for the city's notorious 'building hijackers'. Despite the term's emphasis on violence and forceful theft, building hijacking actually is, generally speaking, a stealthier process. Many residents' committees were persuaded to make payments into alternative trust accounts, which promised to pay for services and maintenance through the funds. However, these accounts were often fraudulent or were taken over by criminal syndicates, who stole the money. Over time, these syndicates came to take control of the buildings, but as they fell into arrears, they were disconnected from water and electricity services due to non-payment, and the legal owners were either threatened or simply gave up on their failed investments.

Although the area is far more stable today, memories of building hijacking endure and become another type of fear that shapes the urban environment. One employee of an SHI makes clear the association between allowing tenant committees and anxieties over losing control over properties. He explains:

> Building hijackings, normally it's not like a car hijacking where someone sticks a gun through the window – it's a process, it's people getting a little bit unhappy, then they form committees and it builds up and builds up until someone convinces them to not pay the rental to the landlord but pay to some other bank account and they will manage the building better.

Another employee from a private affordable housing company explains their stance as follows: 'We don't encourage tenant committees because they tend to flare up when there are service interruptions or difficulties in the buildings and it becomes a platform for a whole variety of a shopping list of issues and it often becomes very political and polarised.'

These intransigent approaches have indeed made inner-city buildings more manageable, as residents have been rendered passive and estranged from one another. Most of the residents I interviewed did not query or complain about the restrictions placed on them. However, those who did pointed out that the lack of committees and opportunities to share concerns contributes to the social distance and lack of interest between people. For instance, one resident complains: 'Everybody minds his business in this building. We are not united as tenants, we don't even have tenant meetings, just in-out, in-out, in-out' (Tenant Four, Greatermans). Another speaks with frustration about the way in which residents are deliberately divided and prevented from having any form of collective representation. He complains that the company managing the building he lives in

> have a policy whereby they don't want their tenants to converge and discuss problems amongst their tenants. They want us, or they expect us, to go to them as individuals, address the problem as individuals; but that's not solving the problem because the problems that we have here in this building, they affect each and every tenant who lives in this building!

ARTICULATING ASPIRATIONS

Combined with residents' temporariness, resignation and desire to live else-where, security and regulation measures create a social landscape in which people are passive and seldom articulate wider demands or aspirations for the area. Because it describes a set of enduring dispositions and conceptions about one's place in society, habitus has also been used to discuss different people's aspirations and abilities to formulate long-term plans (see Bhat and Rather 2013; Bourdieu and Passeron 1990; Gale and Parker 2015; Reay 2004). Appadurai (2004) refers to this as 'the capacity to aspire' – the ability to envision, articulate and pursue future plans and desires. Poor people do not lack dreams and aspirations. However, the horizons of possibility open to them and the material deprivations they face mean that their aspirations are frequently articulated differently and in more limited ways. As with habitus, which, when successfully acquired and performed, confers on people higher distributions of prestige, status, distinction and material wealth (Bourdieu 1984), the capacity to aspire is unevenly distributed. The relatively rich and powerful have 'a more fully developed capacity to aspire' and also possess the means with which to pursue (although not always obtain) their goals (Appadurai 2004, 68).

Residents in inner-city Johannesburg demonstrate limited or constrained capacities to aspire or 'a more brittle horizon of aspirations' (Appadurai 2004, 69). Although they do not lack long-term plans and goals, and engage in activities that are clearly oriented towards the future, such as investing in education, raising their children and saving money where possible, they also confine their hopes to immediate, personal circumstances. When it comes to the area in which they are living, because they see it as a temporary situation, feel detached from those around them, are fearful of public spaces and are pre-vented from engaging in collective organisation in the buildings in which they reside, residents generally do not articulate aspirations or ambitions for long-term or meaningful betterment. These limited aspirations are in sharp contrast to other inner-city areas around the world, where more active and assertive res-ident mobilisations have emerged. For instance, in São Paulo strong housing collectives directly challenge private systems of ownership and adopt insurgent self-help strategies, using occupations of vacant buildings to both secure shel-ter and forge alternative models or conceptions of urban belonging and claims to the city (De Carli and Frediani 2016; Earle 2012). These movements are aided by and operate as part of an active civil society that directly promotes marginalised, low-income communities' rights to the city, again contrasting with inner-city Johannesburg, where civil society and social movements are largely absent and private landlords monopolise political and spatial power.

When asked about possible improvements that could be made to the inner city or to describe what would make their living situations better, residents frequently fell back on narratives centred on crime and fear. The sense of endangerment discussed previously comes to the fore and occupies a decisive role in shaping their horizons of possibility and ideas about 'the good city' (Amin 2006). These expressions are particularly notable given the fact that crime rates, while still relatively high, have fallen in recent years.[6] Residents are aware of this but continue to desire more security, as the following excerpts from interviews show:

> It is much safer but if they could make it more safer it would be better (Tenant One, Lake Success).

> The only thing that can make the building in a better way than it is right now, when the management can keep on having the security tight like this. Everything's going to be fine in the next years, I can say (Tenant One, Rochester).

> If they can also improve security around Hillbrow, so people, they can go out. You know, South Africa sometimes, not only Hillbrow but South Africa generally, is crime-ridden so if they can try by all means just to beef up the security around Hillbrow, then people they can live in safety. But I think now it's more safer. I do feel safe but people outside there, they don't feel safe in Hillbrow; we need that environment where people even outside there they are able to live and say Hillbrow is safe (Tenant Eight, Gaelic Mansions).

> Security [would make Hillbrow a better place to live]: they've tightened it but they must continue (Tenant Five, Lake Success).

These statements are indicative of the fact that fear of crime and feelings of vulnerability are still prominent. Furthermore, because fear dominates narratives about and experiences of the area, it subsumes other aspirations or articulations. Feelings about a lack of stability and belonging in the space are displaced to a generalised fixation on crime or longing for personal safety.

However, this pattern also emerges because residents are placed in situations in which they are rendered relatively powerless. Many interviewees adopted passive stances when responding to questions about improving the area, using the vague third-person pronoun 'they'. Replies such as these were characteristic and frequent:

> I don't know. If they could clean the area it would be fine (Tenant Five, Rochester).

> There are other buildings that are old. If they can renew them it would be better (Tenant Two, Gaelic Mansions).

> There are still some buildings which are neglected. In those there is no law and order, it is too much crowded. If they could modify them so they look nice [that would improve the area] (Tenant Four, Lake Success).

It thus becomes apparent that tenants generally do not see themselves as active members of the inner-city community, and forgo or fail to acknowledge their abilities to actively make and alter spaces. This situation again contrasts with other cities with more established and engaged communities and forms of activism. It reflects and is exacerbated by the unequal distribution of political and spatial power in the area. Housing companies and property developers are the dominant actors and they monopolise governance procedures and processes, often at the expense or to the exclusion of residents (Didier, Peyroux, and Morange 2012; Peyroux 2006). At the same time, residents disengage from public life, both out of fear and owing to the ongoing struggle to get by, which occupies the majority of their time. Urban citizenship is drastically reduced and rights to the city – to access the benefits of urban life, to participate fully in making and shaping urban spaces, and to enjoy collective civil engagement (Harvey 2003; Parnell and Pieterse 2010; Purcell 2014; Simone 2008b) – remain elusive.

CONCLUSION

Anxieties about crime and violence are constitutive parts of lower-income residents' experiences of the inner city. The progressive symbolism of black people now being able to reside in an area that was previously reserved exclusively for white people is sadly tempered by feelings of vulnerability, detachment and longing to be elsewhere. It becomes clear, then, how anxieties about crime reduce the horizons of possibility and forms of urban citizenship which are open to people and which they feel able to pursue. Feelings of endangerment therefore have to be taken seriously as expressing real concerns and fears, and also as political factors. Who is vulnerable to crime, how this vulnerability manifests, and how people deal with it are all questions which shape the landscapes of urban society and forms of citizenship. Suburban communities invest heavily in privatised security and forms of fortification, which drastically reshape the urban environment and restrict others' movements and abilities to use public space (Clarno 2013; Dirsuweit and Wafer 2006). Communities in informal settlements and townships, who often cannot rely on police to protect them, frequently resort to violent forms of vigilantism (Fourchard 2011; Super 2016). Inner-city residents largely retreat from public spaces and confine themselves indoors, particularly at night. They therefore surrender the city to their fears and those who embody them, and the space remains one characterised by hostility and estrangement, where few belong or cultivate any long-term attachments. In the inner city, fear of crime thus causes a disconnection between people and the place in which they are living.

Fear of crime, though, is also a placeholder for other anxieties, forms of stratification and inequality. People's distance from one another contributes to atmospheres of suspicion and distrust. In addition, resignation about living conditions and desires to be elsewhere make the inner city a space to be endured rather than invested in, enjoyed or shared with others. Furthermore, the intense forms of regulation to which people are subjected contribute to feelings of detachment and powerlessness, and reduce the possibilities for forms of collective life to emerge. Recourse to concerns about crime is therefore a substitute for other disconnections and restrictions, and expresses the constrained meaning and experience of urban citizenship in the aftermath of apartheid. The inequalities that define contemporary South African society, in terms of the physical disparities between different residential areas and limited housing options presented to people, as well as in terms of unequal distribution of financial and political power and consequent ability to influence urban environments, play out in residents' narratives and the issues or subjects which concern them. It is therefore important to understand how discussions and fears about crime fill the space left by the absence of more fundamental rights and political identifications, and how the unequal landscape of citizenship in the wake of apartheid is reflected in the anxieties which people hold.

ACKNOWLEDGEMENTS

I would like to thank the editors for their enthusiasm and dedication in putting this collection together as well as their insightful comments and suggestions as to how my chapter could be improved. I would further like to thank the editorial team at Wits University Press for their hard work, the anonymous reviewers who helped shape the chapter, and all those who participated in my research and shared their time and thoughts with me; this work would not be possible without their generosity. Lastly, I would like to thank Mncedisi Siteleki for designing the map that I use as well as Wendy Willems for originally suggesting my work for inclusion in this collection.

NOTES

1   The strict security arrangements in inner-city residential buildings meant that I could only gain access with prearranged approval and subject to building managers being on site. For these reasons, fieldwork usually took place during daytime working hours, although some interviews were conducted over weekends, on public holidays and in the early evening, in order to broaden the sample to include people who would be working during weekdays.

2   Community Policing Forums (CPFs) are formal neighbourhood watch or civilian patrol groups which operate in conjunction with local police services. Although conceived as vehicles to enhance democratic and community-oriented forms of policing, CPFs frequently express the fractures and hostility which pervade contemporary South African society (see Bénit-Gbaffou 2008; Fourchard 2011; Super 2016).

3   RDP communities are large housing settlements constructed as part of the government's National Housing Subsidy Scheme. This project, one of the largest fiscal undertakings of the post-apartheid government, sees the state construct stand-alone, four-room houses which are given to poor households, defined as those earning less than R3500 per month. The project was included in the Reconstruction and Development Programme, the ANC's first macroeconomic policy. Hence, these settlements are colloquially referred to as RDP houses or RDP settlements. While over 3 million houses have been provided so far, this project is frequently criticised for situating poor households on the far-flung peripheries of urban areas, cut off from amenities and access to jobs, schools and health-care facilities (see SERI 2016).

4   Despite the absence of widespread public forms of resistance, there have been successful civil society interventions which have focused on individual eviction cases and have had significant national implications. Litigation brought by occupants of two

inner-city residential buildings helped entrench access to housing as a right which the state is obligated to take meaningful steps to protect and realise (Wilson 2010). These cases also helped establish laws ensuring that evictions cannot proceed if they will result in people being left homeless, and that the state is obliged to provide alternative accommodation for people facing eviction (Tissington and Wilson 2011). However, these court cases stand as relatively isolated incidents and have not inspired broader mobilisations and forms of political engagement in the inner city.

5   In São Paulo, building occupations, while based on cooperation and collective action, construct hierarchies of authority to ensure that members comply with rules, such as not consuming alcohol or drugs inside occupied buildings and mandating members to participate in communal cleaning and maintenance activities (De Carli and Frediani 2016). Communities living in occupied buildings in inner-city Johannesburg have enforced similar rules (see Tissington 2008), indicating that regulation is not always punitive or externally imposed, but is often essential for diverse communities to exist together.

6   For instance, there were 56 murders recorded in Hillbrow in 2012 and 63 in 2013 (the time period in which I was conducting research), compared to 84 in 2008 and 88 in 2009. Significant reductions are also recorded for attempted murder, assault with attempt to inflict grievous bodily harm, common robbery, and robbery with aggravating circumstances between 2008 and 2013. See https://www.crimestatssa. com/precinct.php?id=261 and https://www.saps.gov.za/services/crimestats_ archive.php.

REFERENCES

Amin, Ash. 2006. "The Good City." *Urban Studies* 43 (5–6): 1009–23.

Appadurai, Arjun. 2004. "The Capacity to Aspire: Culture and the Terms of Recognition." In *Culture and Public Action*, edited by Vijayendra Rao and Michael Walton, 59–84. Stanford CA: Stanford University Press.

Bénit-Gbaffou, Claire. 2008. "The Uncertain 'Partnerships' between Police, Communities and Private Security Companies." *Trialog: A Journal for Planning and Building in the Third World* 89: 21–6.

Bhat, Mohd A., and Tanveer A. Rather. 2013. "Youth Transitions in Kashmir: Exploring the Relationships between Habitus, Ambitions and Impediments." *South Asia Research* 33 (3): 185–204.

Bourdieu, Pierre. 1984. *Distinction: A Social Critique of the Judgement of Taste*. Cambridge, MA: Harvard University Press.

———. 1990. *The Logic of Practice*. Stanford CA: Stanford University Press.

———. 2005. "Habitus." In *Habitus: A Sense of Place*, edited by Jean Hillier and Emma Rooksby, 43–9. Farnham: Ashgate Publishing.

Bourdieu, Pierre, and Jean-Claude Passeron. 1990. *Reproduction in Education, Society and Culture*. Newbury Park: Sage.

Butcher, Sian. 2016. "Infrastructures of Property and Debt: Making Affordable Housing, Race and Place in Johannesburg." PhD thesis, University of Minnesota.

CAHF (Centre for Affordable Housing Finance in Africa). 2015. "Understanding the Challenges in South Africa's Gap Housing Market and Opportunities for the RDP Resale Market." Johannesburg: Centre for Affordable Housing Finance in Africa.

Caldeira, Teresa. 2000. *City of Walls: Crime, Segregation, and Citizenship in São Paulo*. Berkeley: University of California Press.

Clarno, Andy. 2013. "Rescaling White Space in Post-Apartheid Johannesburg." *Antipode* 45 (5): 1190–212.

COHRE (Centre on Housing Rights and Evictions). 2005. "Any Room for the Poor? Forced Evictions in Johannesburg, South Africa." Johannesburg: Centre on Housing Rights and Evictions.

Crankshaw, Owen, and Caroline White. 1995. "Racial Desegregation and Inner City Decay in Johannesburg." *International Journal of Urban and Regional Research* 19: 622–38.

Crossley, Nick. 2013. "Habit and Habitus." *Body and Society* 19 (2–3): 136–61.

De Carli, Beatrice, and Alexandre A. Frediani. 2016. "Insurgent Regeneration: Spatial Practices of Citizenship in the Rehabilitation of Inner-City São Paulo." *GeoHumanities* 2 (2): 331–53.

Didier, Sophie, Elisabeth Peyroux, and Marianne Morange. 2012. "The Spreading of the City Improvement District Model in Johannesburg and Cape Town: Urban Regeneration and the Neoliberal Agenda in South Africa." *International Journal of Urban and Regional Research* 36 (5): 915–35.

Dirsuweit, Teresa, and Alex Wafer. 2006. "Scale, Governance and the Maintenance of Privileged Control: The Case of Road Closures in Johannesburg's Northern Suburbs." *Urban Forum* 17 (4): 327–52.

Earle, Lucy. 2012. "From Insurgent to Transgressive Citizenship: Housing, Social Movements and the Politics of Rights in São Paulo." *Journal of Latin American Studies* 44 (1): 97–126.

Everatt, David. 2014. "Poverty and Inequality in the Gauteng City-Region." In *Changing Space, Changing City: Johannesburg after Apartheid*, edited by Philip Harrison, Graeme Gotz, Alison Todes, and Chris Wray, 63–82. Johannesburg: Wits University Press.

Flusty, S. 2002. "The Banality of Interdiction: Surveillance, Control and the Displacement of Diversity." *International Journal of Urban and Regional Research* 25: 658–64.

Fourchard, Laurent. 2011. "The Politics of Mobilization for Security in South African Townships." *African Affairs* 110 (441): 607–27.

Gale, Trevor, and Stephen Parker. 2015. "Calculating Student Aspiration: Bourdieu, Spatiality and the Politics of Recognition." *Cambridge Journal of Education* 45 (1): 81–96.

Goga, Soraya. 2003. "Property Investors and Decentralization: A Case of False Competition?" In *Emerging Johannesburg: Perspectives on the Postapartheid City*, edited by Richard Tomlinson, Robert A. Beauregard, Lindsay Bremner, and Xolela Mangcu, 71–84. London: Routledge.

Gotz, Graeme, and Alison Todes. 2014. "Johannesburg's Urban Space Economy." In *Changing Space, Changing City: Johannesburg after Apartheid*, edited by Philip Harrison, Graeme Gotz, Alison Todes, and Chris Wray, 117–36. Johannesburg: Wits University Press.

Gotz, Graeme, Chris Wray, and Brian Mubiwa. 2014. "The 'Thin Oil of Urbanisation'?" In *Changing Space, Changing City: Johannesburg after Apartheid*, edited by Philip Harrison, Graeme Gotz, Alison Todes, and Chris Wray, 42–62. Johannesburg: Wits University Press.

Harvey, David. 2003. "The Right to the City." *International Journal of Urban and Regional Research* 27 (4): 939–41.

Kihato, Caroline. 2013. *Migrant Women of Johannesburg: Everyday Life in an In-Between City*. Basingstoke: Palgrave Macmillan.

Landau, Loren B. 2006. "Transplants and Transients: Idioms of Belonging and Dislocation in Inner-City Johannesburg." *African Studies Revue* 49 (2): 125–45.

———. 2009. "Living within and beyond Johannesburg: Exclusion, Religion, and Emerging Forms of Being." *African Studies* 68: 197–214.

———. 2018. "Friendship Fears and Communities of Convenience in Africa's Urban Estuaries: Connection as Measure of Urban Condition." *Urban Studies* 55: 505–21.

Landau, Loren B., and Iriann Freemantle. 2010. "Tactical Cosmopolitanism and Idioms of Belonging: Insertion and Self-Exclusion in Johannesburg." *Journal of Ethnic and Migration Studies* 36 (3): 375–90.

Lemanski, Charlotte. 2006. "Residential Responses to Fear (of Crime Plus) in Two Cape Town Suburbs: Implications for the Post-Apartheid City." *Journal of International Development* 18 (6): 787–802.

Le Roux, Hannah. 2014. "The Ethiopian Quarter." In *Changing Space, Changing City: Johannesburg after Apartheid*, edited by Philip Harrison, Graeme Gotz, Alison Todes, and Chris Wray, 498–505. Johannesburg: Wits University Press.

Malcomess, Bettina, and Matthew Wilhelm-Solomon. 2016. "Valleys of Salt in the House of God: Religious Re-Territorialisation and Urban Space." In *Routes and Rites to the City: Mobility, Diversity and Religious Space in Johannesburg*, edited by Matthew Wilhelm-Solomon, Lorena Nunez, Peter Kankonde Bukasa, and Bettina Malcomess, 31–60. London: Palgrave Macmillan.

Matsipa, Mpho. 2017. "Woza! Sweetheart! On Braiding Epistemologies on Bree Street." *Thesis Eleven* 141 (1): 31–48.

Mbembe, Achille, and Sarah Nuttall. 2008. "Introduction: Afropolis." In *Johannesburg: The Elusive Metropolis*, edited by Sarah Nuttall and Achille Mbembe, 1–33. Durham: Duke University Press.

Morris, Alan. 1999a. *Bleakness and Light: Inner-City Transition in Hillbrow, Johannesburg*. Johannesburg: Wits University Press.

———. 1999b. "Tenant-Landlord Relations, the Anti-Apartheid Struggle and Physical Decline in Hillbrow, an Inner-City Neighbourhood in Johannesburg." *Urban Studies* 36: 509–26.

Mosselson, Aidan. 2018. "Everyday Security: Privatized Policing, Local Legitimacy and Atmospheres of Control." *Urban Geography* 40 (1): 1–21.

———. 2019. *Vernacular Regeneration: Low-Income Housing, Private Policing and Urban Transformation in Inner-City Johannesburg*. London: Routledge.

Nuttall, Sarah. 2004. "City Forms and Writing the 'Now' in South Africa." *Journal of Southern African Studies* 30: 731–48.

Parnell, Sue, and Edgar Pieterse. 2010. "'The 'Right to the City': Institutional Imperatives of a Developmental State." *International Journal of Urban and Regional Research* 34: 146–62.

Peyroux, Elisabeth. 2006. "City Improvement Districts (CIDs) in Johannesburg: Assessing the Political and Socio-Spatial Implications of Private-Led Urban Regeneration." *Trialog* 89: 9–14.

Purcell, Mark. 2014. "Possible Worlds: Henri Lefebvre and the Right to the City." *Journal of Urban Affairs* 36 (1): 141–54.

Reay, Diane. 2004. "'It's All Becoming a Habitus': Beyond the Habitual Use of Habitus in Educational Research." *British Journal of the Sociology of Education* 25 (4): 431–44.

———. 2015. "Habitus and the Psychosocial: Bourdieu with Feelings." *Cambridge Journal of Education* 45: 9–23.

Sandercock, L. 2005. "Difference, Fear and Habitus: A Political Economy of Urban Fears." In *Habitus: A Sense of Place*, edited by Jean Hillier and Emma Rooksby, 219–34. Farnham: Ashgate Publishing.

SERI (Socio-Economic Rights Institute of South Africa). 2013. "Minding the Gap: An Analysis of the Supply of and Demand for Low-Income Rental Accommodation in Inner City Johannesburg." Johannesburg: Socio-Economic Rights Institute of South Africa.

———. 2016. "Edged Out: Spatial Mismatch and Spatial Justice in South Africa's Main Urban Areas." Johannesburg: Socio-Economic Rights Institute of South Africa.

Simone, AbdouMaliq. 2008a. "People as Infrastructure: Intersecting Fragments in Johannesburg." In *Johannesburg: The Elusive Metropolis*, edited by Sarah Nuttall and Achille Mbembe, 68–90. Durham: Duke University Press.

———. 2008b. "The Politics of the Possible: Making Urban Life in Phnom Penh." *Singapore Journal of Tropical Geography* 29 (2): 186–204.

Siteleki, Mncedisi, Richard Ballard, and Aidan Mosselson. 2017. "Quality of Life Survey IV: Crime and Perceptions of Safety in Gauteng (No. 7)." *GCRO Data Brief.* Johannesburg: Gauteng City-Region Observatory.

Super, Gail. 2016. "Volatile Sovereignty: Governing Crime through the Community in Khayelitsha." *Law and Society Review* 50 (2): 450–83.

Thrift, Nigel. 2005. "But Malice Aforethought: Cities and the Natural History of Hatred." *Transactions of the Institute of British Geographers* 30 (2): 133–50.

Tissington, Kate. 2008. "Challenging Inner City Evictions before the Constitutional Court of South Africa: The Occupiers of 51 Olivia Road Case." *Housing and ESC Rights Law Quarterly* 1: 3–6.

Tissington, Kate, and Stuart Wilson. 2011. "SCA Upholds Rights of Urban Poor in Blue Moonlight Judgment." *ESR: Review of Economic and Social Rights in South Africa* 12: 3–6.

Wilhelm-Solomon, Matthew. 2016. "Decoding Dispossession: Eviction and Urban Regeneration in Johannesburg's Dark Buildings." *Singapore Journal of Tropical Geography* 37 (3): 378–95.

Wilson, Stuart. 2010. "Breaking the Tie: Evictions from Private Land, Homelessness and a New Normality." *South African Law Journal* 126: 270–90.

Zeiderman, Austin. 2016. *Endangered City: The Politics of Security and Risk in Bogotá.* Durham: Duke University Press.

TAXI DIARIES III: AND NOW YOU ARE IN JOBURG

BAELETSI TSATSI

My aunt gives me the phone and my mom is on the other end of the line. She tells me that she has arranged with Mantsho to come and take me to town by taxi. After this I will go to town on my own using a taxi.

The following day I come back from school, change out of my uniform and wait for Mantsho to come fetch me. She arrives and tells me what we're going to do: I'm going to buy new school shoes and with the change we can buy a treat. She explains the route to me and off we go. We walk past the Cashbuild all the way to the complex and wait there for a taxi. We get in, pay our fare, which is R3.50, and soon we get off at the taxi rank, cross over to the Shoprite Sentrum, which is now Kuruman Mall. We've got only two stops, Pep Store for the shoes and Shoprite for the treat: cinnamon buns and Tropika juice for each of us. We cross the road again, back to the taxi rank and back to Mothibistad we go. That evening my aunt gives me the phone and my mom asks if I'm ready to take the taxi alone and I say yes.

Following that are trips to town on my own to go and buy myself clothes or stationery. Long-distance trips to go and visit uncles and aunts in different towns. My mom hands me over to the taxi driver like he is a trusted uncle and tells him my destination. I trust the taxi driver. When I arrive, he waits with me for my uncle or aunt to fetch me, he lets me use his phone to call my mom, he is friendly and kind.

But then I come to Joburg and the taxi driver doesn't speak the same language as me and mocks me for it and refuses to speak Setswana. So I learn isiZulu to communicate my route to him.

In Joburg the queue marshal isn't my friend from primary school who dropped out of high school, but a man who calls his friend to come and mock me when I refuse his advances. He calls me fat and ugly and asks if I really thought he meant what he said when he made a pass at me. 'I was doing you a favour,' he exclaims. I see right through his sham but that doesn't make me less humiliated.

In Joburg the older women in your taxi aren't your English teacher from Grade 8 or your aunt's colleague or your friend's grandmother. They are women coming from tiring jobs and this is their fourth taxi of the day, so when the taxi driver speaks to one of them about the girl sitting next to her, talking about her short skirt and blonde hair, rubbishing her presence by talking over her and questioning if she is marriage material, the older woman smiles, blames Joburg and doesn't protect you.

In Joburg no one knows you, no one is proud of the book you've written. No one knows your family, no one knows your work. You cross the Mandela Bridge into town from a feminist gathering in Braam[fontein] and the first thing you hear upon entering the taxi rank is 'My size,' from various men. None of them knows or cares that you've been grappling with complex ideas and are determined to make a difference in the lives of black women. Here you have no voice, no power. Here you have a body, and for the taxi driver it is for the taking.

In Joburg I am unsafe, I am anxious and I am angry.

AFTERWORD: URBAN ATMOSPHERES

SARAH NUTTALL

Anxious Joburg is a timely and tantalising book. It contributes significantly to the growing literature on global south city lives and city forms. Analyses of these lives and forms have undergone salient shifts in recent times. The first shift has rendered newly vivid those aspects of the urban social that have long been treated as background: its infrastructural forms, in their violence as well as their sensory dimensions, and their capacities for drawing out the capillaries of the political, of the past and of corporeal life in the city in firmer and more graspable outline. The second shift has focused on the reconfiguration of urban landscapes according to material and biospheric processes under conditions of the Anthropocene. The third shift has emphasised cities as works of imagination, structures of affect and producers of atmosphere. *Anxious Joburg* carries inflections of each, while being compellingly located within this third shift in particular.

Johannesburg, along with Lagos and Kinshasa, is arguably Africa's most widely interpreted urban formation, capable of challenging key tenets of contemporary urban theory in ways that are definitive. This narratively dense African city now weaves its accounts of itself from the multiple intersecting anxieties that inflect its lives and forms. Crime is one of these potent strands; another is the tension identified by the editors between a 'striated' urban landscape that blocks flows and movement but which at the same time offers accelerated forms of mobility and chance encounter if and where you can make it through. So it is that the tension between 'the need for something else and the constant reimposition of the same' connects the disparate anxieties that the book tries to put its finger on.

Anxious Joburg takes the measure of its topic while escalating its condition, writing multiple anxieties into form. Reasons to feel anxious in Johannesburg are 'ubiquitous rather than intermittent', Falkof and Van Staden argue. A city's affective existence – its urban atmospheres, as I will suggest – are shaped and amplified by its physical geographies. Here is a city whose volatile social formations in their productive and destructive dimensions draw it closer to other African cities, even as it pulls away from them in its racial complexity and along its historically specific vectors of accumulation and exclusion. Johannesburg is without doubt, as this book suggests, driven, sustained, undercut and undone by anxiety: this is its local obsession and its global condition in the twenty-first century.

To what anxieties does the book bear witness, which does it draw into narrative form – to the exclusion of which others? How does it make its cut into the culture of this city? What are its collective and often turbulent cumulative effects? Let's turn first to the idea of an urban atmosphere. Affective atmospheres, in their indeterminacy, and in their materialist and phenomenological aspects, 'envelop' or press upon life (Anderson 2009). These sensory ecologies of everyday urban life draw on affective or experienced space to produce the *composition* of an environment such as a city. Urban atmospheres, writes Matthew Gandy, are synesthetic: like sounds, they reverberate within urban subjects (Gandy 2017). Think of the role and history of light in producing such atmospheres. Apartheid Johannesburg, Julia Hornberger (2008) has written, was lit with mercury-based 'white light', while the townships were fitted with sodium lights, producing orange light. The latter were generally used to light motorways because of their low shadow-producing quality. They were monochromatic, rendering everything strange. If the city was bathed in brightness, the township was forcefully unshadowed, making it easier to survey – but also unavailable for hidden histories and forms of self-reflection born of the penumbral. What histories and atmospheres of anxiety did these different light-producing qualities engender? What inflections did they bring to topographies of exclusion and access in the African metropolis? Urban atmospheres can be transpersonal, political, architectural, anthropocentric.

What they collectively amount to, precisely in their multiplicity, is a more complex rendering of the dynamics of urban space.

Anxious Joburg builds on, brokers and cumulatively insists upon the extent to which affective atmospheres such as anxiety may be shared among urban residents yet be differentially inflected via historically inflected geographies and their indices of inequality. The range of affects attended to by this volume is wide: atmospheres of anxiety are shaped by emotions that include anger, despair, fear, dread, panic, powerlessness, distress, ambivalence, desperation, embarrassment, envy, grief, stress, fragility and vulnerability. A number of the chapters focus on people's lived and felt experiences as they witness, endure and traverse forms of precarity and change. The extent to which the body and the voicing of a story is central to many of these chapters is striking. It is as if one experience after another of the body in the city is not only the privileged location of emotions but also the primary site of a particular speech act. The scenes and spaces of emotional investment are carefully described; in turn the careful description of their enactment in everyday life reveals unsuspected layers of the urban fabric.

Anxiety is explored across this work as a psychic state, a state-driven structural condition, a permanent encounter with concern for one's own fatality and in relation to fears of intimacy across class and race, among others. Fascinatingly, while it offers accounts of how specific sets of anxieties play out in one part of a city or in a person or set of people's lives, or indeed in the narrative arc of a single chapter, it also enables us to see how they might cumulatively cut across each other, accrue or intermesh as multiple forms of anxious living, revealing the extent of anxiety's reach – its pervasiveness as an atmosphere – thus making the force field that the book tries to articulate even clearer.

Young women trying to make it in the big city, drawn through need and desire and increasingly enmeshed in compensated relationships with older and more wealthy men, are the focus of Lebohang Masango's chapter. Women, she writes, are both enabled and vulnerable in such situations, susceptible to the intense and volatile conundrums of feeling, sex and money – and anxious about their safety. The city itself, aspirational, trading in the production of desirability and endlessly attempting success in the face of structural precarity, Masango argues, produces the conditions for 'sugaring'. Such urban agonies of anxiety rely on intricate and manifold uses of cellphones as 'weapons of self-defence'.

It is not inconceivable that young women such as those described in Masango's work also attended the Global Citizen Festival in Soweto in 2018, the focus of Cobus van Staden's chapter, producing a sense of compounded anxieties and anxious atmospheres. The concert, attended by 65 000 people, was followed by systemic breakdowns, including lack of street lighting, cellphone signals and adequate public transport, as security was deployed away from the concert-goers to the protection of the elites leaving the concert. Van Staden reads for a 'heightened awareness' of how a single systemic breakdown can reverberate through the larger system – and for how one form of systemic failure can trigger others, in a domino effect. He contrasts the ways in which complex forms of ricocheting and intricate dysfunction and breakdown contrast with narratives of 'liberal philanthropy' and their politics of 'clicktivism'. Here we might think of the ways in which ricocheting anxieties form part of contemporary political atmospheres, or atmospheres of the political in Johannesburg – and in many other cities of the south. Political atmospheres are sometimes engineered (through official denials or fake news) and anxieties multiply according to what is both seen and implicitly felt.

Concerts, load shedding, thunderstorms: atmospheres can be sensory, infrastructural, meteorological; both real and intuited, they can be enveloping and unsettling (see Gandy 2017). While much of the literature on such urban events has drawn on the concept of the crowd, recent work asks us to revisit their affective characteristics through the notion of atmospheres. The Johannesburg artist William Kentridge has often remarked on the city's 'cathedrals': its giant and cascading thunderclouds, spiralling above the city on an afternoon in summer, giving content and form to the riverless city's aerial domes of open sky. As the rains pours, so too the blackouts will often begin – and so the vegetation spills, verdant and green, over curbs and out of gardens and across rickety fences or school courtyards, adding to our sense of urban place, writing its environmental atmospheres – and their complex histories of anxiety.

In the age of the Anthropocene, precisely when matters of environmentalism become urgent, exclusionary urban forms such as gated communities claim 'an environmental stewardship ... that trumps all other claims to land precisely because it is not a claim *to* land, but a claim *on behalf of* the land itself', writes Renugan Raidoo in his chapter. All threats to 'tranquillity' are expunged, he argues, as residents disavow and physically remove themselves from the conditions of the city as such. His chapter joins others in the book in reading for what Nicky Falkof, citing Stuart Hall, refers to as anxieties associated with Johannesburg's 'constitutive outsides'. The lush northern suburbs, she argues, allow privileged city dwellers to avoid or disavow the labour of landscaping and its bodily life and waste – the sweat, blood and sewage of its 'outside'. She discusses the outsize cockroaches, 'monstrous invertebrates' that have long terrified suburbanites as they scuttle like symptoms through suburban houses. Known as 'Parktown prawns', they recall the alien prawns of the iconic Johannesburg film *District 9*, their insectoid other-than-human composite forms exploited by organised crime and subject to the xenophobia and racism of humans.

Derek Hook turns, in the course of his chapter, to a Lacanian parable of a subject who wakes from a dream of the self as a dazed figure wearing a mask (eerily prescient of our current times), and finds before them a giant insect. The parable suggests anxiety or anguish at multiple intersecting levels. The experience of becoming-insect is 'not merely that of death or psychological or symbolic transformation; it is that of existing at a wholly different ontological level, of completely unbecoming one's (physical, psychological) self'. These processes of unbecoming, and the anticipation or dread to which they attach themselves, may sometimes but not always be attached to histories of whiteness and its psychogeographies, and Hook notes how often their narration 'veers' into a different genre, such as science fiction or urban noir. Here, anxiety is a temporal relation, attached to the state of 'waiting for something to happen', and offers fertile ground for the workings of the unconscious. This is especially so in the contexts of the racial city and its colonial aftermaths, where, following Fanon, Hook writes about the anxiety of 'not knowing quite what one represents relative to the opaque desire of the Other' and speaks to the underpinnings of the subject's 'most crucial identifications'.

***

In *Johannesburg: The Elusive Metropolis*, which I edited with Achille Mbembe (2008), we saw the city as a place in which historical structures of racial inequity were simultaneously being sedimented and unbundled; as an urban conurbation that seems to have no fixed parts, no completeness and almost no unique centre. We described it, too, as having a porosity which, released from the iron cage of apartheid, enabled it to fashion and refashion itself. Johannesburg in the aftermath of apartheid was a city in formation, the book a chance to capture a moment in the life of the city 'overwritten with possibility, underwritten with anxiety' (32). Now, it is as if Johannesburg is a city of shuffled parts, reassembled in a related but different sequence – a city, one could say, overwritten with anxiety, underwritten with possibility.

One of the reasons for that, and for the pervasive anxiety that is recounted in this book, relates to the complexity of the concept of freedom in the city. Johannesburg has long, B Camminga points out, been a destination, site of employment and often sanctuary for migrants from all over southern Africa and beyond; its very imagination has been mapped 'by the multiple bodies not born within its physical or imagined limits'. Increased and eruptive tensions between South Africans and migrants, parsed by potent pockets of xenophobia, have made migrant and refugee protection more tenuous. Transgender migrants and 'gender refugees' are especially vulnerable and subject to anxiety, Camminga shows, despite the constitutional freedoms extended to them in South Africa. Returning again to the Soweto concert stadium and its multilayered urban atmospheres, Van Staden captures the ironies and contradictions of the social: many LGBTQ+ people travelled to hear Beyoncé in Soweto (responding to her 'explicit connection between her personal work ethic and that of black women as they strive to overcome structural inequality') and yet, outside the stadium, the space became 'striated by hostile gazes', perhaps even a precursor to the violence that ensued later that day.

Freedom and self-transformation in the city, Njogu Morgan reflects, have been closely tied to the desire for self-directed mobility – the capacity to own a car and drive oneself. 'Status anxiety' is read through the city's transport behaviour, a psychosocial reading which encompasses road rage, crime, potholes, poorly maintained buses and trains, and errant minibus taxi drivers. The piece recalls, and references, Paul Gilroy's (2001) work on 'driving while black', in which histories of propertylessness and material deprivation can be read against investment in the high visibility of the car and the status it infers and confers. The anxieties of freedom are themselves significant here: the difficulties associated with living in a state of apparent political freedom and the un-freedoms attendant on living with ongoing inequality. One might juxtapose the significance of car ownership in social terms with calls for carbon reduction in cities, and the complexity of weighing these forms of new found freedom with calls to address environmental crisis.

Anxieties about contamination and hazardous waste on former mining land where artisanal miners use mercury for processing gold and where uranium breaks down into carcinogenic gas is the subject of Khangelani Moyo's study. Urban histories of tear gas, turning streets from places of protest into toxic chaos, have to date been more fully written than histories of pollution and their political and atmospheric ecologies in the present. As greenhouse gases and other pollutants hover above cities, and in turn dramatically increase the energy available for violent weather events within cities, we could add the multiple, ricocheting anxieties in navigating, sensing and feeling the city's more material atmospherics to our already sensorily overloaded city.

***

If anxiety is an emotion characterised by a state of inner turmoil, nervous behaviour, somatic complaints and rumination, then urban anxiety, as this book multiply defines it, is this condition intensified by its psychogeographies. Anxiety as a state of being unsettled or 'out of place' in the city itself, with a heightened awareness of those who appear as ghosts of the urban, including cleaners who appear in the night only to disappear during the day, is explored by Joel Cabrita and Sabelo Mlangeni. Anxieties about blackness, crime and interracial intimacy manifest in the homes of Chinese traders living in the suburb of Cyrildene, Mingwei Huang writes. Inheriting and refashioning apartheid's political and psychic architectures, these homes rely on domestic service while subtly changing its terms, if not the fact of servitude as such. Hauntingly, as Huang's final sentence puts it, 'the back room intractably remains'.

The city can be written, and overwritten, and rewritten, in a way that itself generates anxiety, but of the kind that pushes the writer forwards, capturing what is seen and felt. Baeletsi Tsatsi reveals the anxiety, let alone the fury, of being read otherwise than one appears to oneself: 'You cross the Mandela Bridge into town from a feminist gathering in Braam[fontein] and the first thing you hear upon entering the taxi rank is "My size" from various men.' Nobody knows her work or cares about the ideas she has been grappling with; here, in the taxi, she is reduced to her body. Yet despite the uneven conditions for doing so, Tsatsi is writing about it, bearing witness in words to her anxiety, describing it in diary form.

Urban anxiety, we could say by way of conclusion, much as we attempt to capture it in writing, and despite its concrete and specific histories, still has something about it that 'hesitates at the edge' (Anderson 2009, 78) of what we can explain. The city's 'collective atmospheres of fear and risk', as Aidan Mosselson's chapter explores, are as unstable, shifting and occasionally as mysterious as the city's towers that Antonia Steyn photographs.

What is it, we might ask again, that is enveloping and pressing upon us from all sides? What are its intensities and auras? How does it emanate from yet exceed both bodies and built structures? The anxious city is constantly an atmosphere in formation. What is it that we sense is about to happen?

REFERENCES

Anderson, Ben. 2009. "Affective Atmospheres." *Emotion, Space and Society* (2): 77–81.

Gandy, Matthew. 2017. "Urban Atmospheres." *Cultural Geographies* 24 (3): 353–74.

Gilroy, Paul. 2001. "Driving while Black." In *Car Cultures*, edited by Daniel Miller. Oxford and New York: Berg.

Hornberger, Julia. 2008. "Nocturnal Johannesburg." In *Johannesburg: The Elusive Metropolis*, edited by Sarah Nuttall and Achille Mbembe, 285–96. Durham: Duke University Press.

Nuttall, Sarah, and Achille Mbembe. 2008. *Johannesburg: The Elusive Metropolis*. Durham: Duke University Press.

CONTRIBUTORS

Joel Cabrita teaches African History in the Department of History at Stanford University, USA. She has held posts at the University of Cambridge and the School of Oriental and African Studies, University of London. Her most recent book is *The People's Zion: Southern Africa, the United States and a Transatlantic Faith-Healing Movement* (2018), which was awarded the American Society of Church History Albert C. Outler Prize for the best book of 2019 on global Christianity.

B Camminga is a postdoctoral fellow in the African Centre for Migration and Society (ACMS) at the University of the Witwatersrand, South Africa. Their work considers the interrelationship between the conceptual journeying of the term 'transgender' from the global north and the physical embodied journeying of African transgender asylum seekers globally. A current book project, *Beyond the Mountain: Queer Life in ' 'Africa's Gay Capital'* (2019), with Dr Zethu Matebeni, explores the conflicting iterations of race, sex, gender and sexuality that mark the city of Cape Town.

Nicky Falkof is an associate professor in Media Studies at the University of the Witwatersrand, South Africa. She holds a PhD in Cultural Studies from the London Consortium, University of London. Her research centres on race and anxiety in the urban global south with a focus on South Africa. She is the author of *The End of Whiteness* (2014/2015), and has been awarded the National Research Foundation's 2017 Excellence Award for Emerging Researchers, a Rockefeller Foundation Bellagio Centre Residency, a Wits University Friedel Sellschop Award, and a fellowship from the African Humanities Programme. She has been a visiting fellow at Sussex University, UK; the University of Dar es Salaam, Tanzania; and the Universidad Nacional Autónoma de México.

Derek Hook is an associate professor of Psychology at Duquesne University, USA, and an extraordinary professor of Psychology at the University of Pretoria, South Africa. He is the author of *Six Moments in Lacan* (2017), *(Post)apartheid Conditions* (2014) and *A Critical Psychology of the Postcolonial* (2011). His most recent book is an edited collection of Robert Mangaliso Sobukwe's prison letters entitled *Lie on Your Wounds* (2019).

Mingwei Huang is an assistant professor of Women's, Gender, and Sexuality Studies at Dartmouth College, USA. She has a PhD in American Studies with a graduate minor in Feminist and Critical Sexuality Studies from the University of Minnesota, Twin Cities, USA. Her research has been supported by the Social Science Research Council, the Wenner-Gren Foundation and the Centre for Indian Studies in Africa at the University of the Witwatersrand, South Africa. She is currently working on her first book project, *The Intimacies of Racial Capitalism*, which explores Sino-African worlds across South Africa and China.

Lebohang Masango is a social anthropologist, poet, UNICEF Volunteer Programme Ambassador and award-winning author of the children's book *Mpumi's Magic Beads* (2018), which is available in all eleven of South Africa's official languages. She has a MA in Social Anthropology from the University of the Witwatersrand, South Africa, and her research interests include love, feminism and digital media.

Sabelo Mlangeni is a photographer whose work has focused on capturing the intimate, everyday moments of communities in contemporary South Africa. He graduated from the Market Photo Workshop, Johannesburg, in 2004. His work has been widely exhibited locally and internationally and has been awarded several prizes, including the Africa MediaWorks Photography Prize (2018), the POPCAP '16 Prize for Contemporary African Photography (2016) and the Tollman Award for Visual Arts (2009).

Njogu Morgan is a postdoctoral researcher in the History Workshop at the University of the Witwatersrand, South Africa. He has a PhD from Wits University, and an undergraduate degree from Northwestern University, USA. His overall research interest pertains to theoretical, conceptual and empirical aspects of urban sustainability transitions from a spatial comparative perspective. His book *Cycling Cities: The Johannesburg Experience* (2019) provides a history of commuting by bicycle in Johannesburg since the late nineteenth century.

Aidan Mosselson is an urban geographer and sociologist. He has a PhD in Social Geography from University College, London, has held positions at the Gauteng

City-Region Observatory and LSE Cities, and is currently a Newton International Fellow based in the Department of Urban Studies and Planning, University of Sheffield, UK. His research contributes new perspectives to comparative urbanism, postcolonial theory, processes of urban regeneration, planning and housing studies, and geographies of infrastructure.

Khangelani Moyo is an associate researcher with the Global Change Institute (GCI) at the University of the Witwatersrand, South Africa. He is a former postdoctoral researcher at the African Centre for Migration and Society (ACMS). He completed his PhD at Wits University in 2017, focusing on Zimbabwean migrants' mobilities in urban spaces and how their spatial identities are negotiated in the city of Johannesburg.

Sisonke Msimang is a fellow at the Wits Institute for Social and Economic Research (WiSER), South Africa, and has held fellowships at Yale University, the Aspen Institute, and the Bellagio Centre of the Rockefeller Foundation, USA. She is the author of two books: *Always Another Country: A Memoir of Exile and Home* (2017) and *The Resurrection of Winnie Mandela* (2018).

Sarah Nuttall is professor of Literary and Cultural Studies and director of the Wits Institute for Social and Economic Research (WiSER), South Africa. She is the author of *Entanglement: Literary and Cultural Reflections on Post-Apartheid* (2009). She has taught at Yale and Duke universities, USA, and in 2016 was an Oppenheimer Fellow at the Du Bois Institute at Harvard University, USA. She has directed WiSER, the largest and most established humanities institute in the global south, for the past seven years.

Renugan Raidoo is a PhD candidate in Social Anthropology at Harvard University, USA. He holds an MPhil in Social Anthropology from Oxford University, where he was a Rhodes Scholar, as well as a BA in Anthropology, and a BS (with honours) in Chemistry from the University of Iowa, USA. His research concerns lifestyle estates in the Gauteng City-Region, their political economic origins, and their social and spatial consequences.

Antonia Steyn is a photographer and portraitist based in Cape Town, South Africa, who works internationally. In 2008 she received an ABSA L'Atelier Merit Award and in 2011 she won the Vuleka Art Award. She was named the Media24 Photographer of the Year in 2014 for her work with satirist Pieter Dirk Uys.

Baeletsi Tsatsi is a storyteller, writer and facilitator based in Johannesburg, South Africa. She has studied at the Market Theatre Laboratory, Johannesburg, and the International School of Storytelling and the Centre for Biographical Storytelling, UK. She won the Basetsana Best Script Award in 2014, and the J.J. Renaux Emerging Storyteller Grant Award in 2018.

Cobus van Staden is a senior researcher at the South African Institute of International Affairs (SAIIA), University of the Witwatersrand, South Africa. He specialises in China–Africa relations as part of SAIIA's African Governance and Diplomacy Programme. He has a PhD in Media Studies from the University of Nagoya, Japan, has worked as a documentary producer and investigative journalist on the award-winning South African television series *Special Assignment*, and has done postdoctoral research at Stellenbosch University and the University of Johannesburg, South Africa.

INDEX

Page numbers in *italics* indicate figures or tables.

2Summers (blog) 120

A

abjection 33–34, 40n4, 121–125
access control 251–253
affective atmospheres 268–269 *see also* emotions
affordable housing 242–243, 250
African Americans 69–70, 72, 74
African king cricket *see* Parktown prawns
African National Congress (ANC) 24, 37, 95–96, 139, 157, 211
Africanness 48, 143
AfriForum 144
'Afropolis' 247
Agamben, Giorgio 119
agency 60, 241, 252–253
agriculture *see* farming
Ahmed, Sara 5–6
AIDS *see* HIV/AIDS
alcohol 88, 89, 252
Alexandra 95
alien vegetation 124–125, 143–144
Allen, Danielle 233
Ally, Shireen 173n8
'amandla' 26
ANC *see* African National Congress
Anglocorp 138
animals 140, 141–142, 147
anonymity 247, 249, 266, 273
anthropocene 145, 267, 270
Antwoord, Die (band) 119–120
anxiety
    apartheid and 6
    asylum seeking and 206–207
    compensated relationships and 46, 52, 60, 269–270
    gated communities and 133–135, 147, 149
    Global Citizen Festival (2018) 12, 23–24, 28, 33, 38–39, 270
    in Johannesburg 4–14, 267–274
    Lacanian conceptualisation of 98–103, 271
    Parktown prawns and 117, 127–128

Sol Plaatje settlement 235–236
transportation and 64–65, 67–68, 76–80, 272–273
white fragility and 6, 10, 92, 94–95, 98–108, 110–112, 271
apartheid
    anxiety and 6
    asylum seeking and 215
    Chinatown 153–155, 170–171
    class and 40n3
    gated communities and 135
    Global Citizen Festival (2018) 34
    inequality and 48–49
    inner city and 245, 247
    lighting and 268
    Parktown prawns and 121–122, 125, 127–128
    spatial segregation due to 9–10
    transportation and 66, 68–69, 79
    white fragility and 105, 109–110
'apartheid remains' 154
Appadurai, Arjun 255
ARC *see* Association for Residential Communities
archaeological sites 146–147
artisanal mining 227–228, 230–233, 235–236, 237n2, 273
Association for Residential Communities (ARC) 141
asylum seeking
    anxiety and 206–207
    in Johannesburg 11, 206, 207–209, 213–219, 272
    Refugee Reception Offices (RROs) 206, 207, 209–213, 220–221
    in South Africa 205–207, 209–211, 219–221
authenticity 8, 12–13
AVBOB 139–140

B

Baartman, Sara ('Saartje') 141
back rooms *see* Chinatown
Bad Boyz Hillbrow 156, *158*, 159, 164
Ballard, Richard 142